CONTENTS

RECORD SHOP IN CHENNAI, INDIA (ROBERT MILLIS)

YETI BACK ISSUES

prices/ordering information at yetipublishing.com

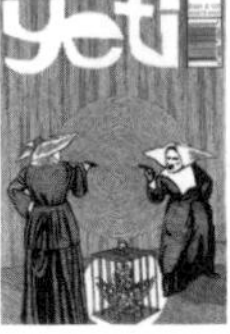

YETI ONE Harry Smith, Terry Riley, James Brown's Original Funky Divas, Alan Greenberg, Califone, Destroy All Monsters, Träd Gräs Och Stenar, Brad Johnson, Pita, Fennesz & Bauer, Robert Walser, Tae Won Yu (photographs), Jana Martin, "A Lo-Fi Metal Primer,"Alphonse Allais, "Downtown 81," James Kochalka. **On the CD:** Iron & Wine (debut recording), Elliott Smith, Nobukazu Takemura, Harry Smith (debut release of his "field recordings"), Califone, Stereolab, L'Altra, Träd Gräs Och Stenar, Screamers, Turn On, Mice Parade, +

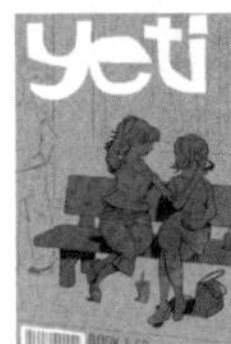

YETI TWO Alfred Jarry, Laura Cantrell, Aceyalone, Luc Sante ("The Birth of the Blues"), Richard Thompson, Trinie Dalton, Steffen Basho-Junghans, Amy Gerstler (poems + interview), Rachel Kushner, Brian Chippendale, Ben Katchor, Marcellus Hall. **On the CD:** Steffen Basho-Junghans, Shins, Keith Fullerton Whitman, Death Cab for Cutie, Califone, White Hassle, Pell Mell, Iron & Wine, Six Organs of Admittance, Takagi Masakatsu, Kill Me Tomorrow, Birdbrain, Carissa's Wierd, The Scene Is Now, +

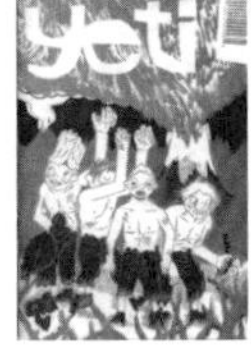

YETI THREE Unpublished William Burroughs interview, Devendra Banhart, Neko Case, Naomi Yang, R.J. Smith, Jason Miles, Michael Galinsky, Erik Davis, BloodNinja, Henry Flynt, Charles Peterson, "The Apes Guide to the Apes," Eileen Myles. **On the CD:** Devendra Banhart, Henry Flynt, Postal Service, Colin Meloy, Iron & Wine, Jolie Holland, I Rowboat, the Mad Scene, the Lights, Dan Melchior, Ian Nagoski, the Apes, the Robot Ate Me, Blues Goblins, Dream Lovers,Timesbold, Washington Phillips, KRMTX, +

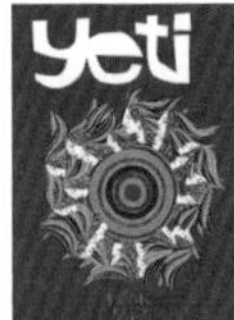

YETI FOUR Fred Tomaselli, Rev. Louis Overstreet, Stacey Levine, "How to sing along to 'Sweet Home Alabama'," Destroyer, Jana Martin, Peter Doyle, Octavia Butler, Sam Lipstyte, Will Sheff, Jason Miles, Melissa Dyne, Khaela Maricich, Peter Lamborn Wilson, Souled American, Vanessa Vaselka. **On the CD:** Destroyer, Califone, Bright, Okkervil River, Michael Hurley w/ Tara Jane O'Neil, Valet, Fly Ashtray, Plants, Rev. E.W. Clayborn, Theo Angell, the Blow, Souled American, Alela Diane, Somos Marquis Homos, +

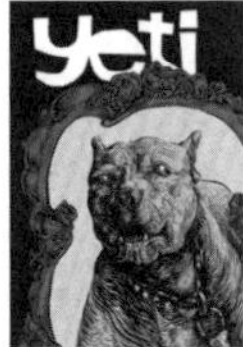

YETI FIVE Jeff Mangum, Will Oldham, Blind Willie Johnson, "The marriage made in hell between folk music, dead cultures, myth, & highly technical modern extreme metal," Nicola Bowery on Leigh Bowery, P.G. Six, Unica Zürn, Meredith Brosnan, Hisham Mayet: travel journals from Western Sahara, Kevin Sampsell, BloodNinja. **On the CD:** Akron/Family, Iron & Wine, Karen Dalton, Dean and Britta, Deerhoof, Vashti Bunyan, Tara Jane O'Neil, Anglin Bros, Grouper, Evolutionary Jass Band, Spiritualaires, Kathryn Williams, Cooper Moore, +

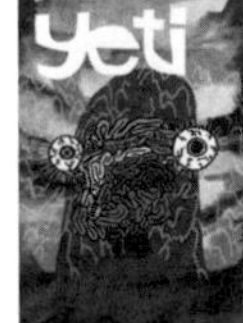

YETI SIX The Clean, Vivian Girls, Sic Alps, Eat Skull, Sun City Girls, Andy Beta's hilarious chat with roots-disco DJ Thom Bullock, Eric Isaacson on Mingering Mike, Luc Sante on folk photography, Tim Lawrence on the neglected role of disco in NYC's '70s downtown scene, David Fair's paper-cut art **On the CD:** Clean/Great Unwashed, Times New Viking, Crystal Stilts, Megapuss, Sun City Girls, Mingering Mike, Cause Co-Motion!, Eat Skull, Blank Dogs, Sad Horse, Ilyas Ahmed, E*Rock & Mat Brinkman, Grass Widow, Way of the Ancients +

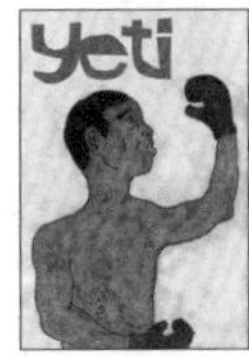

YETI SEVEN Wooden Shjips, Jim Woodring, Black Twig Pickers/Jack Rose, Rudy Wurlitzer, Nancy Dupree, the Nodzzz, Mimi Lipson, Lynne Tillman, Joe Brainard's book designs, Abner Jay on his time at the Stephen Foster Center, Ilyas Ahmed. **On the CD:** Grouper, Abner Jay, Dum Dum Girls, Wooden Shjips, Dutchess & the Duke, Jacuzzi Boys, Great Unwashed, Nodzzz, Zola Jesus, Crystal Stilts, Finally Punk, 39 Clocks, the Bible Aires Spiritual Singers, Fresh + Onlys, Moon Duo, Explode Into Colors, Limes, Eternal Tapestry, Woods +

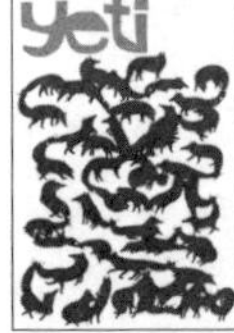

YETI EIGHT Explode into Colors, Zola Jesus, Jim Dickinson, Eliane Radigue, Bishop Perry Tillis, abandoned Japanese amusement parks, Harry Partch's instruments, Johnny Mathis/Chic, Flower Electronics, King Capitol Punishment. **On the CD:** Ty Segall, Woven Bones, Fergus + Geronimo, Zola Jesus, Aran Ruth, Vaselines, Little Claw, Tyvek, Evan Miller, Pigeons, Pete Swanson, Mantles, Jim Dickinson, the Splinters, Brown Recluse, Neverever, Limes, Bishop Perry Tillis, Inca Ore, Vampire Hands, Myelin Sheaths, the Moles +

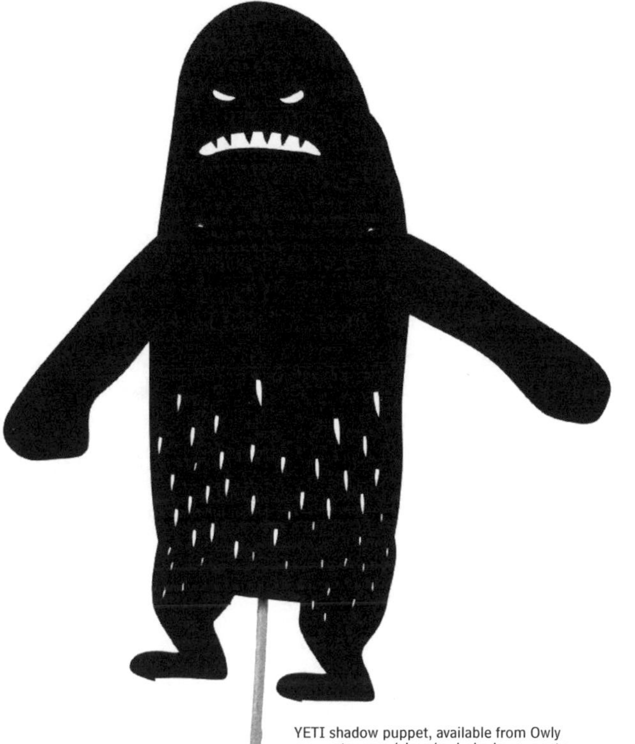
YETI shadow puppet, available from Owly
www.etsy.com/shop/owlyshadowpuppets

yeti

PUBLISHER & EDITOR
Mike McGonigal

MANAGING EDITOR
Steve Connell

CONTRIBUTING EDITOR
Fred Cisterna

COVER IMAGE
Lori D.

COPYEDITOR
Dwight Pavlovic

GRAPHICS GUY
Scott Nasburg

WEBMASTER
Marcus Estes

CD MASTERING
Brian Pyle at the Beach Hut

CD manufactured in Canada by Cravedog
Book printed in Canada by Kromar Printing

This issue is dedicated to all the victims (past and present) of the BP/Halliburton/Transocean oil disaster

Yeti is published 2 to 3 times a year
by Yeti Publishing LLC

CONTACT US
PO Box 14806,
Portland OR 97293
yetipubs@gmail.com
yetipublishing.com

I WAS PAID IN BREAKDANCING LESSONS

An introduction to James Turek's awesome comic strip about *Soylent Green*

YETI: What is your earliest memory of art—making it, seeing it, etc.?
JAMES TUREK: My father always surprised us with a funny hand drawn birthday card, usually a two page gag. With six kids that's a lot of cards over the years. My earliest memory of "art" being created was from watching him draw my brothers' and sisters' cards. My mother also made these giant macramé owls that hung on the wall. They were extremely frightening; it's probably why we never had any guests over.
How long have you been making work yourself?
It really started for me in junior high when I was bullied by my upper classmates to draw their names in bubble letters with a cityscape inside the letters. This was the first taste I had of a real "deadline," and critiques for that matter. I was paid in breakdancing lessons.
Do you see what you're doing as part of a tradition—if so, which one and how?
For sure. I am always reminded of the Kaz strip in which the kid wants to become a cartoonist, but first he has to do ten years of horrible "Kaz-style" living. Only then can he draw Little Bunny Foo Foo.
Any big plans—shows, publications, illustration gigs you're psyched about, etc.—in the future?
Going to Leipzig to hang out, draw some comics—trying to get to the Crack Festival too!

Soilent Groan

turek

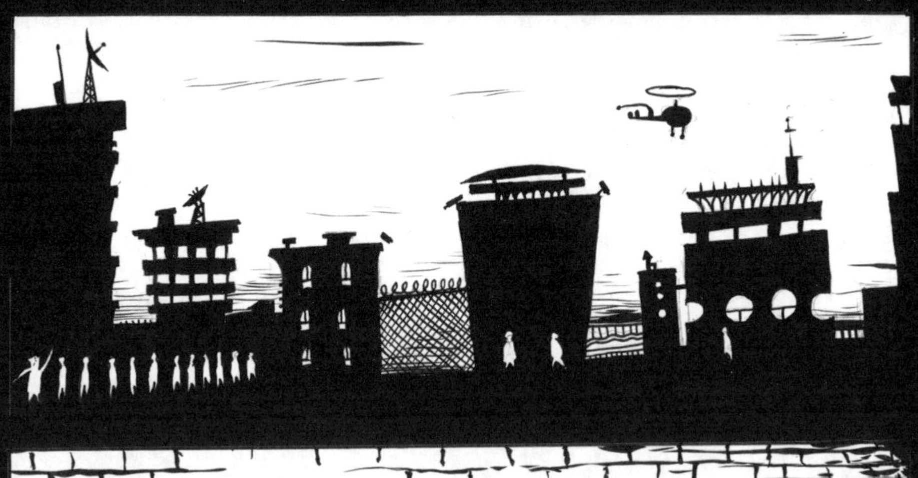

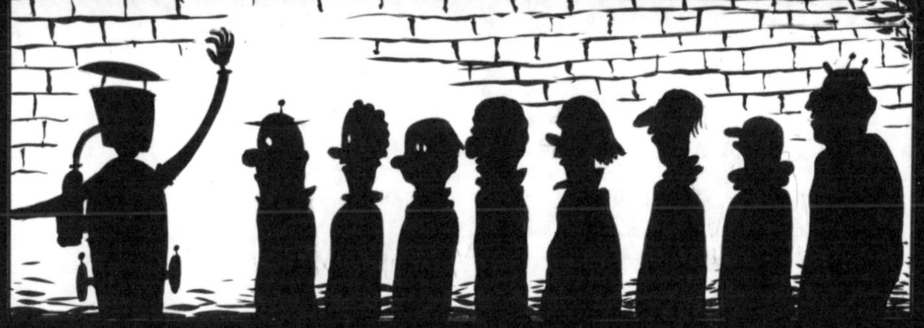

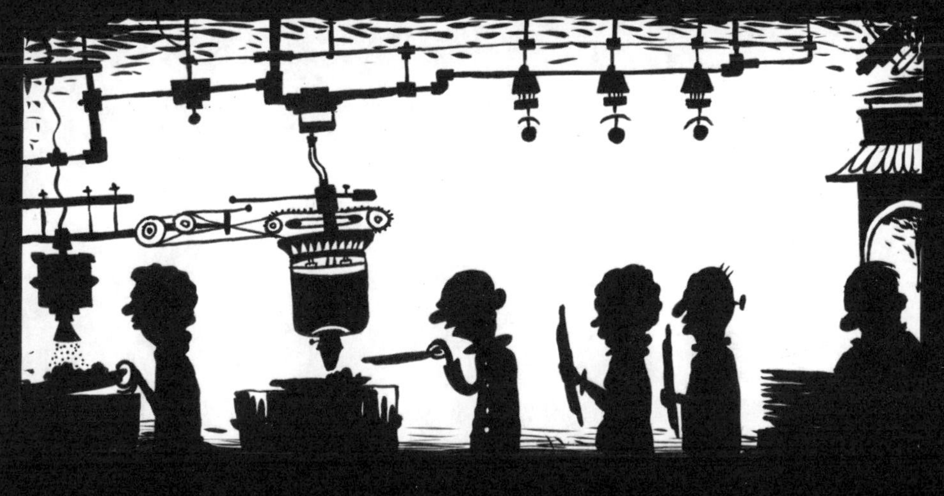

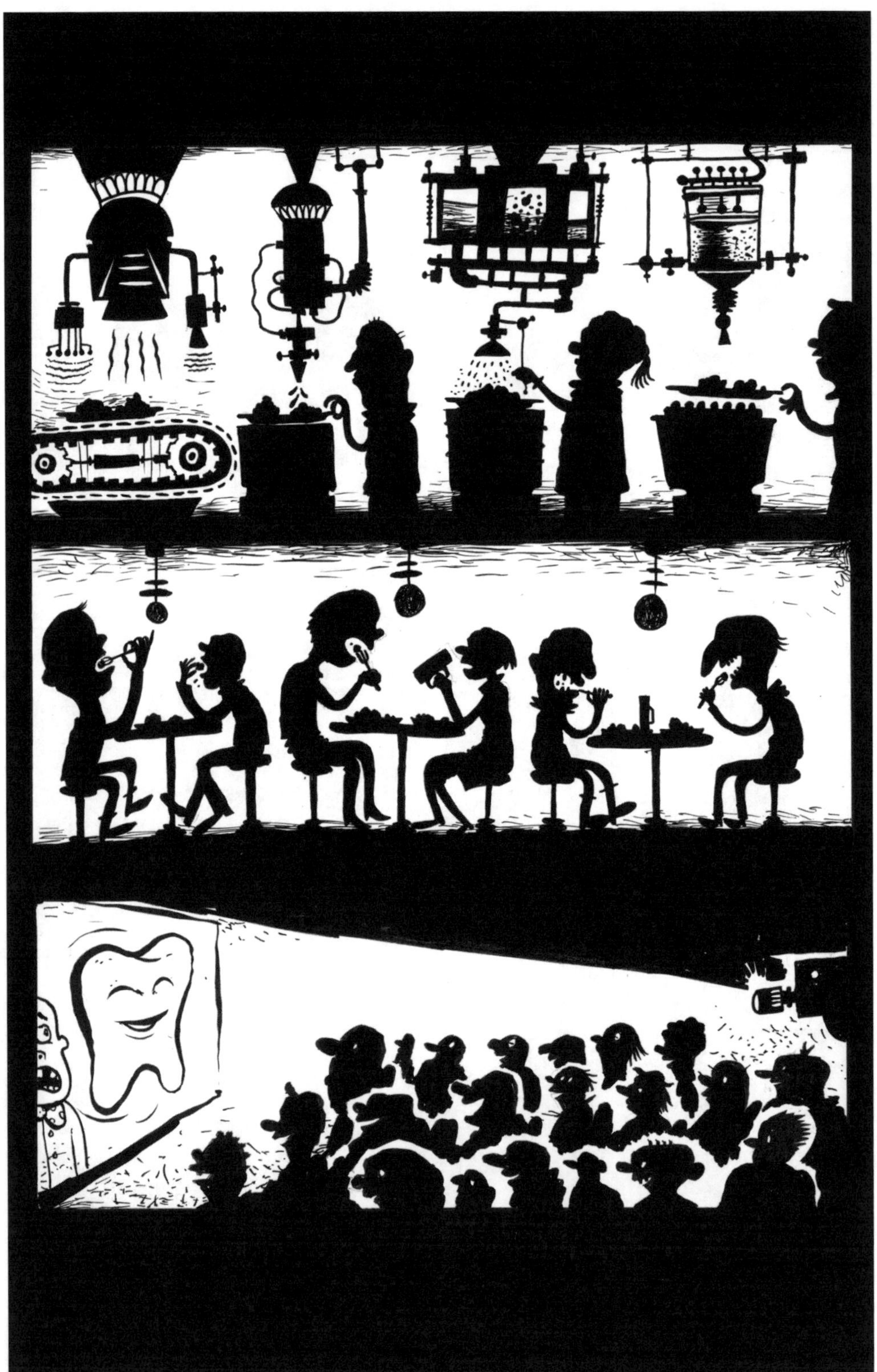

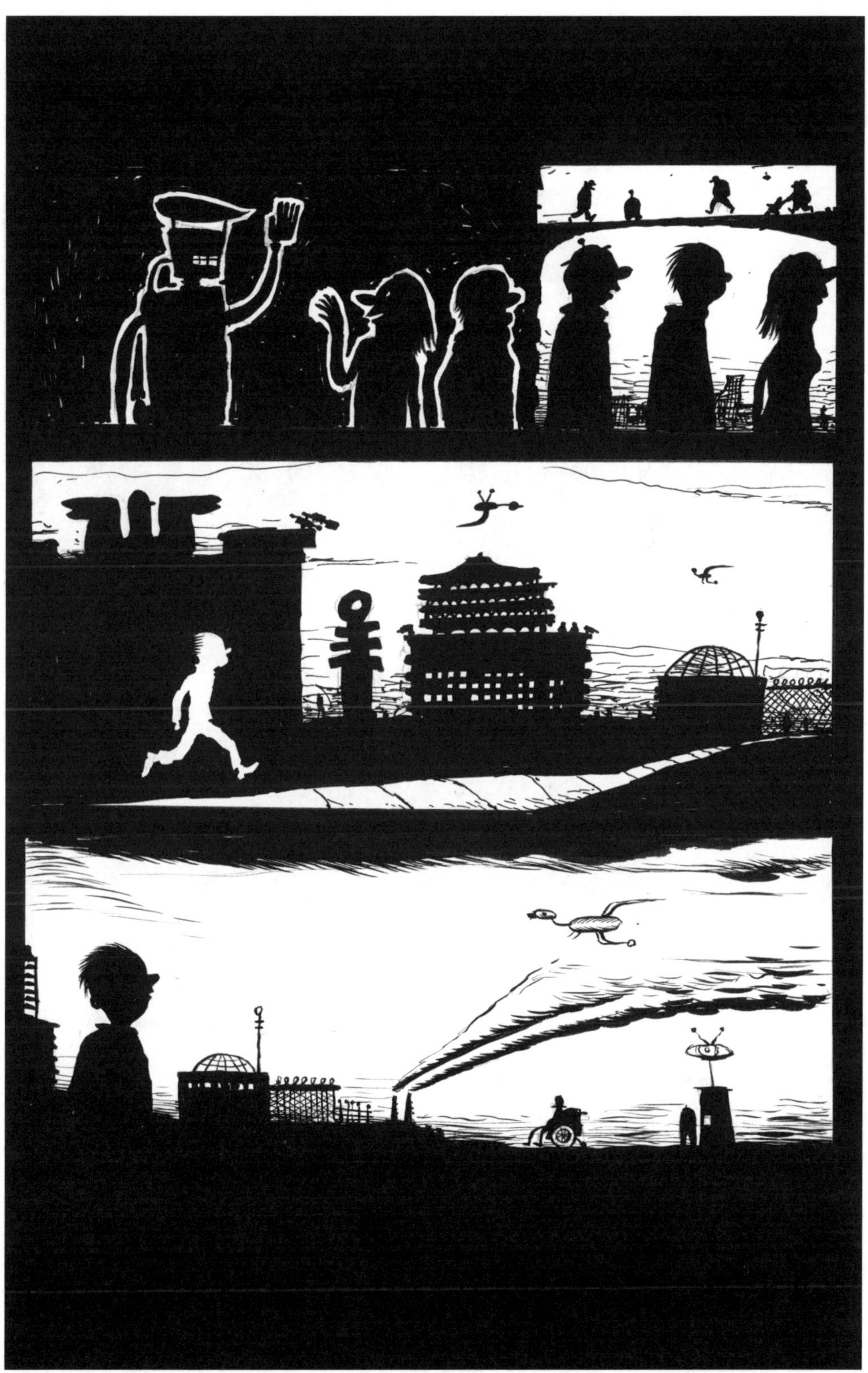

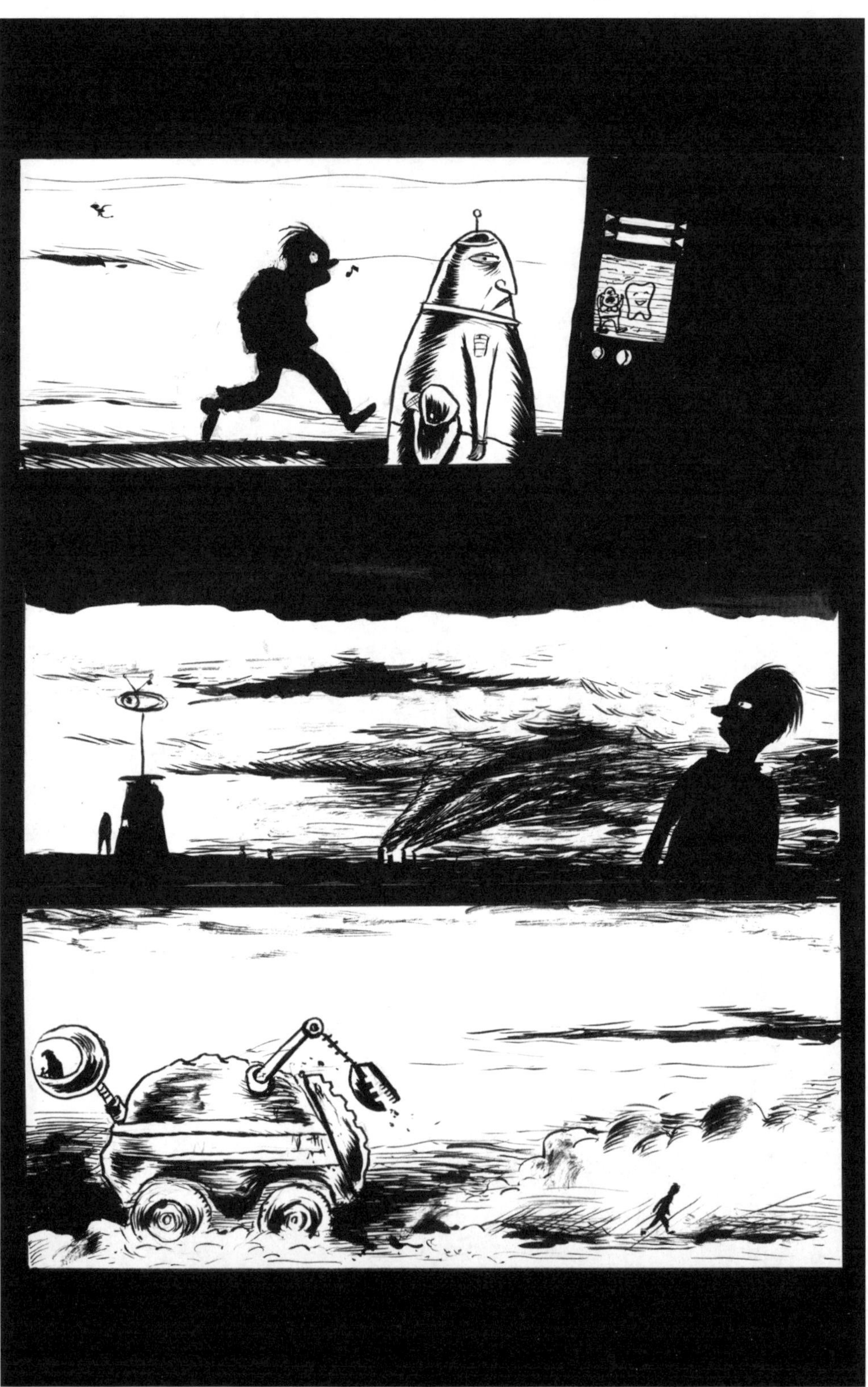

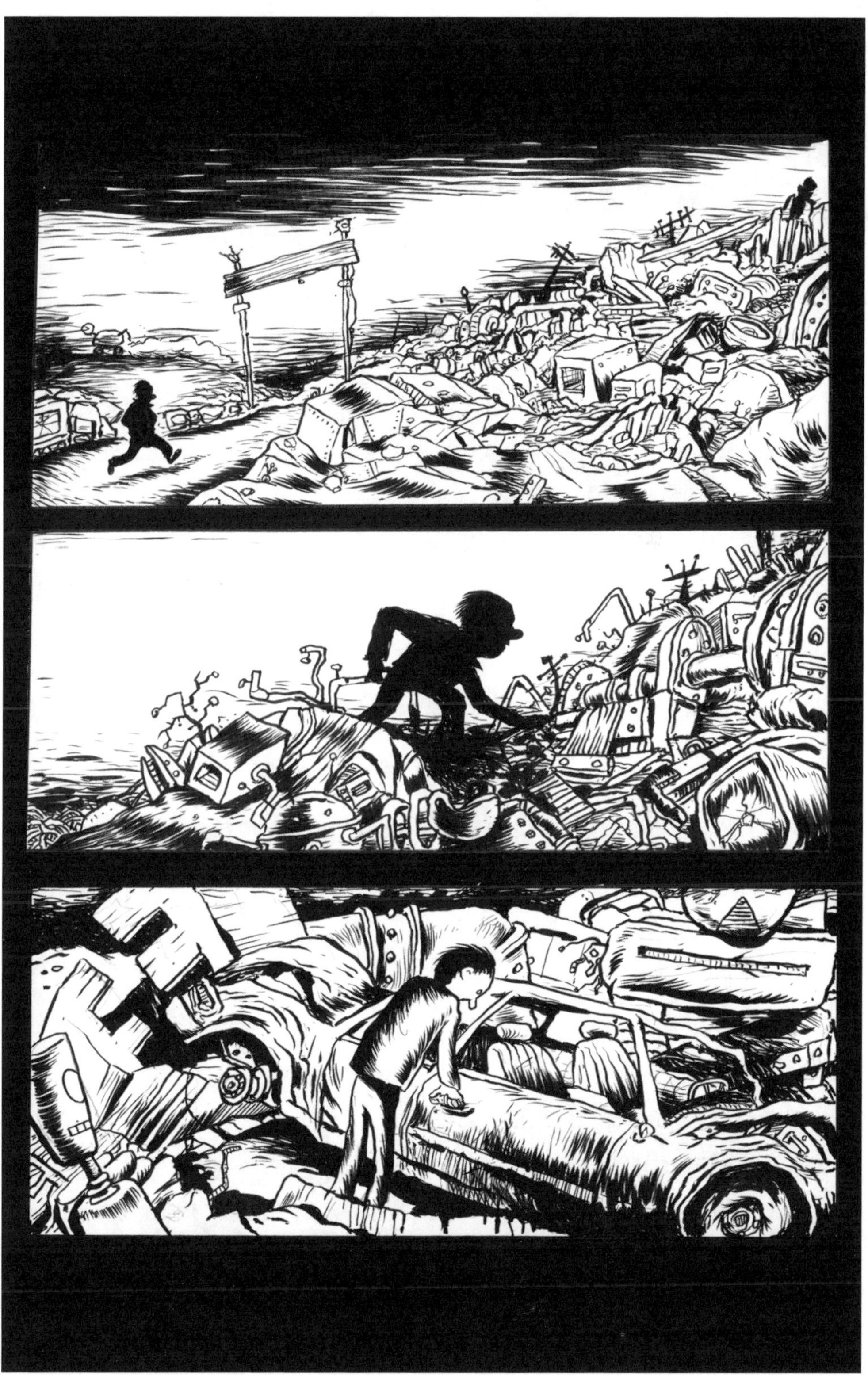

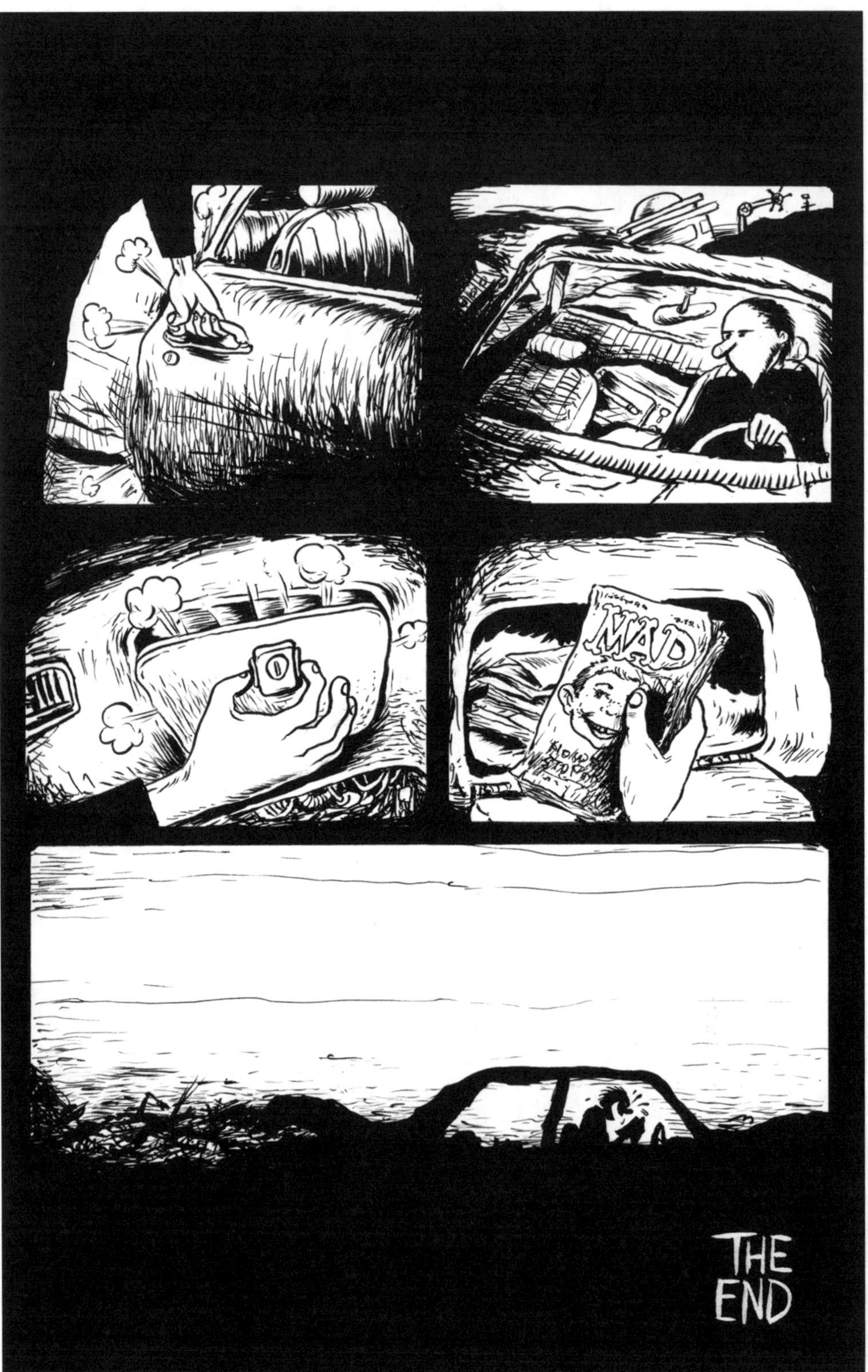
MAD
THE
END

GARBAGE HEAD

by Mimi Lipson

ILLUSTRATION BY E*ROCK

Isaac went north on 42nd Street, conscious of walking *through* the air, which was tangible. Out of the shower for fifteen minutes and already his clothes were stuck to him. Coppery light vibrated on every reflective surface, and the heat that muffled all other sounds somehow amplified the hum of insects in the drooping boughs of the old maples, hummm, hummm, Isaac this, Isaac that, a mocking reference in the call and response of insect noise. He pulled himself out of it, only to realize that he'd walked right past the frat house, the one he usually jogged over to 41st Street to avoid.

But this was exactly the kind of brain pollution that kept him on the hamster wheel: go to work; pick up a stromboli on the way home, eat half of the stromboli for supper, eat the other half for breakfast, then to work again. He'd been on a floor-sanding crew for a few months and he'd put aside three hundred fifty dollars toward a red Aerostar he had his eye on. Today was Saturday, though—payday—so he forced himself out the door and headed up to Killtime to see Poison Idea and get drunk. He had a right.

The sun dropped below the onion domes and dunce caps of Victorian West Philly as he crossed Walnut Street, leaving behind long blocks of front porches and window grates, and entering a zone of drive-by commerce. 7-Eleven, Pep Boys, an aroma of kung pao chicken. From 38th and Lancaster he could see that there was already a small crowd outside Killtime, so he veered diagonally across Lancaster to the liquor store and bought himself a forty, slipping the last wilted bill in his wallet through the little window. Patting the untouched wad of payday twenties in his front pocket, he squared up to face the people out there.

Of course the first person he saw was Kitty's friend Lisa, sitting on the curb outside of Killtime, which put him in danger of thinking about the circumstances under which Kitty moved out, which, if he wanted to think about that he would have picked up a stromboli and stayed home. To make matters worse, Lisa was talking to a beautiful, creamy-skinned girl—Linda? Leena? Lola?—one of those witchypoo girls he kept seeing around West Philly, barefoot girls in velvet elf dresses smelling like hippie candles. He didn't want to risk making eye contact with either of them, so he ducked into the vacant lot next to the liquor store.

He sat down on a truck tire and straightened his legs. His knees ached from squatting with the edge sander. He drank his forty as fast as he could, in gulps that outpaced the garbagy taste of the malt liquor, and waited for full darkness. While he waited, he thought about the Aerostar, its AC and plush velour seats and power windows. He'd seen it parked at the gas station on Baltimore Ave and talked to the mechanic who was selling it, and he was pretty sure he could get it for less than the nine hundred the guy was asking. He let himself imagine loading his own tools in the back: his own sander and edger, a chop saw and a top-nailer, a good compressor. Sam, his boss, had a full-size van, but Isaac had it figured that a minivan was the ideal work truck: comfortable, civilized, easy on the gas. Take out the bench seats and you could fit a sheet of plywood in the back. Best of all, minivans were dismissed—even despised—by your average goon, and therefore stealth.

After a while he heard the first band start up. They sounded thrashy. He stopped in for another forty and then crossed the street. Lisa and the witchypoo girl were gone, thank God. Inside the storefront gallery, an industrial floor fan moved the soggy air around. Bodies lined up against the back wall, faces in shadow, sweat-glazed arms and legs illuminated by street light coming through the big front windows. Numb with malt liquor and cocooned by the noise blasting in from the warehouse next door, Isaac passed safely through the gallery, forked over his dollars, got his hand stamped, and plunged into the sweltering cave beyond.

The warehouse was still nearly empty: just a few guys standing around holding paper bags in front of the low plywood stage at the far end of the room. Onstage, a skinny kid lunged in tight circles, croaking robo-satanically into the mic he held in a white-knuckle grip. He made Isaac think of a ventriloquist's dummy; the sound coming out of him seemed to have nothing to do with his body. Again and again, he narrowly missed collision with the contrastingly large and immobile

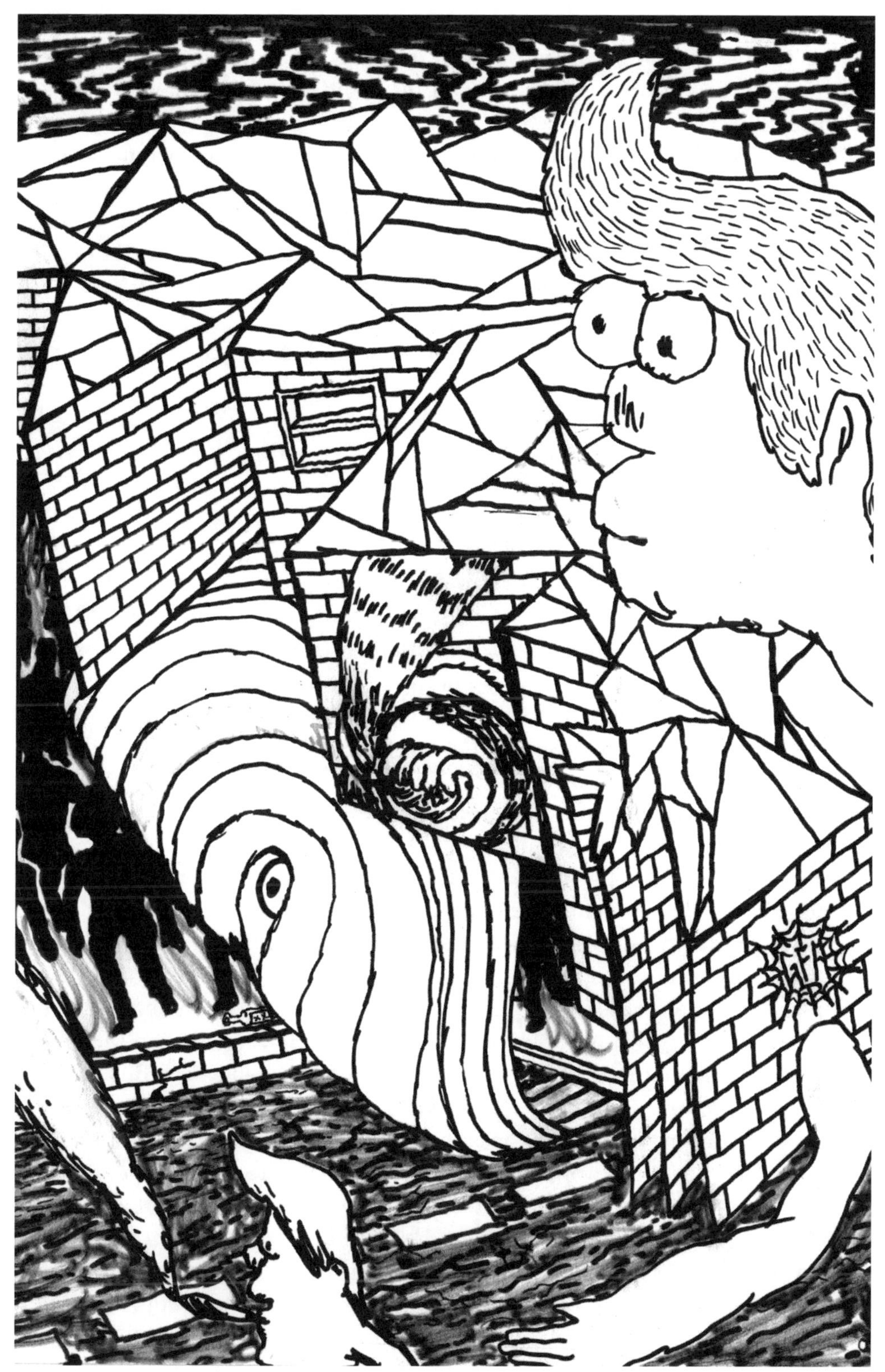

guitar player who was grinding away at a guitar that hung almost to his knees. They were okay. The logo on the kick drum was amateurish, though: the letters "G.F.A," snared in a spider web. Isaac could definitely help them out there.

The back door was propped open to let in some air. When Isaac's eyes had adjusted, he saw a familiar silhouette in the doorway—Greg? Craig? Shit, he was terrible with names—talking to someone he didn't know, huddling in a furtive way that set off his radar. "Hey! Greg!" he yelled to be heard over the satanic croaking as he approached the huddle. "Gimme some of that! What is it?"

Greg and his friend exchanged a look, and Greg leaned in close to Isaac's ear. "NNDM," he yelled.

"What?"

"MNDN."

"*What* is it?"

"NNDN."

"I don't care . . . gimme it."

The three went back out through the storefront and around the corner to a car, where Greg's friend's started explaining about the MNMN. It was a compound he and his partner had just invented. They were Penn students or chemists or something. It was cool what he was saying, actually: if you came up with a new molecule that the government didn't know about, it wasn't technically illegal.

"What do you do, snort it?"

A few minutes later, Isaac was back in the cave watching the first band break down their equipment. He didn't feel much of anything—just maybe a little jittery. It had, if possible, gotten hotter in the warehouse, so he stepped out the back door to wait it out between sets.

Behind the buildings that made up Killtime, the gallery and the warehouse, were the ruins of another warehouse. Gutted by fire, exposed to the elements, overgrown with city fauna, the ruin had become a sort of courtyard. Isaac leaned against the brick wall in the farthest corner and breathed in the sour perfume of the ghetto palms. *Kitty called them "trees of heaven."* This was his favorite part of the complex. If he could get over his shyness, penetrate the scene, he would transform this place. He would make thrones out of the rubble, an amphitheater, organic shapes like Gaudì. And he would paint the back wall white and project movies out here; he would be the king of it out here. He wondered if Lisa had seen him, or if she'd said anything about him to the other Killtime people. He thought now that she *had* seen him, had looked at him without *looking* at him.

Maybe he hadn't done enough of that MMMM. He took out the bindle and snorted half of what was left. There was warm, spreading sensation, like right after you piss your pants, but all over his body. It was interesting, but it only lasted for a few seconds, so he snorted the rest and sank into the deep shadow of the warehouse.

A slow, kicking beat pulled him back to the surface, and then a single bass note in the key of dirge, and a guitar riff that led him back inside where the second band was starting, a riff like a sludgy current on thick, corroded wire, twisting into the shapes of letters he couldn't quite read: H.D.R.? F.D.R.? D.R.I., G.F.A., MMNDMDM. The room had filled with smoke and flesh and sulphurous light, and it was hotter than ever. He felt a splash on his neck. Looking up, he became transfixed by the condensation pooling up on the pipe above him until, suddenly and irrevocably, it occurred to him that he might have puked all over himself. He tried to get closer to the stage so he could see, searched for an opening in the wall of meat and sound, then gave up and fought his way back in the other direction and through the door to the gallery and burst out onto Lancaster Ave, gulping for air but finding only warm gel. There was no puke on him.

He went back across the street to the vacant lot and sat on his truck tire and stared at the throbbing halo around the streetlight. A sludgy drone oozed out through the open doors of Killtime. Gel, throb, sludge. The climate on Lancaster Avenue had achieved a reptilian homeostasis with the climate in his skull. After a while he realized that the music had stopped. He got up too quickly, and his stomach heaved. A flume of malt liquor splattered the weeds and the tire and the brick wall, and when he looked up, the halo around the streetlight had disappeared. *Maybe I should just get another forty and go home*, he thought.

The bum standing in front of the liquor store looked familiar. Something about the way he was hopping from foot to foot, his thin ankles poking out of orthopedic shoes, colorless windbreaker even in this jungle heat. Of course, it was Eddie. Isaac hadn't recognized him here. He knew Eddie from the deli near his house, where he was like part of the street furniture—as fixed to his spot as a mailbox or a streetlight.

"Hello, Picasso! It's you!" said Eddie, his face opening up into a gummy smile. "The artist!"

It occurred to Isaac that he'd been followed.

"What are you doing here, Eddie?"

"What am I doing here? This my old stomping grounds. What are *you* doing here, blessed boy?"

"Right now I'm going to buy myself some beer." Eddie kept on moistly beaming at him. "Aw hell, you want a forty? My treat, buddy. I just got paid."

"You don't have to give me nothing. I ain't ask you for nothing," said Eddie.

"I know," said Isaac, "I want to."

He went inside and asked for two Olde Englishes.

"You gotta take it someplace else though," said the cashier. She must have been watching them outside the store.

Isaac reached in his front pocket, but instead of the roll of twenties he pulled out a wad of Kleenex.

Fuck fuck *fuck*.

He tried his other pockets, and then his wallet. No, his roll was gone. "Forget it," he said, and walked out, and past Eddie, and west on Lancaster Ave.

"Hey! Picasso!" Eddie called after him.

"Sorry, Eddie," Isaac yelled without turning around.

A week, six fucking days on his knees, scraping and edging and sucking in polyurethane fumes. Apparently he'd done all that for free, like the fucking slave that he was. His stomach heaved again, but there was nothing in it. Yuppie bitch telling Sam to "make sure those guys don't go in my kitchen." Drinking out of the fucking hose like a dog. With what he'd had in his pocket he could have paid for the Aerostar.

Six days. Fuck. He thought of the Penn guy, the chemist. He'd paid him with the change in his wallet, but maybe he'd somehow dropped his roll in the car. Then he thought about the other guy, his roommate's friend, lying on the couch in front of the TV when he came home and got in the shower. Of *course.* That piece of shit went through his stuff; Isaac was sure of it.

He turned on 42nd Street, across Walnut and into the green canopy of the old maples. The air was still heavy, but the insects had gone quiet. Listening for them he heard something else, though. Footsteps. He spun around and saw Eddie half a block behind him.

"I'm sorry, Eddie. I lost my money."

"I told you I ain't ask for nothing. I'm headed home just like you are."

"Okay." He waited while Eddie caught up, and they walked together silently.

"I lost my whole paycheck," said Isaac after a bit. "In cash. A roll of twenties."

"I'm sorry."

"Yeah, it pretty much blows, but I know who took it," said Isaac.

"So . . . that's your old stomping grounds? Over there by Lancaster Ave?"

"Ludlow. 37th and Ludlow is where I'm from."

"Isn't that all Penn buildings? I never noticed any houses over there."

"It used to be nothing *but* houses over there before they plowed it all under. That's where I grew up, 37th and Ludlow."

"No shit? Your house got knocked down?"

"Not just *my* house," said Eddie. "We had a—" He waggled his hands. "O-over on 34th and Walnut we had a movie theater, stores, everything you might need right there in the neighborhood. A drug store. I used to run the deliveries after school, take my little money and go to the movies. And they plowed it all under."

"I never heard about that."

"I expect you haven't," he said. "I am not one bit surprised. I call that place Atlantis now. Atlantis, you know? But the real name we called it was Black Bottom, and it was a nice place to grow up. Didn't nobody lock their doors when I was growing up."

Kitty would have wanted to know about that, thought Isaac a little sadly. It was the kind of thing they'd talked about: secret history.

"Penn tore it down so they could build all those labs and shit?"

"Well, that's one thing. The other thing is they ain't want us in a so-called slum. So now everybody living in a worse slum somewhere else, if they living anywhere at all.

"Wait, did Penn tear it down or the city?"

"You tell me the difference."

"You've got a point there," said Isaac.

"Anyhow, it's long gone now."

"How old are you, Eddie?" Isaac asked.

He stopped for a moment. "I'm forty-two years old. Forty-two. Or forty-one or forty-three. One of them."

Wow, thought Isaac. *I thought he was like sixty*.

When they got to his house, Isaac let himself in, and Eddie waited outside until the light went on in the attic window. He waited until it went out again. Stepping onto Chester Ave, he saw something under the tire of a car and leaned over to pick it up. Yes it was: a roll of twenty-dollar bills. ✪

KNIGHTS IN YELLOW ARMOUR

Pip Proud in the 1960s

by David Nichols

ILLUSTRATION BY E*ROCK

The visionary pop music of Australian singer-songwriter Pip Proud is uncompromising and honest, beautiful and unrestrained—especially on his three albums from the late 1960s (the first a private pressing of 50 copies, the other two on Phillips). Proud's songs sound like they're about to crack open and fall apart; you can almost feel the yolk rolling about inside. He is way too strange to be "twee," although you could say that he's twee in the sense that you could say that Merzbow is loud. What follows is an extract from David Nichols's forthcoming history of Australian rock and pop music, the first volume of which (covering the years 1960-85) will be published by Verse Chorus Press in 2011.

my music has brought young people to tears, to exclaims of 'genius', yet, still, there are these incredible people who think im a child. Gosh, i was screwed up too, i used to cry at night, but i got out of it, i created my self out of the mess my parents manufactured, but it seems theres not many like me. isnt there anyone who values truth before pleasure? i have no resentment, only a rather compassionate repulsion, and hence, a lonliness.

—Pip Proud, circa 1967

While much of the flowery, celebratory puff which seems unavoidable in writing about the sixties should be viewed skeptically, the short public career of Pip Proud between 1967 and 1969 demonstrates that, at

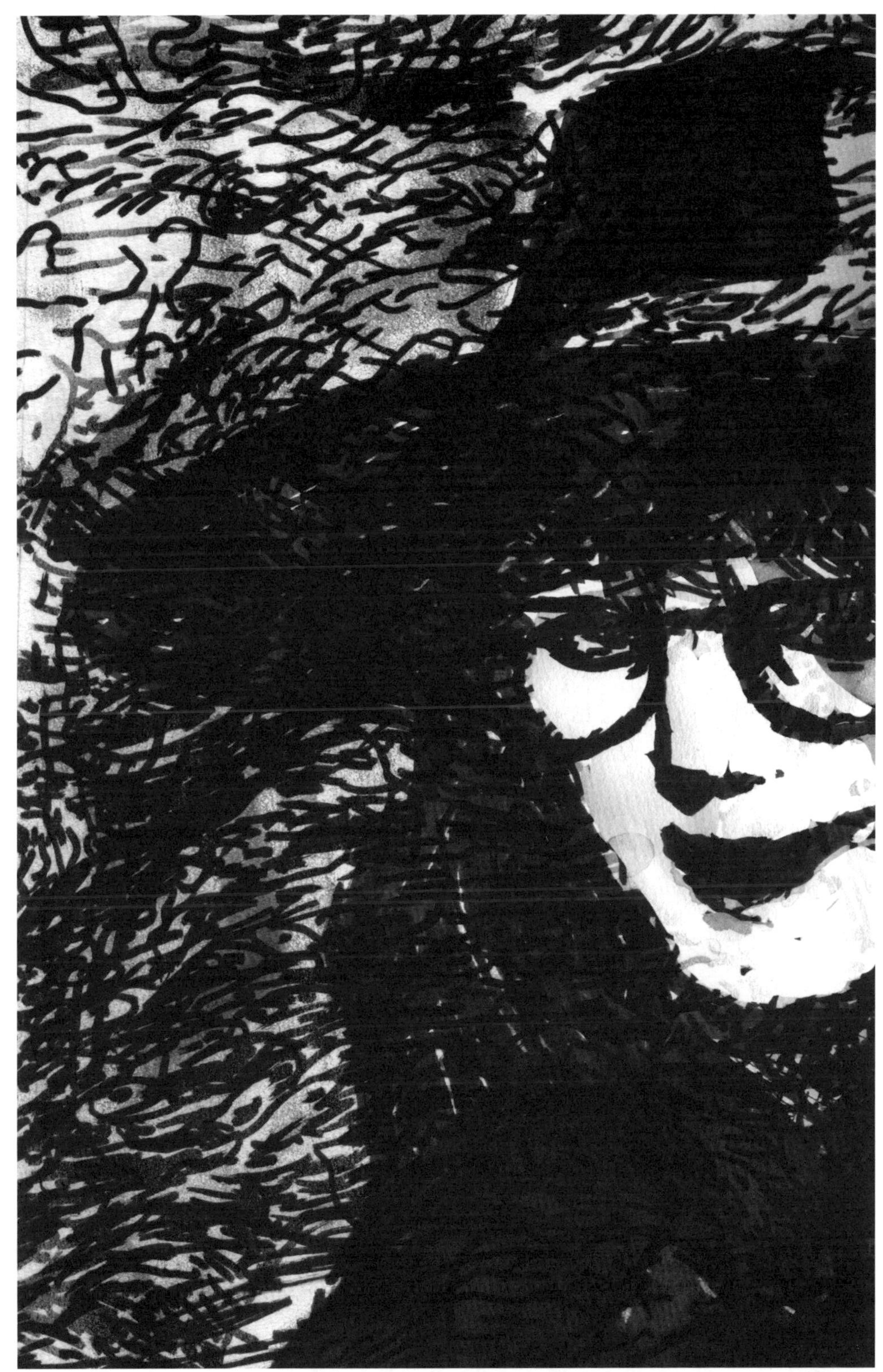

very least, major record companies of the period were happy and even eager to release experimental and entirely original music however possibly harrowing and uncomfortable (or, for that matter, valid and rich) it might have been for some. No doubt this was on the principle that the hippie and/or rock market was too difficult to understand, and that therefore anything might sell (the punk/new wave market was deemed to be much the same a decade later), and this could include albums of strange, surreal, whimsical-cum-scary songs sung in a hesitant but eloquent way, accompanied by a solitary unplugged electric guitar.

Philip Proud was born in 1947 in South Australia; his father was a state public servant and, occasionally, a failed businessman whose work required that the family—Pip, his parents, older brother Geoffrey and a number of Aboriginal foster children who might now be classed as members of the "stolen generation"—move around the state to river towns like Berri and new industrial towns like Elizabeth.

Proud introduced himself to the readers of *Australian Poetry Now!*, an anthology of work by new poets including his friend Michael Dransfield (through whose influence he was included in the book) as follows:

> My name is Phillip John Proud, and this was naturally shortened to Pip Proud a few years ago . . . My parents are middle class and so on, and so on.

The "middle class" admission might indicate a desire to avoid the kind of exposé Bob Dylan suffered in 1963 when *Newsweek* revealed he was merely "a Jewish kid from the suburbs," though Proud had made no outlandish claims like Dylan; he had, like many others, reinvented himself as transcending class, time and material considerations. As mentioned previously, the Proud family had lived for some time in working-class Elizabeth; Proud was a contemporary of such fellow Elizabethans who would later become major Australian (and international) pop stars as Glenn Shorrock (Little River Band), Doc Neeson (The Angels) and Jimmy Barnes (Cold Chisel), though he did not know them.

Pip and his brother Geoff were creative; Geoff would become a very well-known and successful painter. Pip, diagnosed with motor coordination difficulties at a young age, prescribed guitar for himself as therapy. During his mid-teens, as an apprentice radio technician in Cowra, NSW, he was taught some chords by a friend. The therapy worked. As a teenager he was anti-authoritarian (he enticed an early girlfriend to run away from home with him; the experience is explored in a masked fashion in one of his early songs, "Latin version") but never anti-knowledge; he had a strong interest in science both theoretical and practical. He abandoned his apprenticeship to live with Geoff in Sydney, where the brothers endured poverty for some time until the elder Proud began to find mentors and some recognition for his art. Forty years later, Pip wrote:

> All this lugging my guitar around trying to figure an E chord from an A chord. My brother trying to paint pictures. Once we rented a laundry to live in. It had a sloping cement floor with a big old cement laundry tub and a bunsen burner for a stove, but somehow we didn't mind. We had our dreams of fame and wealth one day, but the pleasure was from the sheer iconoclasm of it all. It was bloody hard and cold but each day seemed new. I liked pissing out the window or in the laundry tub. It was cool to see how many days we could stay awake without sleep. We used to compete like that. I think five was our record though I'm not sure who won. My brother painting and me trying to figure out how a damn guitar works.

Geoff's rising star aided Pip in another way, as two men stepped in to further his career. Garry Shead, a painter but also a cartoonist (for *Oz,* the satirical Sydney forerunner to the late '60s London counterculture organ) and a maker of experimental short films, directed the 20-minute *De Da De Dum.* And one of Geoff's patrons, a stockbroker named Michael Hobbs, purchased a tape recorder for Pip and then, on hearing the songs he recorded on it, paid for 50 (some sources say 20) copies of an album, *De Da De Dum* to be pressed on a pretend label called Grendel.

Proud wrote many times to Michael Hobbs in the years 1967-70. The letters were written to reinforce the Medici-like relationship. Proud assumes throughout that Hobbs has his best interests at heart, but does not wish to trespass on his good will more than necessary. He also, plainly, intends to use Hobbs' monetary gifts and/or loans as an "in" to the conventional pop industry in Australia; the letters refer to important industry figures of the day, such as Ivan Dayman, Jim Sharman and Harry M. Miller. Hobbs was apparently interested not just in Proud's musical career but in his overall development as an artist, so the letters also refer to books Proud is writing; he completed numerous novels (most of which he later destroyed), film scripts, and his play *Almond,* which was performed in Sydney in 1968. Usually, though, the letters are about Proud's music. They begin at the time Garry Shead embarked on the *De Da De Dum* film (Garry Shead also wrote to Hobbs with a recommendation that "I think Pip's music is so authentic and good that he is potentially the most original pop musician in Australia.") and occasionally refer to recent phone calls or interactions between Proud and Hobbs. One letter discusses the kinds of records that Proud might go on to make, one of which appears to place him in a writer/producer position rather than a performer role:

> Well, Mr Hobbs, i have two kinds of music that are possibly capable of getting the success we want.
>
> the first kind of music is the kind on the film, and this is very simple to produce in all respects, but, as it is, if i am to continue with the sole guitar and my voice, nothing much can come from this, save a small name and following. to escape this nothingness and still keep the words to this type of song, i must orchestrate that the music has a beauty of its own, with the words and their feeling still guiding the melody this would require harpsichords and the like. there is no hope, and indeed, i feel, very little point in doing this, as i would produce only a very weird and beautiful sound. i think people would have to be led to like it, and i would have nothing to lead them with, except the film-type songs, but as i said, the following would be too small to bother leading. of course, business would improve as the word spread, but i am too impatient to wait for that sort of thing.
>
> the other type of music i have is a gentle but earthy sort of pop music. this would be very lucrative from near the beginning, after i had made the necessary adjustments to my self and thinking, which would be no trouble. the difficulties in doing this are these. firstly, i would need a very obedient group who were paid a regular wage, and this would be fairly impossible to get, as well as bringing many new problems such as where to practice etc.
>
> the second difficulty is brought with the second possibility, and this concerns musicians also. for, i could write out each song in full detail, hire musicians from their union for an initial charge of $20 a piece, and get them to play it whilst it was recorded. there are a few singers who do this. of course money is the problem.

In *De Da De Dum,* Proud holds up the record of the same name, so it plainly existed prior to filming. However, the versions of the songs that are heard in the film are not those on the album (some of them are not on the album at all). A letter to Hobbs claims that EMI had the "record

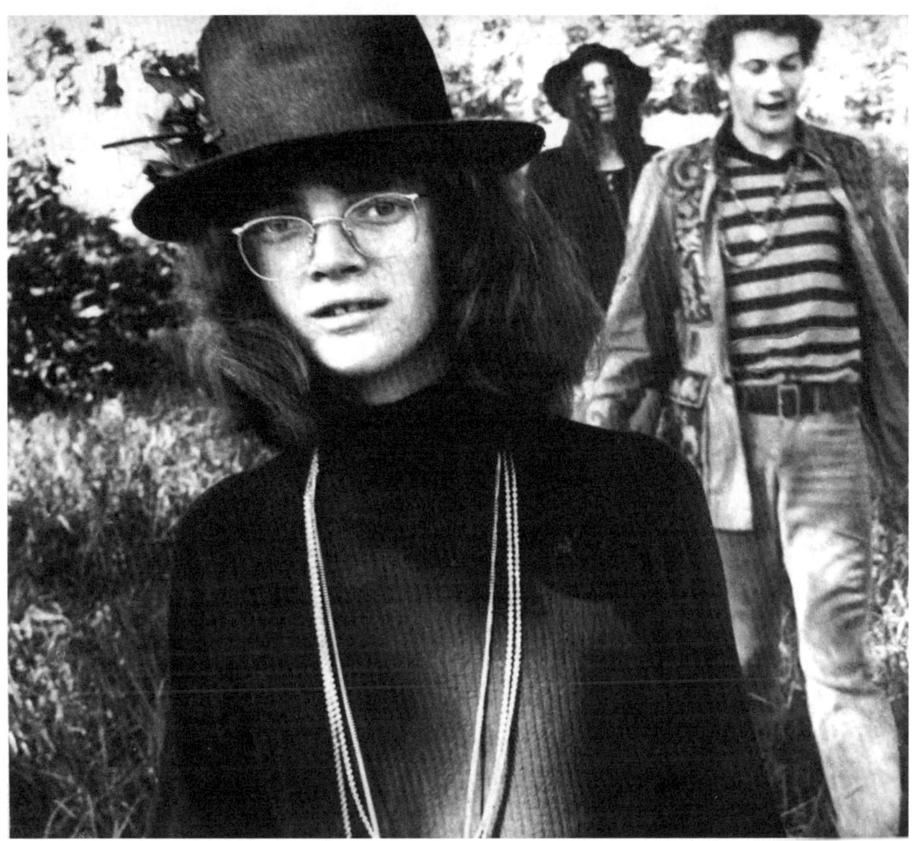

of the film music" though whether this refers to *De Da De Dum,* to the recordings in the film, or something else is unclear. The same letter suggests the promoter Ivan Dayman as a possible industry contact, and Proud indicates he is on the verge of hitchhiking to Brisbane to introduce himself to Dayman.

During the short and heady period in which he began his musical forays (probably around August 1967), Proud met Alison Burns. "She had on a purple, woven dress and a hat, with thick, long, dark hair, and purple stockings. We started talking and she showed me her poetry," he told *Australian Women's Weekly.* The two of them (with another friend) appear on the cover of the album and in extensive scenes in the film, strolling around exploring the beauty and horror of late 1960s Sydney to the backdrop of Proud songs like "An Old Servant" and "De Da De Dum" itself. In a short interview segment, Proud claims his inspiration as "knights in yellow armour."

It is clear that the film—which was made available as part of the Ubu Collective experimental and low-budget film distribution concern—brought no small amount of publicity to Proud, though whether it was seen in any broad forum (television, for instance) is uncertain. An

A&R man at Philips, Bob Cooley, was alerted to the Proud phenomenon by the film and arranged to re-record the album with a slightly altered tracklisting. In 1968 magazine writer James Oram quizzed Cooley on Proud and reported:

> "He is," said Cooley, "either a genius or an oddball."
>
> "I am," said Pip Proud, "a romanticist, an idealist, a writer of fantasy."
>
> Whatever he is, Pip Proud is in danger of becoming one of Australia's biggest singing sensations. I shouldn't use the word "singing," for he recites rather than sings and does it to a badly played guitar and a cowbell tinkled by his girlfriend.

It may be that Cooley anticipated hiring session musicians to work in the studio with Proud but that his erratic timing and inability to record his guitar and vocal separately made this impossible. In the end, only two tracks were given additional instrumentation: the feminist parable "Adreneline and Richard" (which became the title of the new version of the album) and "Purple Boy Gang," which Proud had originally written for the Aboriginal singer Black Allen and which was transformed into a rollicking R&B number. Proud did not hear these transformed tracks until the album was released.

Philips allowed (indeed, required) him to appear on television, where he was periodically ridiculed by smarmy hosts and where the freedoms of live TV allowed him to turn the tables on producers and cameramen who tried to make him stay in shot and play particular songs. In July 1968, he wrote to Hobbs from Melbourne, where he may have travelled specifically to appear on *Uptight.* "If you wish to see the fulfillment of your ambitions concerning my abilities then you could tune into channel 10 on saturday morning on the 5th of July at 10 AM. I do not know precisely at what time "I" shall be on."

He was in some respects an early example of a music phenomenon suited better to television—he was quietly spoken and needed strong, separate amplification on his vocals—than to live performance, though he did not shy away from live appearances entirely.

Gil Wahlquist, music writer for the Sydney *Sun Herald* (also widely available in Melbourne, which at that time lacked its own Sunday papers) praised the album considerably, concluding with the rousing: "If he can keep it up (he's only 21) he'll go places. If he doesn't, his contribution so far is considerable." But much of the press coverage from this time expresses undeniable ambivalence regarding Proud's quavering style. *Go-Set,* for example, only referred to the album at arm's length, as "described as the most poetic disc ever made in Australia." Proud clearly felt that *Go-Set* owed him support; given the general sycophancy and uncritical outlook of most of its editorial staff, he certainly could feel unjustly singled out that it did not. David Elfick, who ran Sydney *Go-Set,* was less than thrilled, in Proud's estimation. He wrote to Hobbs:

> The man from the *Go Set* magazine simply doubted his own judgement with the songs it seems. we were foolish in that we mentioned andrew loogold ham and his rejection of us, and the go set man brought a tired looking beatnick around to listen to the songs, he undoubtedly didnt like it, and so Mr david elfick simply became shy with us . . .

Proud and some friends had visited the Small Faces at their Sydney hotel in January 1968, and he had tried to talk to Andrew Loog Oldham. The wider meaning was clear: Elfick was kowtowing to what he saw as an international arbiter of opinion. On the other hand, says Proud:

> Some people who came to our house on friday heard the music and began exclaiming and laughing, they said i had a "whole metaphysical complex," what ever that means, and they became quite elated, so isn't that good?

He continues, baffled:

> People who meet us seem to get initially very excited, as david elfick, who then suddenly withdraw, and im not sure what this is. we think it may be due to the personal neurosis of inadequacy with some, whilst with others its perhaps a contempt derived from their inabilities they discover from comparing.

Proud told Oram that if the public decided "it's a send-up . . . well, all right. I will be disappointed, but there's nothing I can do about it." At the same time, he mixed an insistent dedication to success with despondency: "there is no market that can be easily reached. i do not wish to spend this year cultivating one." Similarly, he schemed:

> There are probably 50 people just like me in Australia, all saying the same things in different ways, and so how I am to succeed

> is by working into areas where they would not go.—The first album was a good example of this.

And:

> For, you see, the artist sets the fashion in music and so people buy his music, which has made itself fashionable. If i cannot succeed in making myself fashionable, then some one else will make me unfashionable.

"I am already regarded as Australia's top underground singer," he told Hobbs. Proud was in his early twenties at this time, and it's possible his arch style was working against him in a scene which prided itself on being both mellow and unassuming. Penniless—he often did not have enough to eat—he boasted of a largesse that was plainly beyond his wildest dreams. David Elfick reported in *Go-Set* that Proud had "tried to go into the Sydney Public Library last week but was barred because he had no shoes on" and quoted Proud declaring he had "decided to offer the director of the library $1,000 if he would allow bare feet into libraries."

The Australian arm of Philips was one label that did not seem to object to fairly low record sales; furthermore, *Adreneline and Richard* must have been extremely cheap to make—the product of less than a day's recording, and very little mixing. While it is uncertain how well it sold, it was sufficient for them to consider more product from this source. Proud wrote to Hobbs that he had written a song he thought appropriate for a single, and "We took a tape to Philips—they liked the song very much but will not record it until we get a drummer. This could be recorded privately for about $50 . , ." Elfick wrote that the song was "one of a series of songs that Pip wrote on the Titanic disaster," an unintentionally amusing garbling, but telling nonetheless (although there are no songs on the second album, *A Bird in the Engine,* that obviously fit this bill). In March 1969, *The Bulletin* told its readers that "his new records will have the music of bass, drums, and even a cello, so perhaps some musicianship will be managed without the pretentiousness he says he dreads so much. Certainly, if he's only feigning his dread, he's taking a lot of trouble to maintain the pose." (Of his fans, Proud apparently said: "I think half of them come along to see how bad I am.")

The short-lived Pip Proud Group featured two young men he met at a party: John Black on bass and Peter Fairlie on drums. "Tomorrow," wrote Michael Symons in *The Australian,* "he spends five hours at another studio recording four possible singles and a fifth if he has learnt piano in time." He might have done so, and he might have involved Black and Fairlie, but no single or Pip Proud Group recording emerged and the Group dissolved.

In 1969 Proud recorded a second album accompanying himself on guitar in a small, cheap studio in the inner-city Sydney suburb of Darlinghurst. Most of the tracks on this album were sufficiently similar (and of similar high quality) to have appeared on the first; there was, however, a truly extraordinary title track in which Proud was accompanied by a friend, Harry Parsons, banging a microphone on a cardboard box to create a thunderous, evil sound which presaged art-punk by a decade.

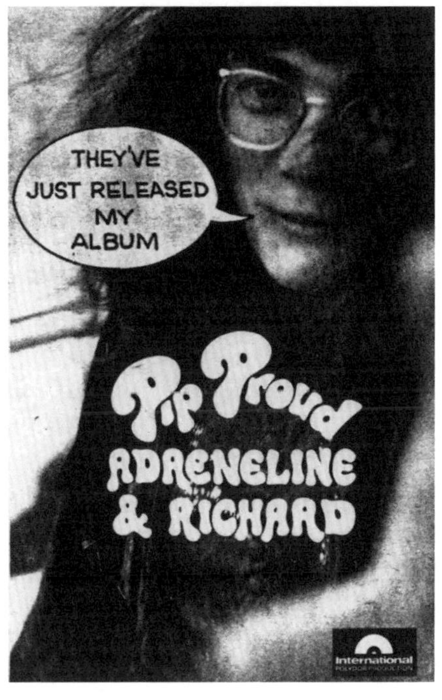

Proud played very few live shows in Sydney in the late 1960s. His debut was at one of a series of anti-war concerts presented by Arts Vietnam at Paddington Town Hall on October 3, 1968, along with Nutwood Rug and Peter Anson's group, the Id. The following February, Proud presented his play, *Al mond*, "involving four characters. They are Ellis, who is the protagonist, a girl named Madrid, her sister Ruth and another character of doubtful definition called Osborne." This production was not, from all reports, a major success, and audience members booed during its performance. In April 1969, he organised two concerts under the title The Best in the World. This was the name of a new song he had written (not about himself), but the use of the title in this context was, of course, provocative. He told Hobbs that "over a thousand people attended both concerts." One of these people was Michael Dransfield, an up and coming poet who was besotted by Proud's music and introduced himself backstage. The two would become inseparable for a time, Dransfield going out with Alison Burns' sister Hilary and the four of them flatting together in the six months before Proud and Burns left.

In October 1968, with no obvious impetus from Proud himself, *Go-Set* had used a picture of the singer in a competition they were running, irresponsibly offering one lucky reader the chance to "Win a one way ticket anywhere." Even more ridiculous than usual for *Go-Set*, the competition—which does not appear to have had a winner—was described as "for people who want to pursue their groove. Once you find your groove, you probably won't want to come back." In late 1969, Proud worked to find his groove, mending washing machines and saving money to go to Europe. In November, *Go-Set* readers were told:

> Pip has left for England where he hopes to crack the big time. He already has a couple of people interested in his work and has a contact in Apple records. Pip has become very interested in Archeology and hopes to do some field work on the subject when he goes to Abyssinia.

London was, however, a disappointment. Apple were, of course, deluged with tapes from hopefuls. The BBC DJ John Peel was more encouraging; he had a label, Dandelion, at this time. Accessing a golfball typewriter with only capital letters, Proud wrote to Alison Burns' mother:

> I WENT AND SAW JOHN PEEL, AND HE IS VERY KEEN ON MY MUSIC AND ONLY APOLOGISED THAT HE COULDN'T GIVE ME A RECORD CONTRACT STRAIGHT OFF, BUT HE SAID HE'D SEE WHAT HE CAN DO, AND I'LL RING HIM TOMORROW. NOT WISHING TO SOUND TOO CASUAL, ACTUALLY IM IN UTTER EXCITEMENT.

"I AM REALLY TRYING FOR A HIT SINGLE," he bellowed across two continents and an ocean. "IF I GET THAT, JUST ONCE, WE CAN ALL RETIRE... THIS ISNT AUSTRALIA."

Burns joined him in London, but the trip was a dud. Proud finished a novel, *The White Forest,* which Dransfield was going to publish (but didn't). Starving in London is much like starving in Sydney, only much colder; the pair began their return to Australia, traveling across Europe and Asia (no Abyssinian archaeology is known to have been undertaken). It was in India that they discovered that Proud's adoptive sister had killed herself; his parents flew him back to Australia. It was an ignoble and tragic end to a great adventure. Pip wrote some more songs—recorded at home—and would go on to write poetry and plays for radio station 2JJ, but the initial reach for the stars was at an end. The death of his sister was also the beginning of the alcoholism he battled for the remaining forty years of his life.

In the late '70s, Proud wrote to Michael Hobbs. He'd just heard the Clash on the radio: "'I have no will to survive, i cheat if i can't win' . . . That's a line out of a "punk rock" song I'm listening to. You know, I'm starting to get this feeling of "what are the young coming to?" I say all of this to you because you thought maybe I was worth encouragement or something." Forty years later, a few months before his death in 2010, Proud contacted Hobbs again to apologise for his inability to pay him back.

Pip Proud was a unique and unusual artist. It would be easy to dismiss him, and many have. British "psychedelia" expert Vernon Joynson, for instance, brays his ignorance with a curt "Both albums are reputedly awful." It would also be simple to write off his work from this time as being of interest merely as an example of how far "out there" major record labels were willing to go in the late 1960s. This is true as far as it goes, but what is more important about Proud's work is that, regardless of when it happened, he was reinventing pop in a way that injected artistic and literary experiment and a brash, rebellious attitude.

Proud's work in the late 1960s demonstrates one of the core truths of Australian music history but also of the history of all art, everywhere—great visionaries are not always recognised in their time and great art is not always rewarded, but this neither enhances nor detracts from the value of their art. Pip Proud's biggest error—though it is an entirely understandable one—was to quit so early in the piece and let circumstances, together with others' ignorant low estimation of his abilities and his own doubts, take over.

His provocative 1970 "bio" in *Australian Poetry Now!* had cajoled and taunted its readers, whom he took to be eggheads. "Any displeasure," he wrote, "is due to your blindness or illusion." This statement could serve as an epitaph to his 1960s career.

Following the reissue of his Phillips albums by Nic Dalton's Half a Cow label in 1995, Pip Proud began writing and releasing music again in the late 1990s, primarily via the Austin label Emperor Jones. He released four albums—a compilation of unreleased 1970s and 1990s material, *One of These Days* (1998); two solo albums, *Oncer* (2000) and *A Yellow Flower* (2001) and a collaboration with Tom Carter, *Catch a Cherub* (2002). He suffered a stroke in 2002 which left him blind and partially paralyzed, at which point he moved from Tenterfield, in northern NSW, to Melbourne. He died in early 2010 from throat cancer.

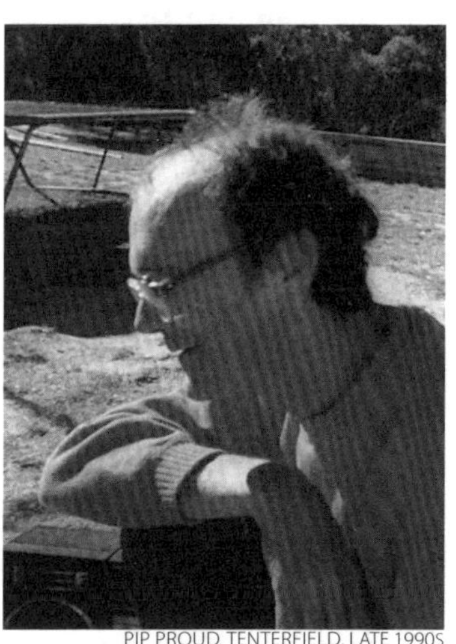
PIP PROUD. TENTERFIELD, LATE 1990S

THIRD EAR MUSIC

Two interviews with Maryanne Amacher

ILLUSTRATION BY SYLVIE SPENCER

The American musician/installation artist Maryanne Amacher was one of our favorite composers. When she died last year at the age of 71, we cast about to find some worthy interviews with her. The tough part of writing even the most brief introduction is describing her work to someone who's never heard it before. If you've ever been to La Monte Young and Marian Zazeela's "Dream House" installation, you know how the sound is pitched so that it sounds different depending on which way you turn your head. Amacher's work can employ similar sonic feats, but it goes much deeper, into the very architecture of the listener's skull and/or the space it's presented in.

As the Wikipedia robots describe, "she worked extensively with the physiological (not psychoacoustic) phenomenon called otoacoustic emission, in which the ears themselves act as sound generating devices. Amacher composed several 'ear dances' designed to stimulate clear 'third' tones coming from the listener's ears," and "her major pieces have almost exclusively been site specific, often using many loudspeakers to create what she called 'structure borne sound'... By using many diffuse sound sources (either not in the space or speakers facing at the walls or floors) she would create the psychoacoustic illusions of sound shapes."

I LIKE TO MAKE SHAPES IN THE HEAD AND IN THE EARS, AND I ALSO LIKE TO MAKE THEM IN THE ROOM

The following interview excerpt from ca. 1991 was found recently in Dr. Eliot Handelman's basement—typewritten and held together with a rusty paperclip. It was done for *Mondo2000* magazine (remember that?) but never published.

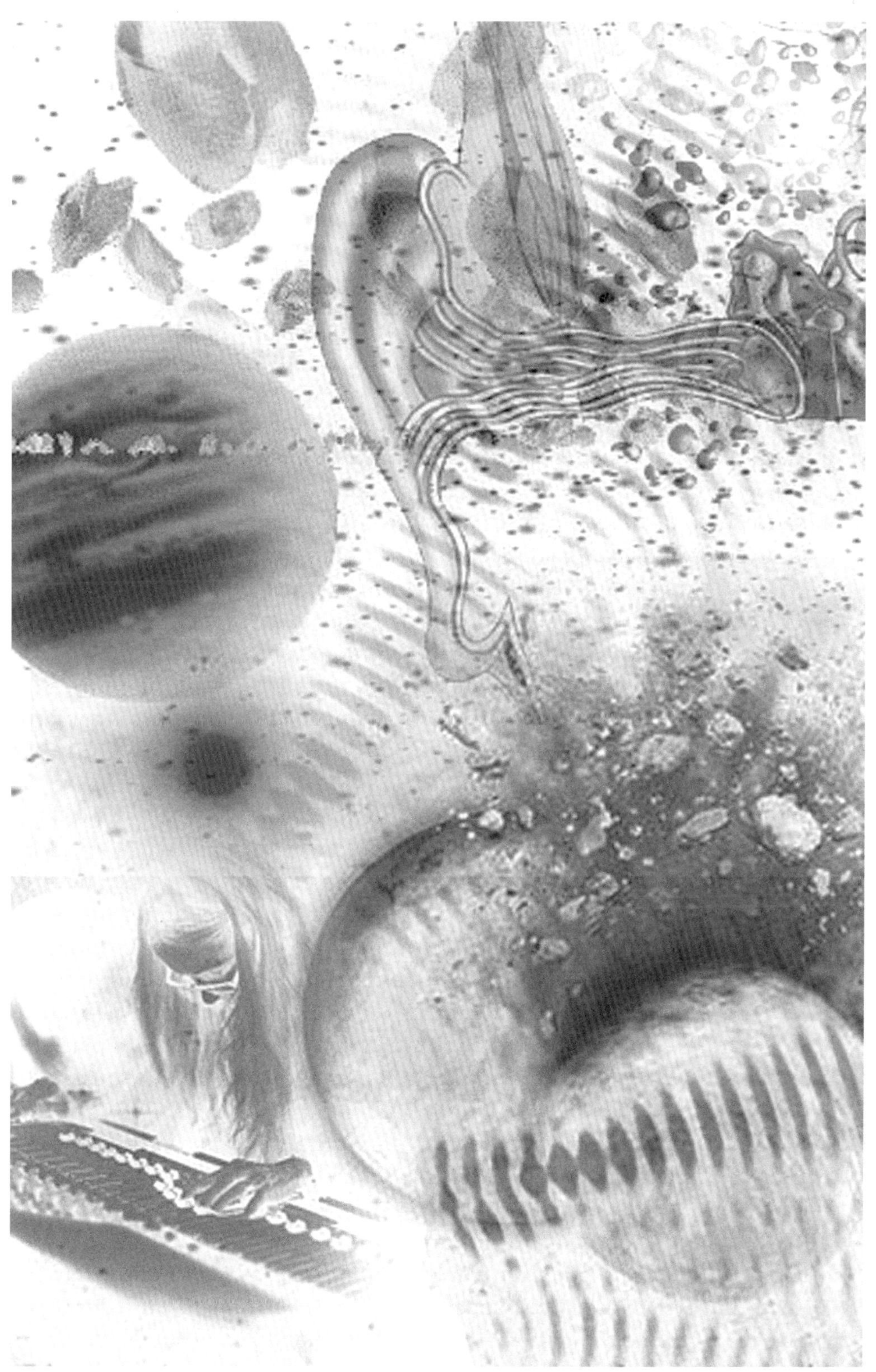

DR. ELIOT HANDELMAN: When I hear your music, sounds are streaming out of my head. What's going on?
MARYANNE AMACHER: Our ears act as instruments in responding to music, sounding their own tones in addition to the music in the room, like another instrument joining the orchestra. Neuroanatomy responds and gives shape to the most subtle traces of acoustic information. We hear tones other than the given acoustic tones taking their shape *inside* our ears, as the membrane vibrates in response to the given acoustic tones.

In music as we know it, such tone responses have been repressed. They have a subliminal existence, suppressed within the complex timbres of music. We're not aware that they exist, or that we're actually creating them as listeners. The experience of our own processing isn't available to us. I want to *release* this music, bring it out of subliminal existence. I want to make a music that is directed past the processing and control of acoustic information, into the network of the nervous system to what we do with this information perceptually.

I like to think of the listener responding to certain extremely sensitive resonant instruments within the anatomical structures of the inner ears. In effect, we 'listen' to what our auditory system perceives, detecting extremely subtle changes in the form of the vibration pattern. We 'hear' the coding response of an evolved sensitivity extracting information on details of the vibration pattern. That's where subjective pitch originates.
Are the auditory effects in your music precisely planned? If so, how do you plan them?
In my most recent music, I'm concentrating on explorations of our perceptual responses to music—tones and melodic patterns taking shape inside our ears and neuroanatomy—interaural rhythms, colors and spatial imaging, a 'virtual' sound world the listener crates in response to music. These virtual sounds and patterns originate in ears and neuroanatomy. I call them "ear-born sound" and "head-born sound." In planning these effects, an important part is to distinguish, first of all, *where* the music is to originate.

It might originate in acoustic space—out there in the room around us, as in a multi-speaker configuration, where you might have distant sound: sounds moving around the room in circles, spirals, squares, or other shapes. Or it might be intense close-up, concrete, locatable. It might come from the stage in front of us, as is usually the case. And then we have the interaural space, and that's here within us. That's what I characterize as "ear-born sound" and "head-born sound." What excites me musically is the interplay of aural and interaural sonic imaging. The convergence of these perceptual dimensions is really the main idea, a multi-dimensional construct. As yet I don't know what to call it. For now I call it "psybertonal topology"—the mapping of interaural spatial imaging with acoustic spatial imaging.

In your Music for Sound-Joined Rooms, *sound seems to become tactile. Why do I sense shapes in space?*

That work deals specifically with architecture: the music is staged architecturally. I mean that I don't just use a combination of speakers, although Naut Humon [aka Mark Sprague] and I gave a concert in Japan last summer, in Panasonic Hall, where there were 750 speakers, and we were able to make quite wonderful spatial configurations of sound. Staging music architecturally is quite different. It's allowing sound to become structure-borne. Sound travels much faster through structure than through air, so a normal middle C is going to be about 4'4". If that middle C is travelling through a structure it suddenly becomes 20'. The wavelength is so much larger that you can have quite a different energy, and the shapes take on a kind of presence which I'm not able to achieve with sound transmitted through the air.

Is composing for the architecture of the ear and brain anything like composing for spatial architectures?

These are quite different situations. I like to make shapes in the head and in the ears, and I also like to make them in the room. In these architecturally-staged works the idea is to create a world where architecture magnifies the expressive dimensions of music, diving down deep into the music in a way that is not so artificial as other ways of presenting music. The audience can walk into it as though they were walking into a cinematic close-up. Unlike a stage concert, where you just watch, you enter and become immersed in this close-up. And I discovered, while doing this architecture, that, to my amazement, an ordinary phrase could create such a dramatic effect, that you could almost *animate* this phrase as a sound character.

So my next step was to adopt the sequel format of the TV miniseries. And I created a new form that I called the "mini-sound series." I create an evolving context for these sound characters. They even have names, like "The Fright," or "The Hardbeat Force." I'm able to make intrigues, suspense, the whole story, in a serialized narrative form, which up to now has only been developed in TV and in comic books. What happens to "Wave #4" when it's set up to meet "The Fright"? "Deep and Deepest Tone" disappears. Was it really shot down by "The Hardbeat Force"? When it reappears two weeks later, it's supporting

"The Coast," who we know has fallen in love with "God's Big Noise." It's serialized musical continuity, in consecutive episodes.

It can sometimes take you days to set up a cinematic architecture, during which time you hardly sleep. What are you doing when you set up one of these rooms?

I'm learning the characteristics of the space. In Japan, recently, at Tokushima, where I presented *Synaptic Islands: a Psybertonal Topology*, I was mixing sounds staged in two totally different rooms. One of the rooms was a curved stone passageway that was like an old Gothic castle. It was a fantastic space acoustically, but there was a clear 10 decibel difference from the main space, where I was mixing. You can make spectacular acoustic effects with these different acoustics, if the audience is listening for a time in one space and suddenly the sound begins making something in the other. The two may interact, or fuse, or be utterly separate, or melodies may drift between the two. Sometimes the sound was not locatable, sometimes above you, on top of your head, directly inside your ears, inside your head.

Does the way in which virtual reality is currently expressed interest you?

I've always been interested in VR. Scott Fischer and I taught a course together many years ago at MIT called "Live Space." I taught the sound part, and Scott taught 3D imagery. At the time I was very much involved in creating *City Links*, a series of sonic telepresence works. I placed microphones in remote locations, in one city, sometimes between cities and even countries. I had an installation at MIT where the mike had been placed in Boston Harbor, using a dedicated telelink that was hooked into my studio for three years, going into my mixer. I could play the space. That is how I learned about the perception of dimension in sound, because there is very little experience of that in music.

Music is usually presented frontally, you don't hear sound a great, great distance away or very, very close. In the harbor, boats would enter and disappear. And that's a very exciting thing to apply to music. It was fascinating to realize that Boston Harbor had a basic tonality of f#, about 93 Hz., and in New York Harbor, where I also had a link, the basic tonality was an E, about 82 Hz.

Do you see any possibility with virtual technology for creating transportable environments, recordable to disc, which can be entered by anyone with the appropriate technology? You seem to be ambivalent about recording.

I haven't made recordings because it's very difficult to reproduce the kind of sound levels I use. My music is not conceived for playing in your living room, although I'm working on the kind of experience that *would* be good for your living room. The architectural element could not be

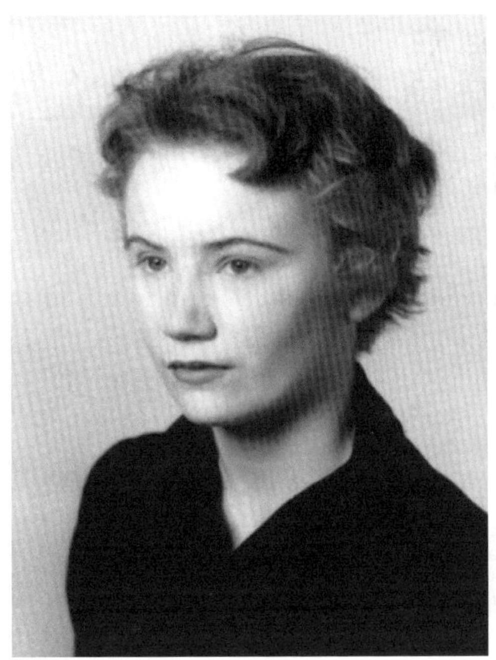

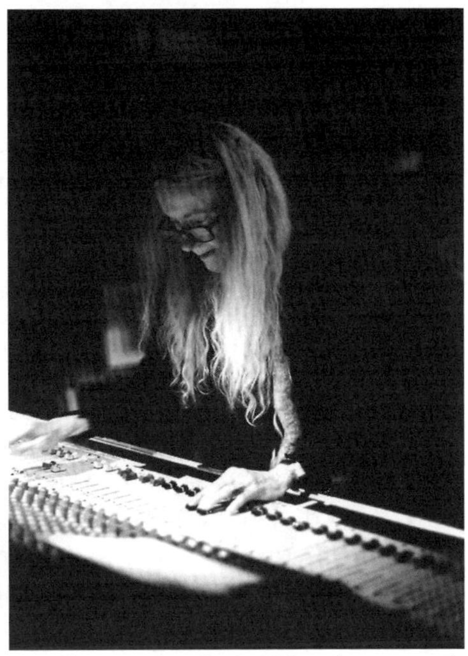

Maryanne Amacher in 1953, and more recently

recorded in 3D sound unless you had an enormous budget.

It doesn't excite me to be listening with headphones because I like to be standing, moving. When you move, your body hears differently: your skin, your ears, the whole neural-processing apparatus functions differently. The effect of sound streaming out of your head is lessened with headphones. I love the sensation that sound is coming with you, and at the same time you're hearing sound elsewhere in the room, like a sonic wrap.

Doesn't recording—even, potentially, virtual technology—unnecessarily confine *listeners to their living rooms? That this confinement, which, not coincidentally, ensures the repression of certain political energies, is a consequence of the 19th-century division of musical labor: active performer, passive listener?*

It's unfortunate that music is still presented as it was in the 19th century, frontally, instead of finding new ways of presenting events. There should be fantastic buildings for musical and sound productions. Not just a lot of speakers, but a really extraordinary architecture that you find your way in, that evolves. This will happen because there is a need for it.

Is the technology of the psybertonal topology therefore opposed to the technology of the HMD [head-mounted displays—remember those*]?*

It seems you're very interested in the technology, whereas, knowing that all early technologies are quite terminal, I'm more interested in perception. I think that VR will come to include physical architecture, where you could make 3D visual and physical sound productions, which you could be a part of with your body, and you no longer would have to wear a helmet.

But isn't that just what you're doing?

Yes, but my visual installations aren't 3D. Scott Fischer, who is also an artist, did incredible 3D photography, and my idea really arises from that. We need to use all of our technology in an exciting way, instead of mounting it as a one-night show.

Isn't it a bit utopian to imagine that architecture will come to substitute for VR? VR might eventually become a way of forgoing architecture, creating fantastic spaces which no one can afford to build.

Both are unique in their own way. In architecture you can create sound effects that can't be created any other way.

You want the most advanced means available of representing or constructing experience inside, whether in the home or within the body, with the alternative, the 'event,' occurring on the outside. But an 'event' is something unpredictable, like an earthquake.

What you say about events interests me very much, because by 1994 or 1995 there will be so many more wonderful ways to experience music and sound in your own living room. These outside events will become something very special. Naut Humon is also thinking in this way, trying to prepare events that are of a spectacular and extraordinary nature, so that if you're going to leave home you can actually experience something worthwhile. That's a consequence of technology that people will explore much deeper. Software will eventually be developed that generates variations of all music, and you'll have to ask yourself, "What am I doing as a musician?" If a variation of your music can be made five minutes after you've composed it, then you'll be forced to imagine much further. Most music amounts to a rearrangement of the figures and patterns of other men's music, in a personalized sequence of time. In order to go beyond that, you'll need to begin with the physical spectrum itself, with effects based on a very precise knowledge of the listening mind.

NOTHING WITHOUT THE OOMPH

Here we have Maryanne Amacher in conversation with Frank J. Oteri. This interview was done on April 16, 2004, in Kingston, New York. It was videotaped by Randy Nordschow then transcribed by Molly Sheridan and Randy Nordschow and later published on the NewMusicBox website (the web magazine from the American Music Center, http://newmusicbox.org) and reprinted here with their kind permission.

FRANK J. OTERI: The work you do inhabits its own unique realm that is sometimes quite at odds with most of the presentational aspects we take for granted with most music: it's really not meant to be listened to the same way in time, in space or in volume . . . So, how you feel about describing your work as music? How does it fit in with the history of music of the past and how it points to the music of the future?

MARYANNE AMACHER: Well that's a difficult question [*laughs*]. Are you thinking of concert music?

I'm thinking of the role that music has had in society, the relationship people have to it as listeners, the context of concerts, recordings, how it's assimilated, how it's taught, how it's learned, how it's acculturated in different societies. What you're doing seems to be somehow beyond that. Obviously it uses sound, tone, and timbre, but it's doing something else.

I think I know how I can discuss that with you, but first I'm wondering if you're thinking more of concerts because occasionally people react and say, "Oh, this is a *real* experience . . ." because of the staging and presentation. I guess it's also because of the music, but I'm interested in making a very different situation for people. From the very beginning, I wanted to do experiential work. I was working with electronic means, therefore I could sit and observe various things. I could try to understand more about what was happening to my ears, to my body, all over.

I think I do music because I'm trying to understand. The ear-tones that I played for you are referred to as otoacoustic emissions. I heard those very early on when I was beginning to work, so I wanted to create a kind of music where the listener actually has vivid experiences of contributing this other sonic dimension to the music that their ears are making. I've become very involved with situations like that. My approach is more like in science, although music is emotional and everything else. I sit and listen and I hear things, then I discover how I can expand them or increase them and try to understand them. I think of them as perceptual geographies actually.

"Ways of hearing"—how we hear things far away; how we hear things close. How suddenly in your head there almost is sound, continuing and continuing. It's particularly effective after very strong sections with enormously long fades, but it has to be done in such a way that the sonic shapes are lingering in your mind afterwards. I believe a lot of music, particularly as it developed from the past, was really a rearrangement of the figures of other men's music—I'm not talking about sampling—but it's just snatching little things and doing your own personalized sequence in time. Whereas, I think my tendency was

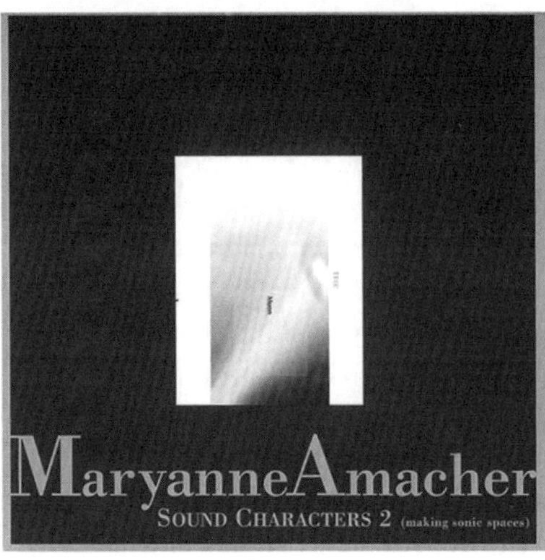

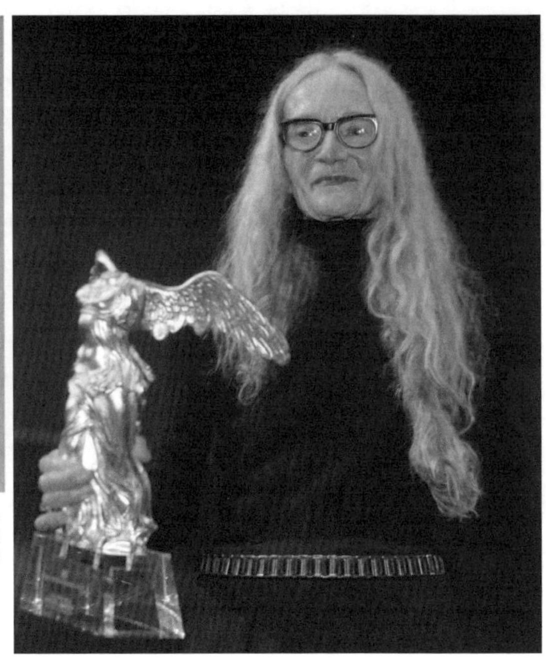

Left: cover of Amacher's 1999 release on Tzadik, *Sound Characters*; right: holding the prestigious "Golden Nica" award for Digital Music in 2005 (Eliane Radigue won the following year)

to become much more involved in the so-called physics—I don't like the word psychoacoustics— both of music and how our perceptual experience changes when sounds are just traveling around here and it sounds like it's miles away, when it seems like it's only in your head...

You studied with Stockhausen; he was certainly a forerunner of the work you do. He was one of the pioneers of having multiple speakers and later, he did a work that was an entire house, every room had different music happening on it.

I was fortunate in that the first electronic music I heard was in Cologne on multiple speakers. Being a fan of Varèse, I immediately connected to imagining the spacialization of sound, and then to have had the wonderful opportunity to study a little bit with Stockhausen, it was just incredible.

At the same time, there's something so human about the music that you're creating and how people's ears are responding. It's so fundamentally human even though it's all created with machines, with electronics; there's something wonderfully contradictory and beautiful about that. And this is a music that could only be created in our lifetime. Maybe you could get strings or the human voice to do this...

Of course.

But that's not what you do. Is that something you'd be interested in doing?

Well, of course I could. But the advantage for me is I don't care. It doesn't matter to me that they're machines or computers. I think what was of value was the possibility of being able to work this way, that you could sit and listen and observe things, observe shapes.

There is a situation when you have architecture as I'm describing it—physical architecture, these larger spaces. It is a very communal thing and because of the dimensions of the space itself connecting to the music in the way it does, it creates a very liberating experience. I mean, people dance. It's very different than if you're in a small place or particularly if you're keeping your seat. I think it's known that you actually experience sound better when you move, which also connects to dancing.

So what constitutes a performance?

It's just me mixing. Of course there are visual elements, and the performance with the people: I'm mixing live and I'm connecting with an audience rather than just having this on a hard drive.

And the mixing that you're doing, you're responding to the audience as they are there, so there is an element of improvisation to it, if you would? How much of it is predetermined?

See that's when you get into this funny area. [*laughs*] Music is crazy... it's insane. Of course I'm improvising. But I'm not improvising the notes.

Right. The notes are there, prerecorded.

Yes, or else I might be making them with samplers or something, but I'm not having the notes come out of my head. What I'm doing is dealing with these perceptual degrees, degrees of sensitivity, degrees of intensity, and things like that. Not the notes because you can play something a million different ways.

In a weird sort of way you're almost doing what a conductor does with an orchestra. Bringing out the woodwinds in a certain passage, etc...

Yes. I never thought of it that way, but it is like that because the basic music is in a way very raw. It's nothing without the oomph. I mean I've come back from these works to where we're sitting now and it takes me over a month to be able to even hear. I have learned what I've been able to learn because I have worked in these situations.

You formulate ideas in your studio before they ever have a life as a work in the space they are intended for. What sort of process generates the decisions that you make here about the pitch content, let's say?

Well, I'm concerned with various tunings. That's one thing.

Microtonal scales?

Sure. And I'm very interested in what are called second order effects in psychoacoustics, which are not the ear phenomena when you tune very close—when you do it with unison it has to be binaural or else you just get beats—but when the beats disappear and you get closer and closer to the 3rd or the 5th or whatever interval and it turns into a shape. I've always been very preoccupied with these different shapes, and of course I have particular frequencies I like, too. But it's the shapes, when it gets really slow and huge, and you're not hearing the beats but it is a beat frequency that's producing the shape. It's something that I've experienced, again, only because I work experientially.

I used to move from studio to studio always trying to tune these oscillators to get these things. [*Sigh*] They would drift and it was making me crazy. Once I got locked into the Queens studio all weekend and it was 98 degrees. After that I thought I was never going to do this kind of work again until I had my own setup.

Shortly after that it was great to read this article in *Scientific American* called "Auditory Beats in the Brain" [October 1973]. The author, biophysicist Gerald Oster, did many experiments and people experienced these different shapes as spirals... They perceived them in the experiments he made. It was really helpful to me. I later met him in New York.

Now, in terms of perception, most of the music around us these days—whether it's commercial popular music or classical music, jazz, or even most experimental music—is created within a pitch grid of twelve-tone equal temperament and anything else is somehow alien. The ear can hear so much more than that, yet if you're not acclimated, you might perceive anything else as indistinguishable or as being out of tune. How important for you is audience perception? Is it important to you that they hear what you're hearing?

I'm not sure we always hear the same things, but I think what I was just talking about with pattern modulation, when you get these shapes, I think everyone experiences that. I don't know if it's so much a matter of everyone experiencing what I'm experiencing. But I would like it, whatever it is, to be vivid and have a kind of reality to it. It's not based on some kind of habit. These are vivid experiences. Yours might be different than mine... I don't think I could do it with two speakers. I don't even like to do it with multi-speakers, with 15 speakers all around because all this direct sound loses a kind of magic.

In a book about John Cage that you contributed an essay to, you brought up something that I thought was so interesting about how music is packaged. We have this notion that everybody has to have the same experience of a pop song or a Mozart recording. You have a big audience that comes to hear a performance and they all should be hearing the same thing, but in fact no one hears the exact same thing. Each person is different and does not hear things the same way. As you said, a work of art, a painting, or a sculpture, is a singularity, only one of it exists. You might reproduce it in a book, but it's not the work. Whereas with music, we have a notion that it's reproducible. There can be 1,000 copies of a recording of Mozart's Jupiter Symphony or the latest Ricky Martin pop single, and they're exactly the same. But the reality is much subtler than that. Each person has his or her own music and that is something that hasn't really been addressed in the history of music.

I have no doubt that will be one part of music in the future. Today with all the customization and tailoring, you no longer have to necessarily think about music for millions. Music can be for millions, but it can actually be tailored for a specific individual. Just yesterday a chemist at UCLA who used techniques from nanotechnology took yeast cells and made a nano device which he used to discover that the cells produce sounds. It's not proven yet. These were just yeast cells, which were supposedly emitting a frequency that could be heard. The frequency was about a C-sharp or D one octave about middle C. They're very hopeful that if it's proven, it could be very beneficial for health purposes. This connection of music to certain cells is basically what I talked about in the article about Cage. The person creating the music may eventually be able to create certain movements in the cells themselves. *Living Sound, Patent Pending*, which I made in 1980, was one of the projections.

Not too long ago there was a microbiologist in San Diego and he spilled this sample on a CD, a music CD. He didn't realize it right away and he tried to put it in the player and of course it didn't play. Because he was very clever he worked out this whole idea—which I can't explain well right now—of the genetic detecting of the protein molecules, which is an expensive operation. These machines are like $300,000 in each lab. He was able to do that, maybe not quite as exact, but using this crazy technique and an ink jet printer that he got at a garage sale for $20. He wasn't talking about it producing sounds, see that's the catch. I just made my first work in this futurist projection, which is really just quite fun. I didn't have anything else, so I put my blood on the CD, and of course I put some sound. I called it *Interactive Precursor, First Protein Modulation.*

But then I thought more and more about it. Won't it be fantastic because everyone says, "Oh, CDs. We're just going to get everything from streaming live." So this will be a great use for a CD. Then, you know, you can mix different things like our bloods and so on and see how that interacts with the music [*laughs*].

In terms of the physical nature of different people responding to sound in different ways and it being a personalized experience for everybody, you discovered something very early on that's been a very key part of your vocabulary, and this is this music for the "third ear." As I listened I actually felt something; I felt my ear vibrating. It was startling.

It was a very intense physical experience. I think the only other time I'd ever felt it was when music had been too loud and it was painful. It's something we're actually taught to avoid. But this wasn't painful. This was something else. It was actually rather the opposite of painful. It felt like my ears were being tickled. It is a very, very interesting phenomenon. How did you first stumble upon these sounds? How do you use them? Why do they do that? How did you get my ears to do that?

It's another one of those things that I observed very early. It was all part of this notion of perceptual geographies. In 1977, the theory was proven—even though this was postulated by Thomas Gold in 1948—that the ear actually emits sound as well as receives it. So there are laboratories all over the world dedicated to this. Now see, this is what I think is funny about music—none of us know this. What in the world are we doing? I mean really to compose consciously.

I've been trying half of my life to get this program where I can really know that if I choose a second combination of tones that this low D-sharp is going to have a certain kind of timbre that my ear is making, a certain quality, rather than if I choose another one. I really want to know this, because this same low D-sharp of 77hz will sound from many different intervals. You know it's a bit obscured by the timbres, right? But our ears are doing this all the time. So these things can be reinforced or they can be enhanced for a more vivid experience in the music you create.

You played us a QuickTime file of an organist playing the famous Bach Toccata and Fugue in D minor, with video of what it was doing to someone's ear. The more voices that were added to that famous chord in the beginning, the more things started appearing in the ear as a response. So if this has been a part of all the music we hear, why is it that until I heard your music this afternoon, I wasn't aware of it?

I guess that's what fascinates me with it because this is a very fundamental thing. And, not only that, in laboratories they test hearing this way and they test babies—and you can actually listen to another person's ear, even. These are called otoacoustic emissions or SOAEs. If you're in a quiet enough place some people actually are able to hear the sound that's coming out of another person and this is not stimulated by sound.

But this has never been part of the vocabulary. This is not part of the vo-

cabulary of music in any culture, or at least not the conscious vocabulary as far as I know...

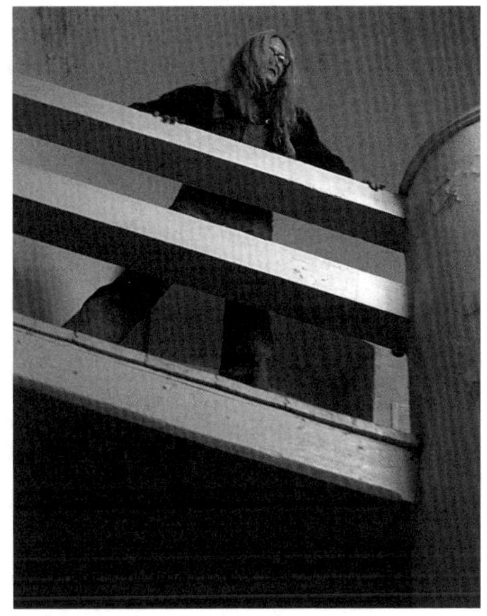

Not so true, I mean look at all the Tibetan and Mongolian people singing to make those results. I'm sure they know what they want to make and they have conscious effects. Maybe they don't think about it the same way. It's even speculated that in really vivid performances of, you know, concertos or what have you, people are bringing out some of these qualities. What's exciting for me is because all this has sort of been subliminally experienced in our music, because of the complexity of the overtones and everything, it's exciting to think of the kind of energy that could be released when it's not suppressed anymore. Imagine an audience in a concert hall just creating this music that's a part of the string quartet at the same time.

I'd like to get back to your essay in the book about Cage after what you just said about listening to something for 24 hours. This is one of the things that really got me very excited about talking to you and there's this quote that appears in that same essay that reinforced it. You wrote: "As the possibilities of all-sound music of the future were to Cage, the possibilities of alltime music are to me. In theory, years, weeks, days minutes, seconds will be possible." So there no longer needs to be this notion of a piece of music, a string quartet that's half an hour long, or a three-minute pop song, or a two or three-hour opera. Your music seems to exist beyond time; it's not really about time, at least not in a metrical sense...

Not that kind of time, it's more like the time in life when something appears and disappears and maybe you don't hear it again for a half hour, you may not hear it for an hour. Suddenly a boat appears after five hours and it gets closer and closer, you know, and makes an approach. It's time like that because we have the means now to do that.

But when you create a work you don't think about whether something is going to last 20 minutes or 2 hours. Or do you?

Well, as a composer I am fascinated by this. I see what I wrote about in that article as really an expansion of classical music, of phrase structure. We used to call it the elemental line. It's like you're trapped, one thing has to come after another. It was always my obsession to get out of the elemental line. I studied medieval metaphysics and I used to try to think of ways of making a macrostructure. Particularly, if you're trained as a musician you do this or that because this is the right note to play and it's all based on habit. I did a psycho-analysis of all my musical habits in order to try to stretch them.

You played us some excerpts and they were these cyclical things that happened and we didn't hear it in its entirety. Is it important to hear the entire thing?

Well I don't know if it is on the CD. It certainly is in the actual hall. Some people relate to CDs better than me. I have a little problem with it... My music is so dense and has so many parts that to me it sounds like all these spirits are trapped in these boxes [gestures to a speaker] trying to get out and it sounds very harsh. Right now I'm very excited because I've never heard any of my music at the higher sampling rates and I think that will make a difference. It's never going to be the same as architecture but at least maybe these parts won't be so trapped and you'll be hearing some of the dimension.

Let's talk then about live performances where people will go and hear this work that exists in four rooms. Does this work then have a beginning, middle, and end? Do people show up at a certain time?

No, they show up at the beginning. For awhile I did another series called the *Mini-Sound Series*. It got more and more interesting the more I did it in different places because the idea was like television where the story continues the next week, and it was a fascinating involvement with the audience. It was not continuous music. We can make sounds go on for as long as we want. I'm more interested in making appearances and things like that.

My first work was doing more or less pure installation work with these *City Links* pieces in which I brought in remote sounds. I had microphones in different remote environments and brought up those sounds in the gallery or museum or wherever. It also involved performance. The sound was alive and it came through high quality telephone lines— people always thought I was playing a cassette. It was just hard for them to realize at that time that this was actually live sound. It was also very interesting to have more than one location and the kind of simultaneous synchronic things that would happen. You know, there are no laws. ✪

TULI KUPFERBERG'S BIRTH PRESS

With selections from some hard-to-find publications

ILLUSTRATION BY DREW CHRISTIE

Eighty-seven-year-old writer, cartoonist, publisher and singer Tuli Kupferberg is best known as co-founder of the rock band the Fugs, or perhaps (now that it's attained Criterion Collection status) for his role as the crazy longhair running about with a rifle in Dusan Makavejev's polemical 1971 masterpiece *W.R.: Mysteries of the Organism*. For many years Kupferberg was a highly prolific publisher and writer of screeds and rants that remain funny as fuck.

Where in the great cultural card catalog of the world does Tuli fit? He's always had the comedic timing and an aesthetic sensibility that is aligned as closely to the Borscht Belt as it is to the Beats with whom he was lumped. And you could call him a beatnik—many have, after all—but he feels more Beat-by-association, or latter-day Beat. His work is closer to Peter Orlovsky's and Taylor Mead's than to Gregory Corso's and Herbert Huncke's, either way. He was not serious, except when he was being serious about not being serious. A book from 1961 is called *3,000,000,000,000,000,000,000,000,000,000,000,000,000 Beatniks: or, The War Against the Beats*, which is hugely awesome. Another book, from 1994, is called *I Hate Poems About Poems About Poems*. In conclusion: he doesn't really fit anywhere. If you're writing him up for an alt-weekly and have very few words, it'd be fair to say his schtick is both post-Beat and proto-punk. Be sure to mention that one of his books is called *My*

Prick is Bigger Than Yours. And there, you're over your word count already, bub.

When Tuli sang . . . well, he never could really sing. And he could rarely afford typesetting back in the pre-desktop publishing days. His stuff has always been highly accessible, in its own way. If only he'd been just a tad less crude, or better looking, or sonorous, or a tad less crude, he'd have been hugely popular, a regular on *Laugh-In*, at the very least. Consider the career of Tiny Tim: Tuli would have been a millionaire if he could've only just not said "fuck" so much, or if his song titles had been a little different than "Kill for Peace." Thank Yahweh, Kupferberg used the prism of crudeness to convey his thoughts; generations of weirdos have rightfully claimed this filthy old man as *ours*.

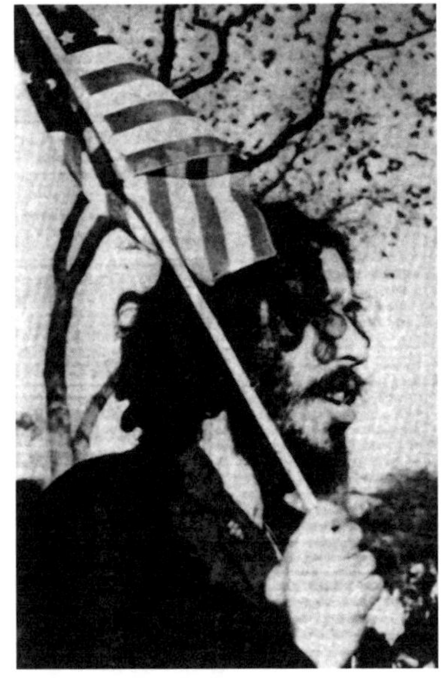

A few of his efforts were decent moneymakers, notably the groundbreaking pacifist tract he co-authored with Robert Bashlow, *1001 Ways to Beat the Draft*, which was reprinted several times, and the *As They Were* books he edited with his longtime companion and collaborator Sylvia Toop. Those books, which sold tens of thousands of copies, consisted of images of famous people early on: a simple concept, but done really well. The two also published the anonymous art and writings of children at a time when most people paid no heed to such work (in 1959).

In the next issue we'll be publishing an awesome interview with Kupferberg that was conducted for public access cable about fifteen years ago by the aunt of a friend of ours. Right now we'd like to praise Kupferberg's work as compiler and publisher for Birth Press, which got started in 1958. I think of the Birth Press titles that I own, many of which hew to one subject—death, sex, stimulants, the hilarious 1962 *The Mississippi (A Study of the White Race)*—as miniature alternative encyclopedias. They're a lot like a great web site, one you can hold in your hand and that smells funny because it's been sitting in the back of a used record shop for many years before you lucked out and found a copy.

Kupferberg's health has been in decline the last few years. Recently, the producer Hal Wilner held a benefit to help offset some of the costs associated with his care. One way to keep up with him is via his youtube channel, http://www.youtube.com/tulifuli.—*MM*

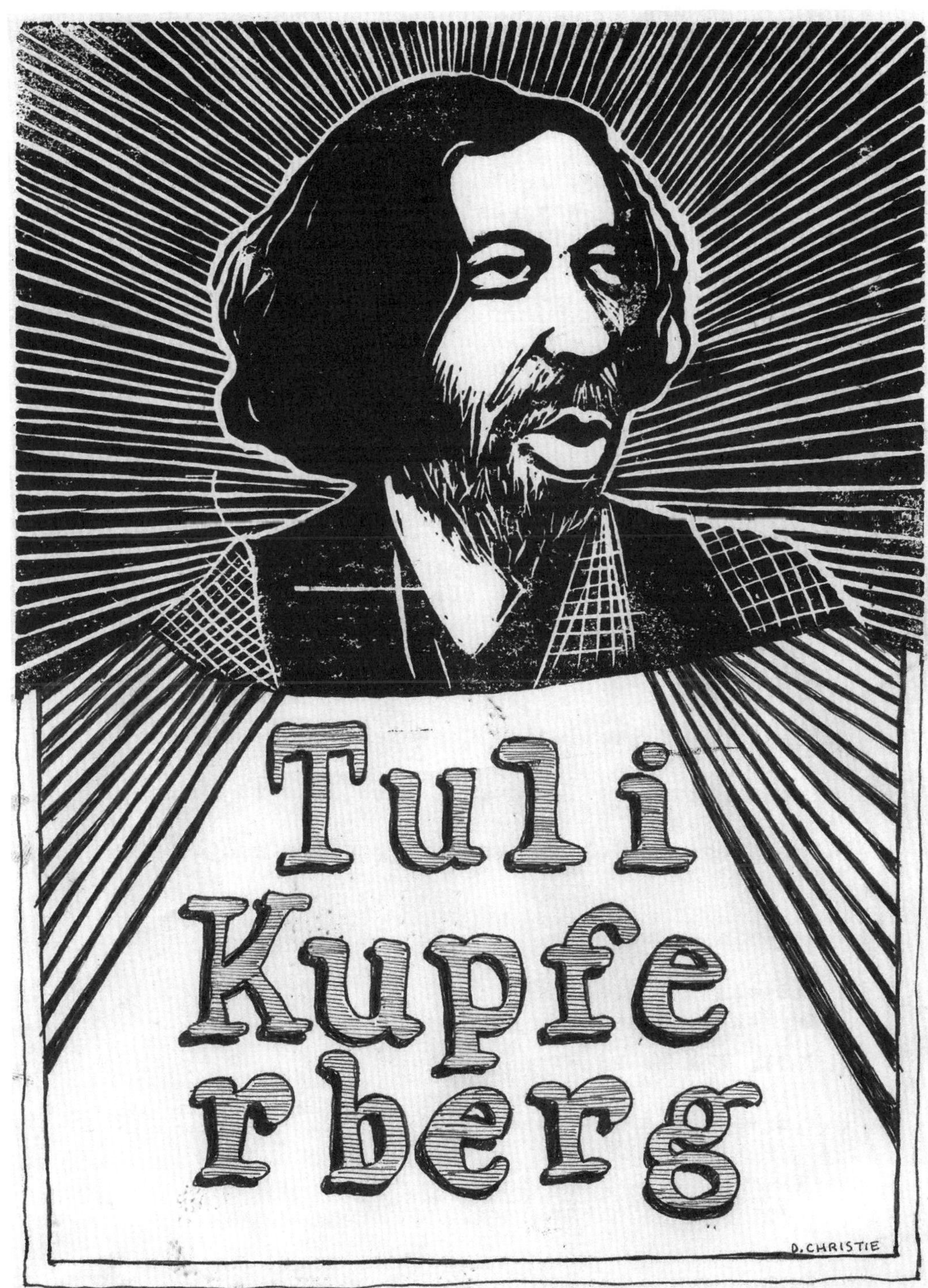
Tuli
Kupfe
rberg
D. CHRISTIE

If I do not believe that reality is in
any way real
How shall I say that dreams are dreams
Japanese

I BOHEMIA

1.A country without boundaries or inhabitants. Everyone is on a tourist visa. Although the terrain is monotonous there are those who claim to have seen a world in a grain of opium. Sex is admired but no one speaks the language.
Bring your own heart.

2.There are many roads to paradise.
The Bohemian stands at the crossroads and stares.

3.The candidate is young.
Bohemia is old.

4.Sometimes I capitalize Bohemianism, sometimes I do not.
Sometimes it is important, sometimes it is not.

5.The Kings of Bohemia are kings whose subjects are kings.

6.Bohemia is now.

7.Between the idea
And the reality

Falls the bookdealer

8.I dreamt I dwelt in Bohemia.

9."Hobohemia"
I dreamt I woke up in Hobohemia.

3

From *Birth* No. 1 (1958)

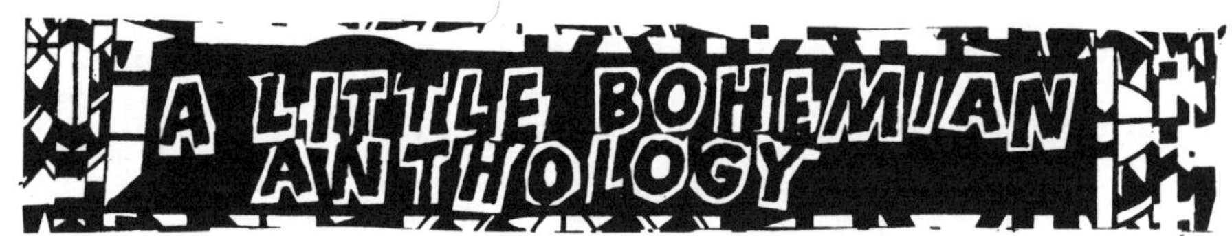

Our ship hath touch'd upon
the desarts of Bohemia.
WINTER'S TALE,III,iii,1.

...if out of dust and grime
Impossible beauty flamed and flowered
once upon a time
If a boy and a girl for a year and a day
laughed bravely at despair
No one will know in Christopher Street
and certainly none will care.
FLOYD DELL

1.Joyeux enfants de la Boheme
Rions du sort et de ses coups!
La societe qui nous aime,
Nous garde, pour l'heure supreme,
Quand meme,
A tous,
Un lit a l'hopital des fous.
CHARLES BATAILLE
(qui donna raison a ces vers en mourant fou

2.J'entends par bohemiens cette classe d'individus dont l'existence est un probleme, la condition un mythe, la fortune une enigme, qui n'ont aucune demeure stable, aucun asile reconnu, qui ne se trouvent nulle part et que l'on rencontre partout, qui n'ont pas un seul etat et qui exercent cinquante professions, dont la plupart se levent le matin sans savoir ou ils dinerat le soir, riches aujourd'hui, affames demain, prets a vivre honnetement s'ils le peuvent, et autrement s'ils ne peuvent pas.
MONTORQUEIL,in Les Bohemiens de Paris,
Adolphe d'Ensernet Grange,1843.

59

HOW TO

D.—AGREEABLENESS.

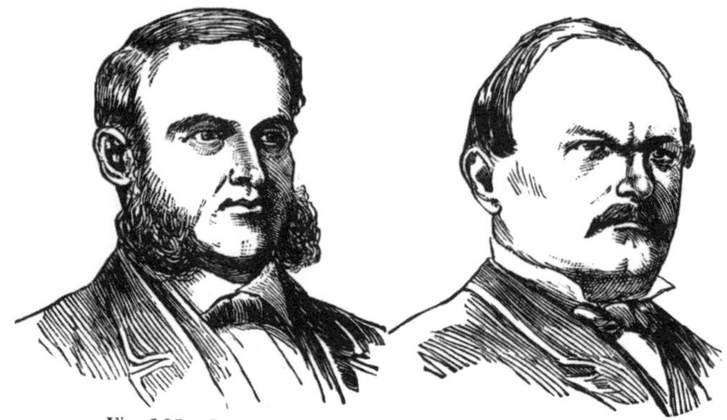

Fig. 103.—LARGE. Fig. 104.—SMALL.

2.—PARENTAL LOVE.

(Philoprogenitiveness.)

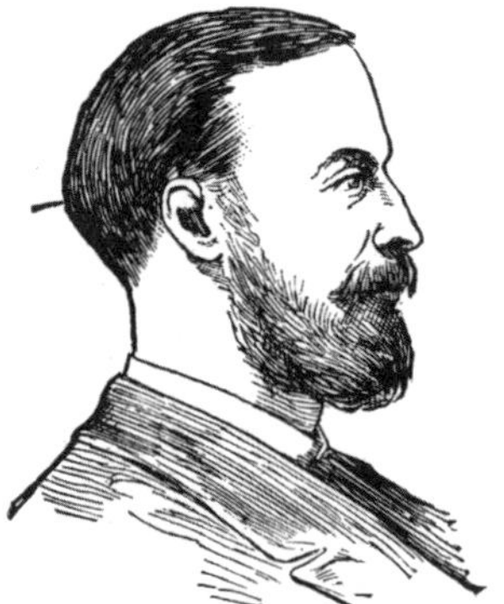

Fig. 25.—LARGE.

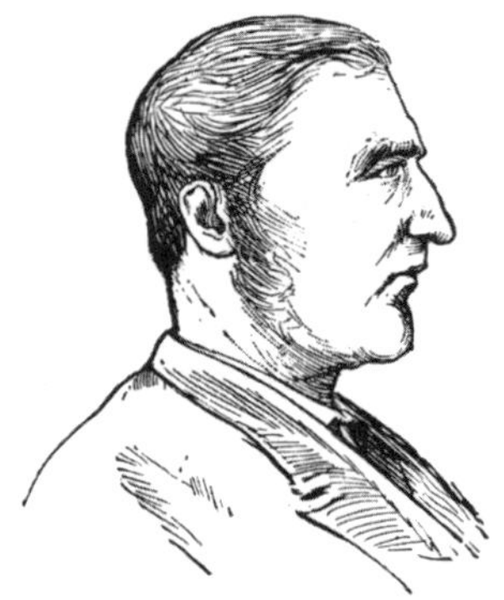

Fig. 26.—SMALL.

LARGE.

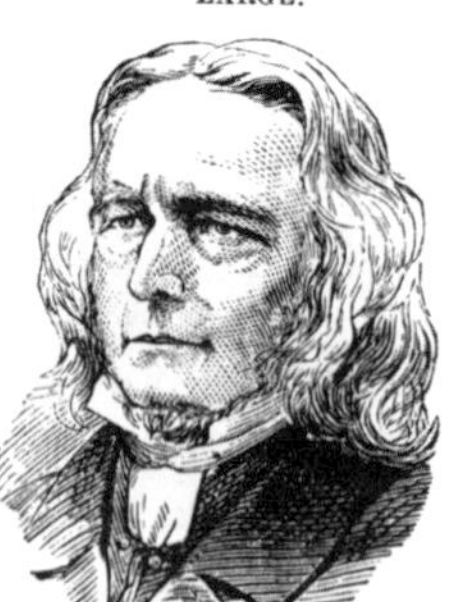

FIG. 13.—T. WORCESTER, D.D.

SMALL.

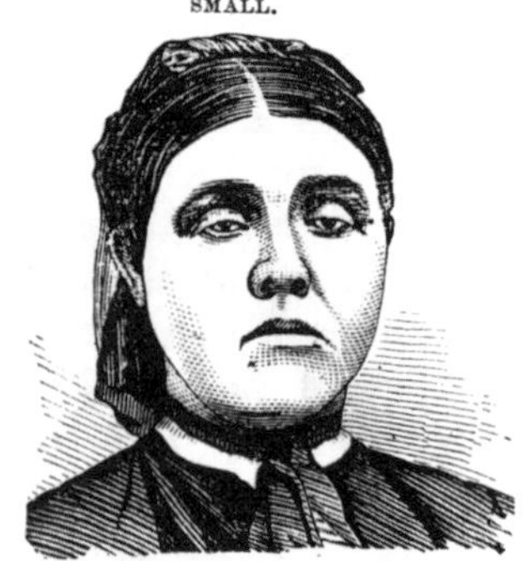

FIG. 14.—BRIDGET DURGAN.

THE MORAL SENTIMENTS.

From *The Grace & Beauty of the Human Form, Tastefully Selected and Arranged by Tuli Kupferberg* (1961)

SMALL.

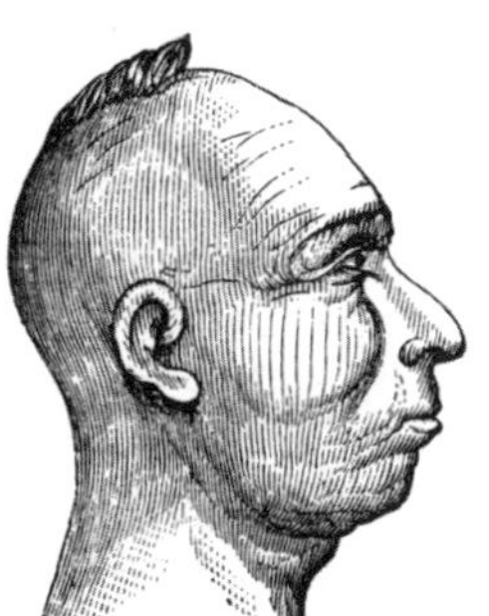

Fig. 16.—Black Hawk.

LARGE.

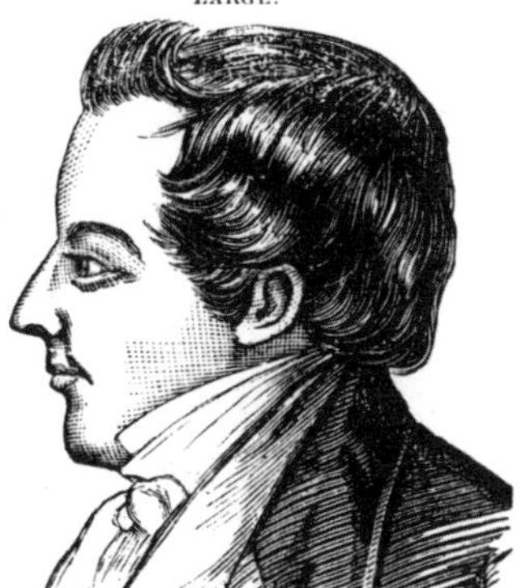

Fig. 17.—Joseph Smith.

THE SOCIAL GROUP.

11. CAUTIOUSNESS

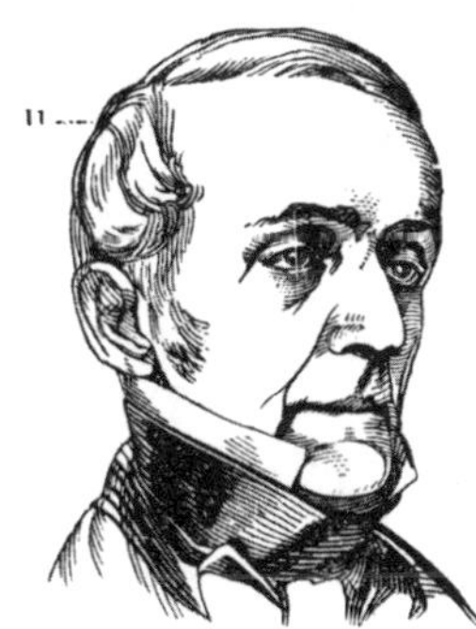

No. 65. Large.

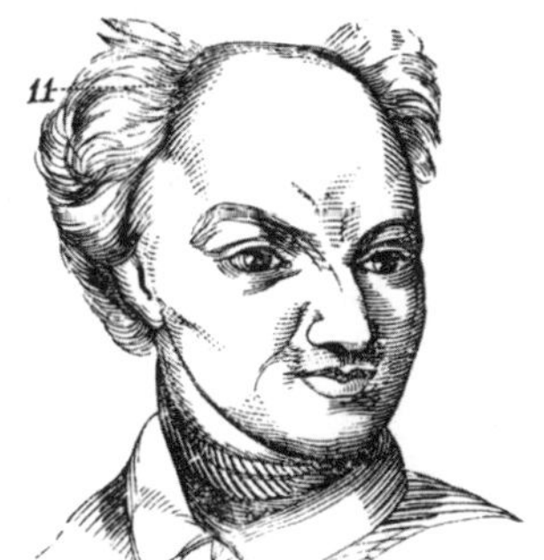

No. 66. Small.

LOW QUALITY.

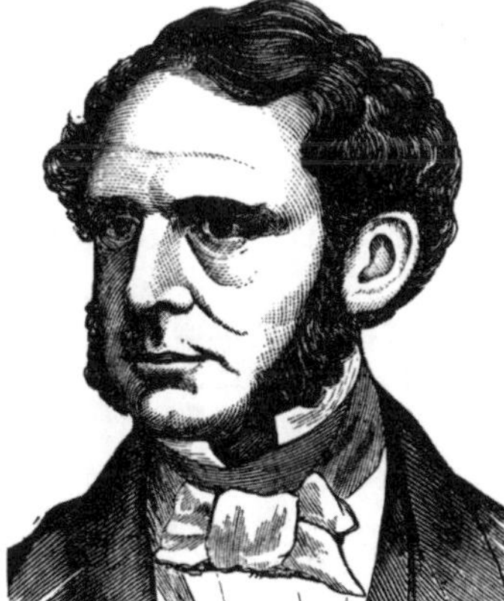

Fig. 7.—Antoine Probst.†

HIGH QUALITY.

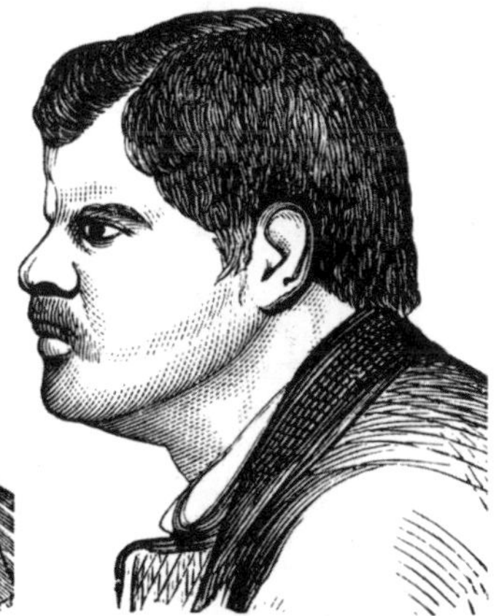

Fig. 6.—Rev. F. W. Robertson.*

* An English clergyman who resided in Brighton, of singularly refined tastes, fervent piety, and impressive eloquence. He died in 1863.

† Antoine Probst, a brutal murderer, confessed that he killed seven persons—the Deering Family. He was executed in Philadelphia in 1866.

MORE FROM THE GUIDE

We mean also to expose the fear of joy which interferes with the rational (and joyous irrational) evaluation of many of these substances. (See Ralph article,Book I,p48.)

Those who cry murder when they mean love are not happy people. Neither do they wish the joy of others to express itself.

Our society (in general) suffers from a complete depression punctuated by insane eruptions of violence: Aggressive juvenile delinquency, authoritarian schools, war, obsolete family, class and industrial structures, corrupt police forces, mechanical medicines etc etc: all these are symbols of our depression.

Repressed hostility to depression to hate (especially of those in love and joy): this is the terrible cycle.

This is the price we pay for the suppression of joy and love.

(I mean PHYSICAL AND SPIRITUAL TRUE JOY & love)

This is the terrible crime against ourselves

ACTING OUT

"But the initiate "acts out" & this is dangerous"

Admittedly this may be so: murder, car murder, physical violence, suicide, schizophrenia all may develop "when the super ego dissolves in alcohol" or some other releaser of the "upper" brain controls. But why is this necessarily so? No it aint necessarily so. Why is there that much suppressed hate lieing around? Why isnt love released?

(Of course love is sometimes released too but those who fear the violence so much also hate the love so

2

From *Birth* No. 3: Stimulants, an Exhibition (1960)

TOBACCO

My doctor has always told me to smoke. To this advice he adds, "Smoke, my friend: if it weren't for that, another would be smoking in your place."

Erik Satie

They (the users of tobacco) frequent soda fountains, and from soda water set to drinking beer, and then brandy, and finally whiskey.

19th century American

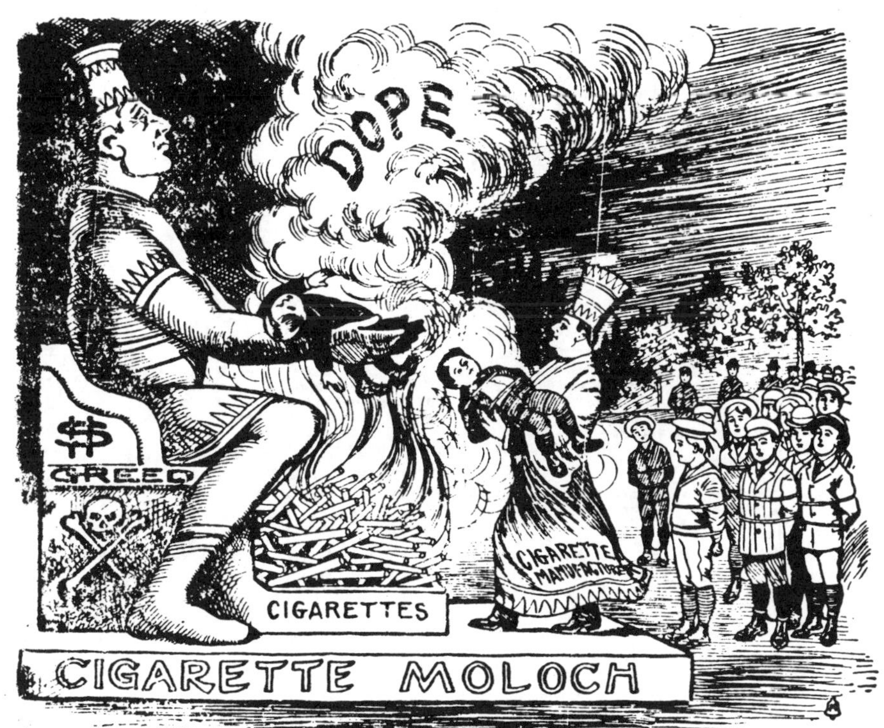

26 The sacrifice of American youth. How long will this abomination be tolerated?

The story of a madman who tried to destroy the armies of the world and outlaw war!

P.S. Why don't
terest for us, you
ers, by printing
rious stages of m
to enjoy mascu
too!!!

Russian Thistle Growing At U.S. Atom Test Site

§§ 1136–1139 *CLEVENGER'S SUPREME COURT PRACTICE*

§ 1136. Action to annul marriage where party was an idiot. An action to annu
marriage on the ground that one of the parties thereto was an idiot may be ma

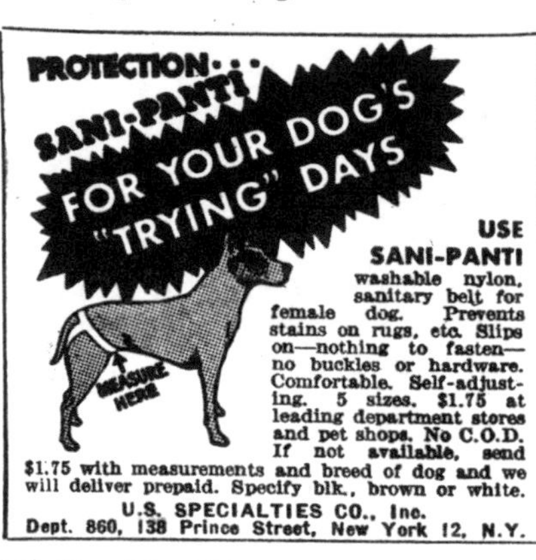

SATURDAY NIGHT AND SUNDAY MORNING—The non-hero type so prevalent in British films of late used to be called a slob. True, as acted by Albert Finney, this one has his attractive side—he has zest, is a good worker and looks clean. In other words, he is not a beatnik. But his callous love-making with the wife of a fellow worker, his constant lying and beer guzzling make him a poor object for sympathy, though he is supposed to represent the "dead end" offered by society to factory workers. With his obvious intelligence there is no reason why he couldn't be bossing the factory in another ten years. Perhaps that is the end the film implies when he finally gets himself led to the altar by a girl with her eye on a brand new house. Acting and direction are superior. A-Very good. Y&C-No. (Continental)

MOSCOW, March 3—A Soviet "lipstick king" who ran a private cosmetics business has

HOSPITALS in America are installing devices rather like taxi meters so that when a patient is supplied with life-saving oxygen the doctors can know exactly how much gas is used — and charge accordingly.

מזל טוב

FIELD'S

MOST RELIABLE
MATRIMONIAL SERVICE
516—5th Ave., Cor. 43rd St.
New York — Room 702
ESTABLISHED 1928

Successful Marriage

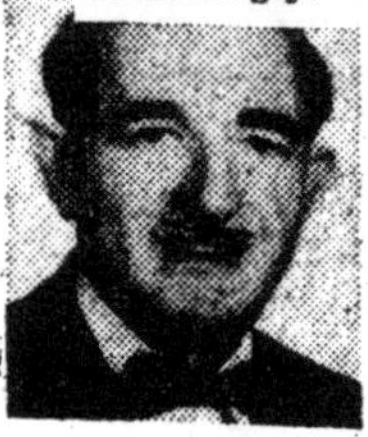

We arrange suitable appointments for your daughter without her knowledge until her happy marriage.

מיר פירען דורך פאסענדע אפאינטמענטס פאר אייער טאכטער אהן איר וויסען ביז איר הייראט.

Free Consultation
CALL MU 7-3885

WIDOW, 56 large mfg. worth $300,000
WIDOW, 60, attractive, worth $500,000
WIDOW, 48, real estate, $200,000
WIDOW, 54, hotel business, $250,000
WIDOW, 58, wholesale bus., $400,000
WIDOW, 50, shoe mfg'ers, $350,000
WIDOW, 52, large hotel, $300,000
WIDOW, 54, refined, worth $250,000
WIDOW, 59, refined, big Real Estate
WIDOW, 55, refined, worth $100,000
WIDOW, 48, will take into diam. bus.
WIDOW, 38, attr., $35,000 dowry
WIDOW, 51, bus. prop., wth. $400,000

MISS, 17, will take in R. E. business
MISS, 27, alone, worth $100,000
MISS, 22, will take into whol. bus.
MISS, 31, pretty, $40,000 dowry
MISS, 28, will take into textile bus.
MISS, 25, attr., father M. D., wealthy
MISS, 30, will take in mfg. business
MISS, 23, parents worth $300,000

LADIES, don't worry if you are Single, divorced, widows, NOT financially secure — come in and you will get your life-time companion JUST AS WELL.

WIDOWERS, all ages, healthy, earners, sincere, with good income, looking for refined ladies to marry soon. Means not necessary.

DOCTORS, dentists, engineers, lawyers, manufacturers, chemists, pharmacists, druggists and businessmen. All ages, all established, wealthy, looking for refined ladies who need not have money.

YOUNG LADIES, 17-38, parents are able and willing to give from $5,000 up to $100,000 dowry.

Open Daily 9:30 a. m. to 6:30 p. m. — Sunday 9:30 a. m. to 2 p. m.
Call: **MU 7-3885** Special Appointments for Out-of-Towners

TOKYO, April 6 (AP)—The highest United States award given to foreigners was presented today to Japan's retiring air force chief, who helped plan the attack on Pearl Harbor.

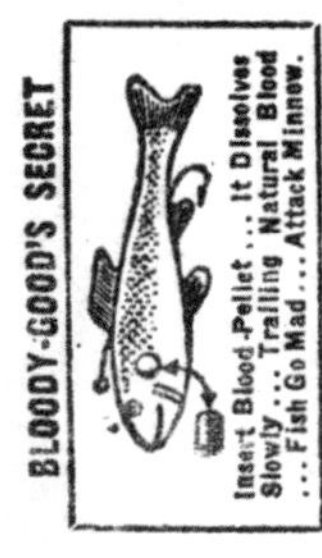

In th
that pa
F. Ken
used w
times
word h
One of
same c
robbed.
sense b
favored
of sayi
mal lu
he wo
shafted

Now
strange
Americ
Pacific.
and w
birds
toos, t
But r
memor
as utte
ton-Ha
gered i
broad
breeze,
so dee
of th
inevit
Kenne
"Shaf

From *Yeah* No. 3 (1962)

l up more in-
l female read-
of men in va-
/e women like
ysique photos

By a WALL STREET JOURNAL *Staff Reporter*

DALLAS—Private survey crews working for the State of Texas have found that all seven out of seven oil wells they have tested in the East Texas Field were slanted illegally to tap oil from under adjoining leases.

TO DEFEAT NATURALIZATION, ALLEGED ACTS OF FORNICATION MUST BE ESTABLISHED. NUMEROUS TRAFFIC TICKETS MAY ALSO BE EXCUSED UNDER SPECIAL CIRCUMSTANCES.

A naturalization petition was opposed on the ground that the petitioner lacked the required good moral character, in that he allegedly had committed fornication, and in that he had received 16 traffic tickets in a period of less than two years. It appeared that no proof of fornication could be shown, only the fact that an unmarried woman had stayed overnight in the apartment of the petitioner, an unmarried male. The traffic tickets were acquired during a period when the petitioner

We are a small but growing company. In the course of trying to build a strong nucleus of talented, hard working men, we've had to let several people go. As president, I know the job of firing a man rests on my shoulders. Frankly, I hate it. Do you know of a smooth, effective way I can let a man out?

A donation by the three major religious faiths in this country of 2,000 cartons of Bibles and prayer books to the Office of Civil and Defense Mobilization will be ready in case of attack on the U.S. One carton is stockpiled in each of 1,931 civil defense portable emergency hospitals. Each carton contains 166 items—10 copies of the Catholic "Prayer Book for Our Times," five copies of "Prayer Book for Jews" and the following American Bible Society items: one New Testament and Psalms, 10 booklets of Psalms, 14 reprints each of several N.T. books. L-r: Rev. Maurus Fitzgerald, Franciscan Fathers, Dr. Fred Kern, OCDM Religious Affairs office, Samuel Rubiner, Nat'l Jewish Welfare Board and Dr. Frank Laugham, American Bible Society.

**r at least in
which John
ed, a much-
ose historic
afted." The
l meanings.
roughly the
as "We wuz
ed" in this
word greatly
edy. Instead
had had dis-
ot a raw deal,
ter, "I was**

**were many
hat fell upon
n the South
were parrots
and mynah
ming cocka-
only a few.
was more
"shafted,"
nnedy's Bos-
ent. It lin-
ong after the
l away in the
bedded itself
consciousness
eard it that
ch things go,
e known as**

The bureaucracy was said to fall well short of the ideal. Polityka cited the complaint of a man who had been summoned to receive a merit award. The invitation was written on the form of a court order, which bore the printed words at the bottom: "Failure to comply with this notice renders the receiver liable to appropriate punishment."

In Washington Undersecretary of State George W. Ball branded the ransom demand as "the most monstrous thing that one could think"—a demand prompted by Castro's critical need for hard currency for Cuba's economy.

"Any man who would sell human beings would sell anything," Mr. Ball charged on television.

However, he said, those who oppose Federal legislation in the field "fail to recognize that * * * something like three or four times as much is spent in advertising by the pharmaceutical houses than for research."

MR. KHRUSHCHEV: RETURN OUR FLYERS AND KEEP OUR QUEERS!

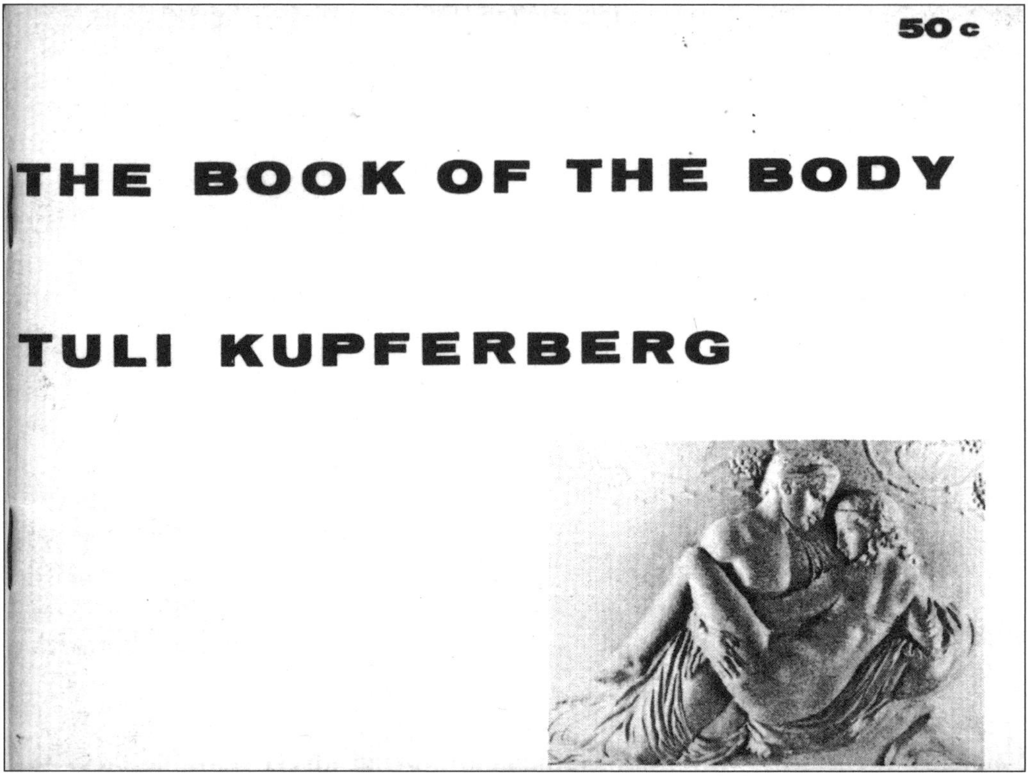

50c

THE BOOK OF THE BODY

TULI KUPFERBERG

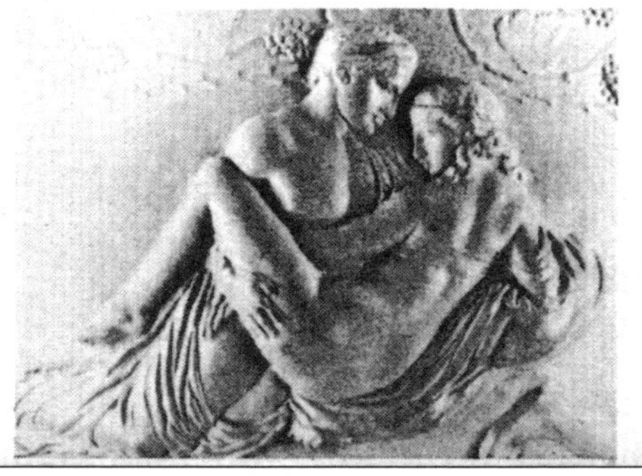

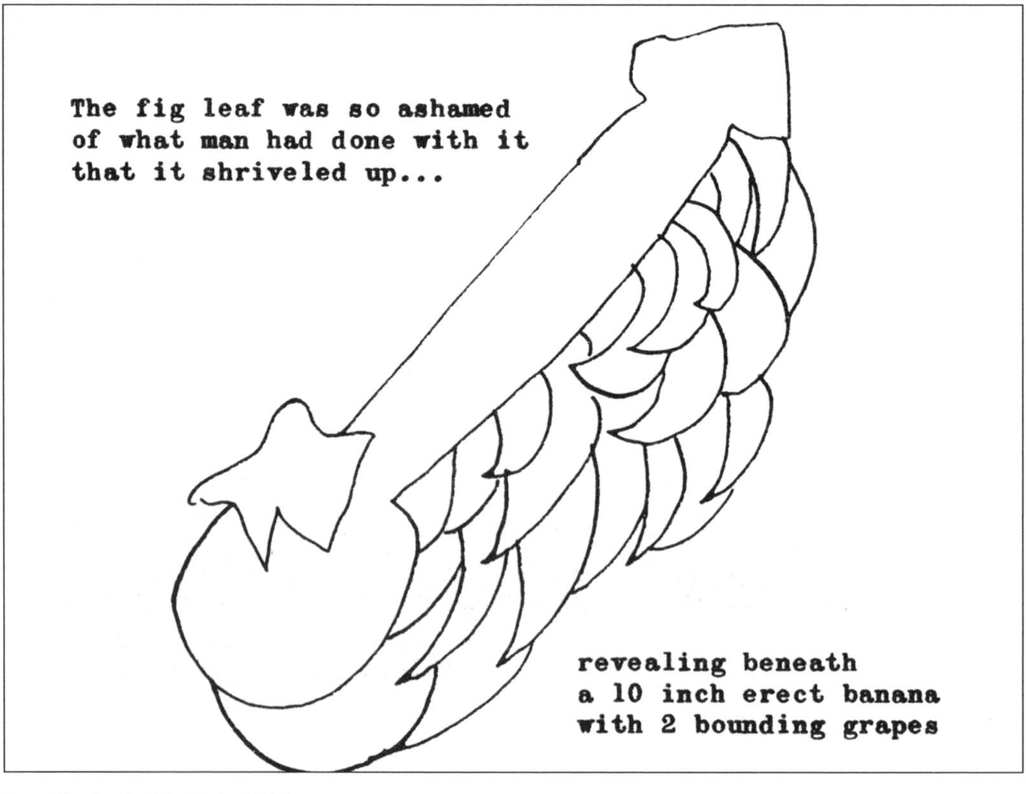

The fig leaf was so ashamed
of what man had done with it
that it shriveled up...

revealing beneath
a 10 inch erect banana
with 2 bounding grapes

From *The Book of the Body* (1966)

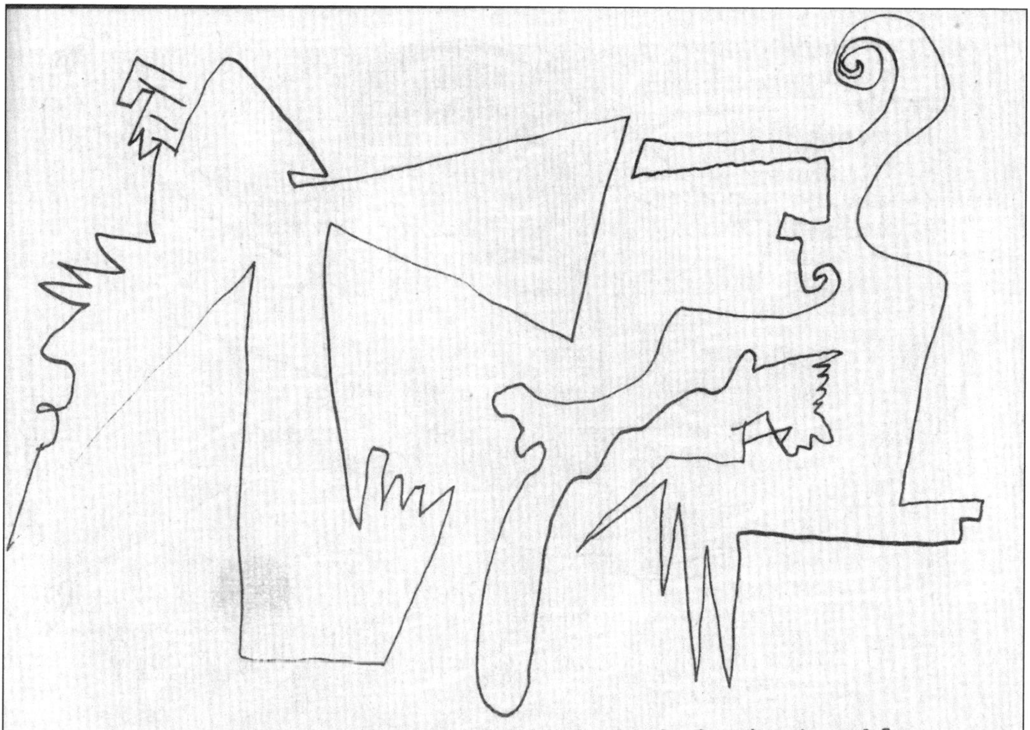

If a person does not fit his body he's in trouble

Filthy mind—filthy body

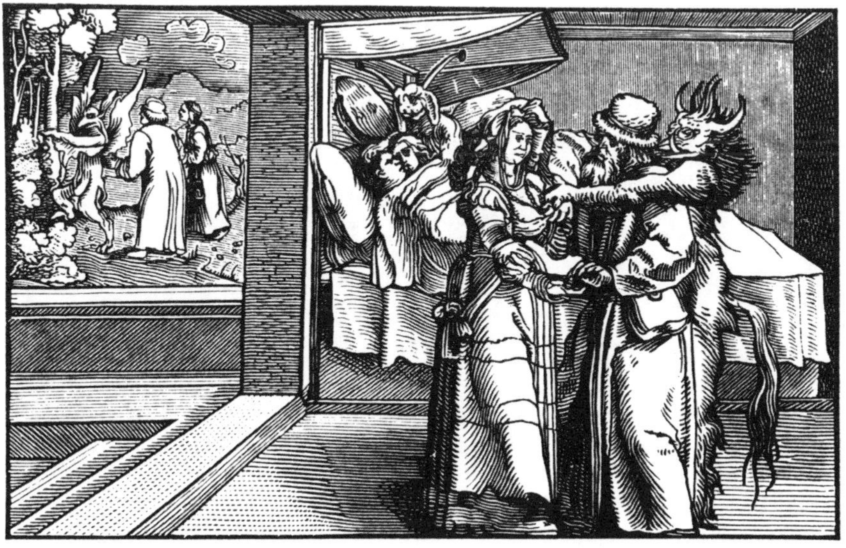

Fig. 486.—Lewdness. (After Petrarca, *Trostspiegel*, 1584.)

SCENES FROM THE ROAD

by Dean Wareham

I've been traveling an awful lot the last two years, performing *Thirteen Most Beautiful: Songs for Andy Warhol's Screen Tests.* This show has taken me to venues I never would have dreamed of playing—the Sydney Opera House; the Town Hall in my home town of Wellington, New Zealand; and the Eglise St Eustache in Paris, where Louis XIV took communion. I have taken to carrying a small Lumix digital camera, the kind that fits in a pocket, because I have been told that the best camera is one you always have with you. You never know when you'll see something sad or lonely, a new flavor of donut, an odd juxtaposition of magazines, a Danish cigarette pack designed by Paul Smith. I confess I arranged a couple of the still-lifes, and I am not sure what *Rygning can draebe* means, though I can guess.

D.W., May 2010

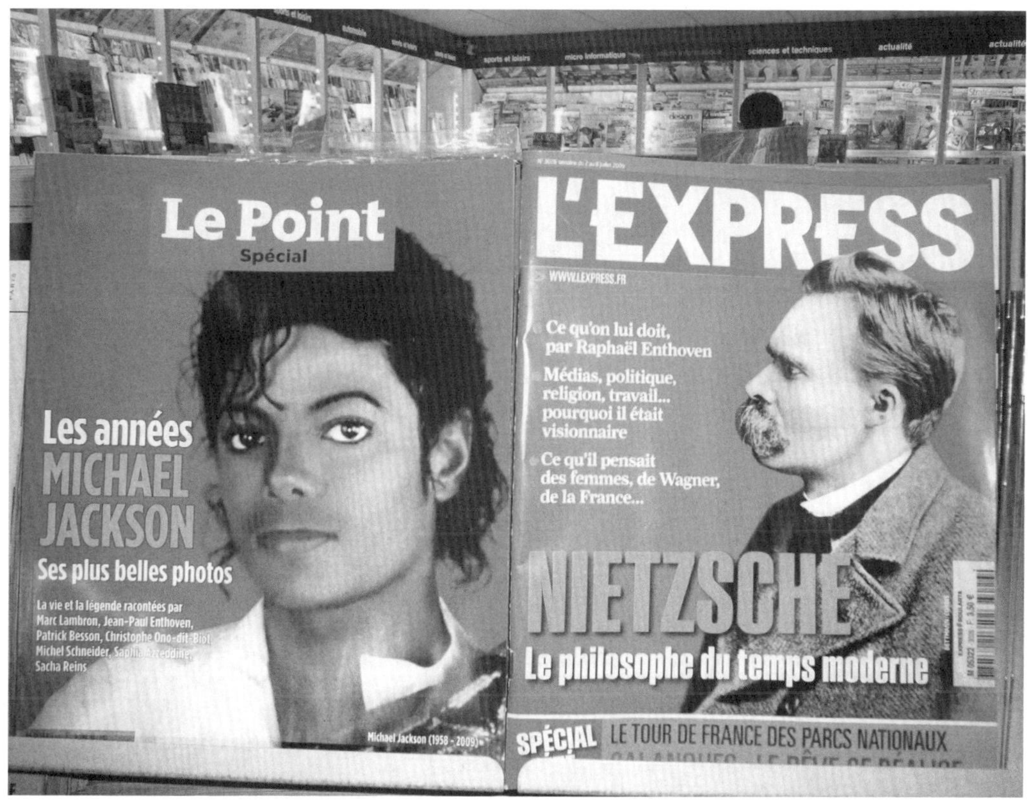

1. **Nietzsche & MJ at the Charles de Gaulle RELAY, Paris. July 2009.**

Le Point has Michael Jackson, *L'Express* goes with Friedrich Nietzsche. I imagine Friedrich and Michael talking.

FN: Be on your guard against the learned! They hate you: for they are unfruitful.
MJ: Lies run sprints, but the truth runs marathons.
FN: In every real man a child is hidden that wants to play.
MJ: There's a Mother's Day and a Father's Day but there's no Children's Day. It would mean a lot. World peace.
FN: I would believe only in a God that knows how to dance.

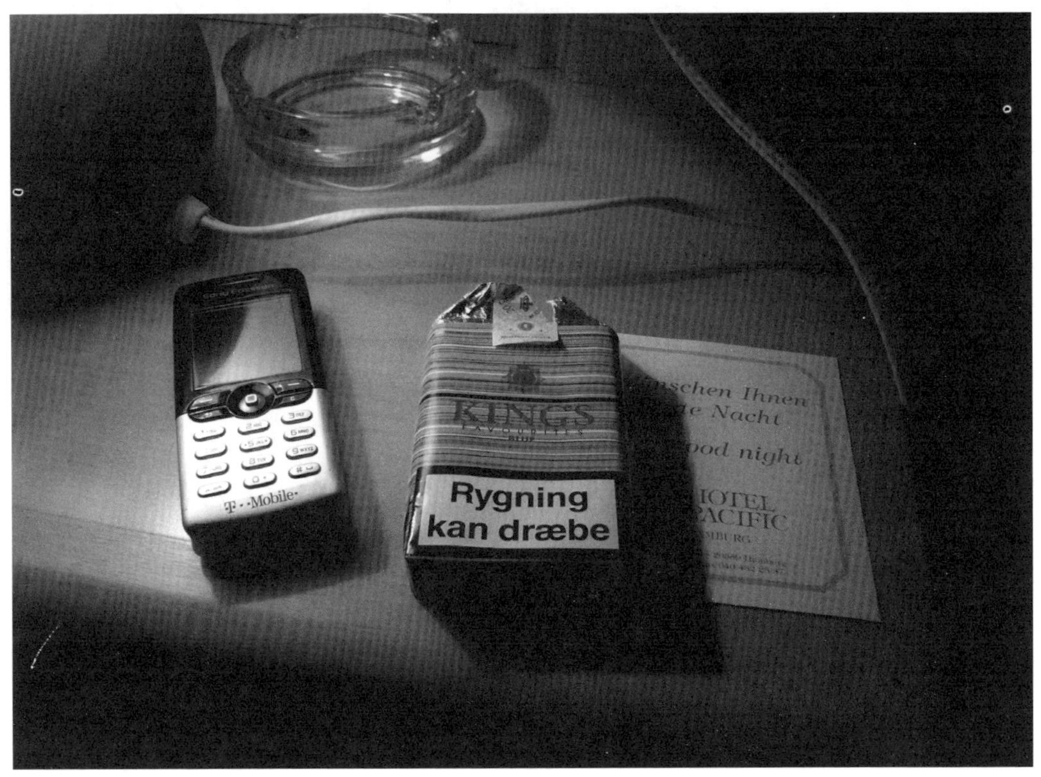

2. Hotel Pacific, Hamburg. November 2007.

The Beatles lived here in December of 1962 and it has not changed much since then, though they now offer in-room showers, which means a shower in a closet next to the desk. WCs are still down the hall.

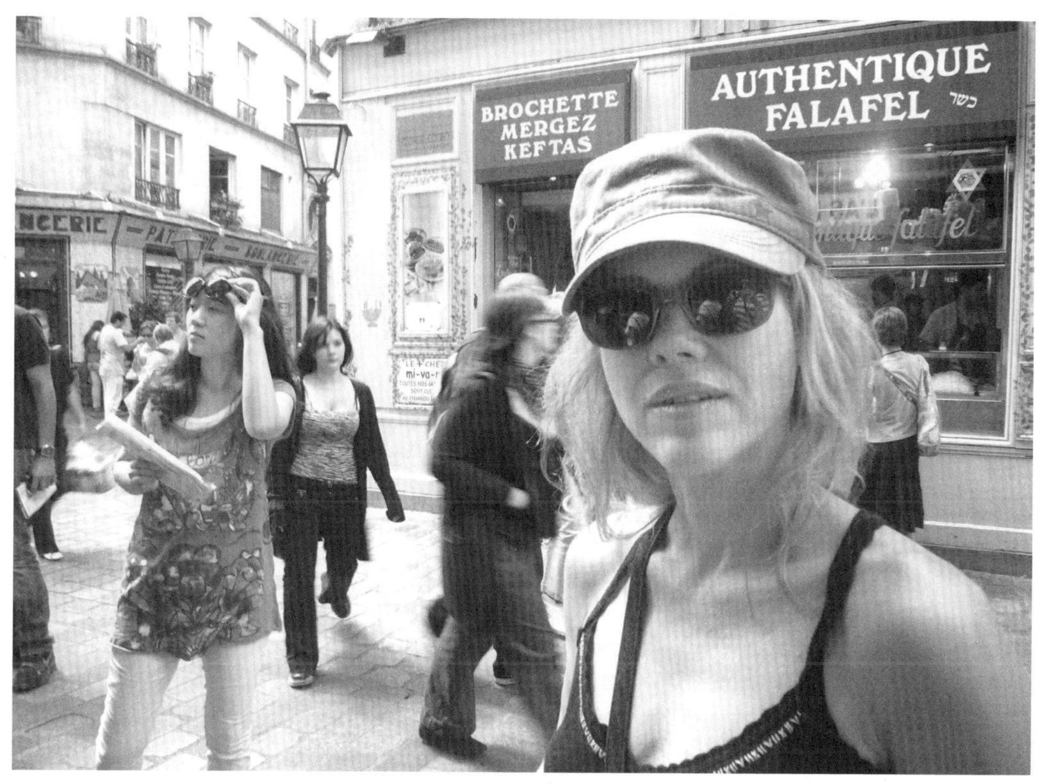

3. The Marais, Paris. July 2009.

In Paris they put eggplant in the falafel.

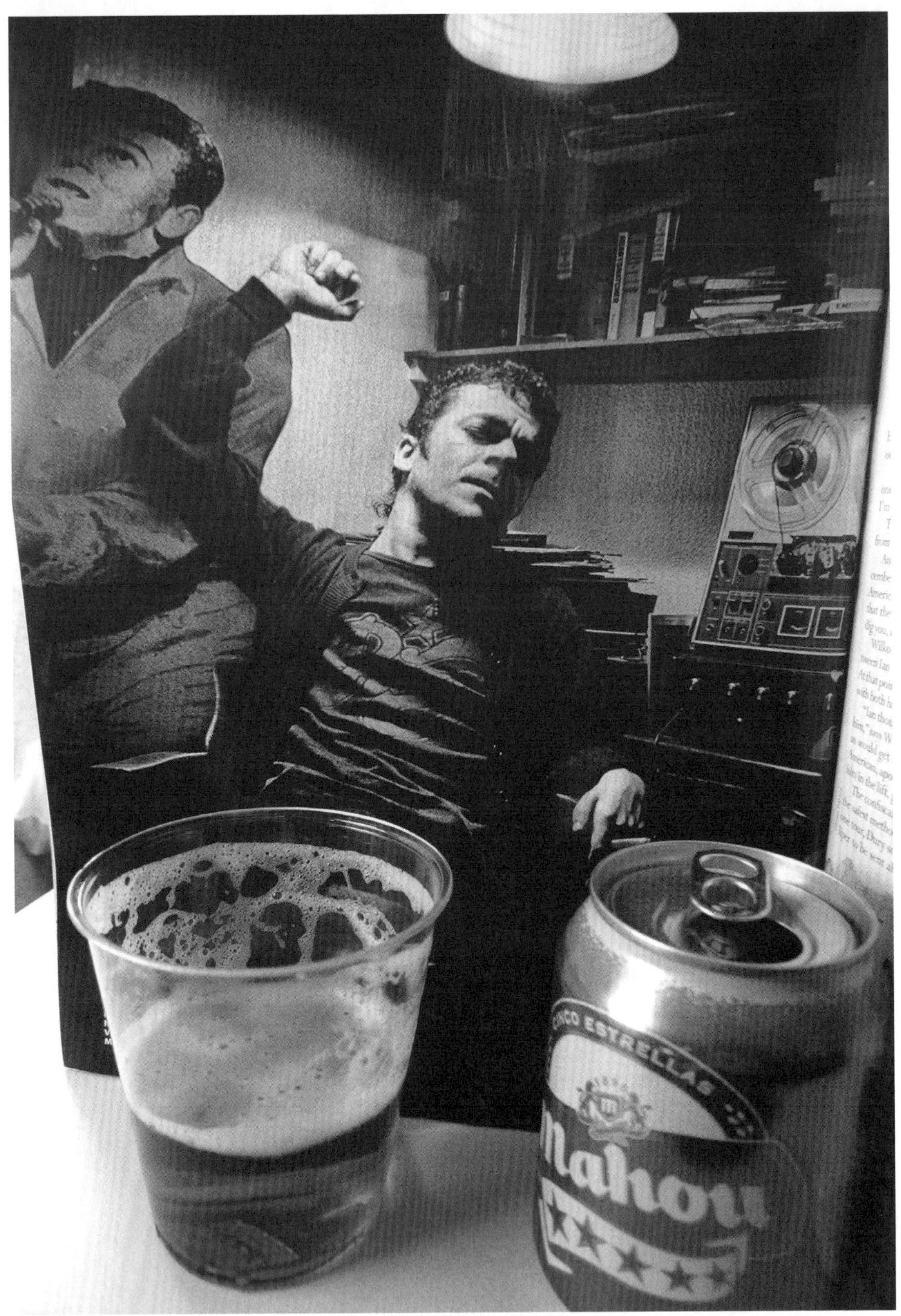

4. Air Iberia Still Life. January 2010.

Flying to Valencia, enjoying a cold Mahou and reading about Ian Dury, remembering "Wake Up and Make Love with Me": *I come awake / with a gift for womankind / You're still asleep / but the gift don't seem to mind . . .*

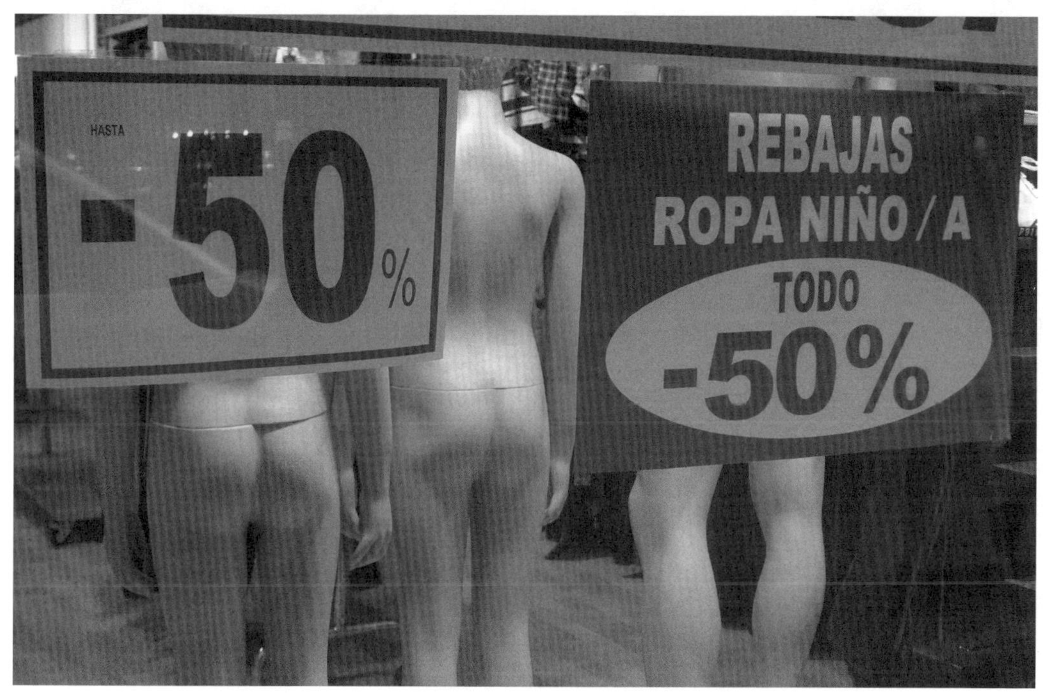

5. Rebajas 50%. January 2010.

In Spain to play the Tanned Tin festival. Everything is on sale in the town of Castellon, as these bare mannequin cheeks prove.

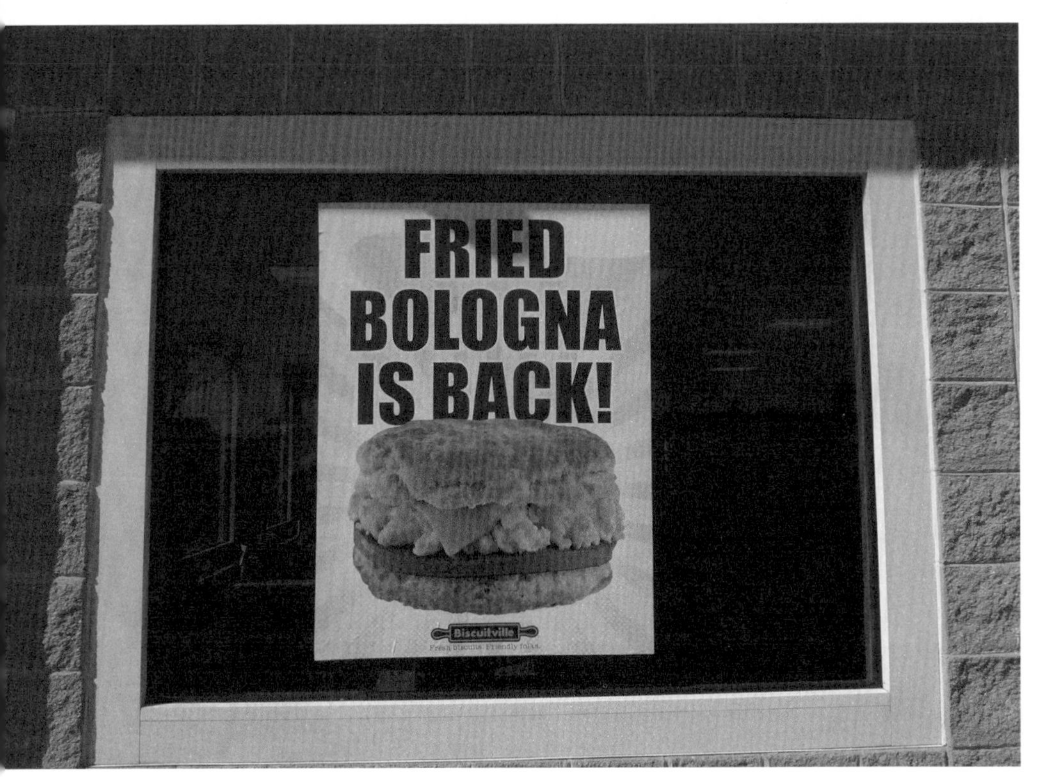

6. Fried Bologna Is Back. Haw River, NC. February 2010

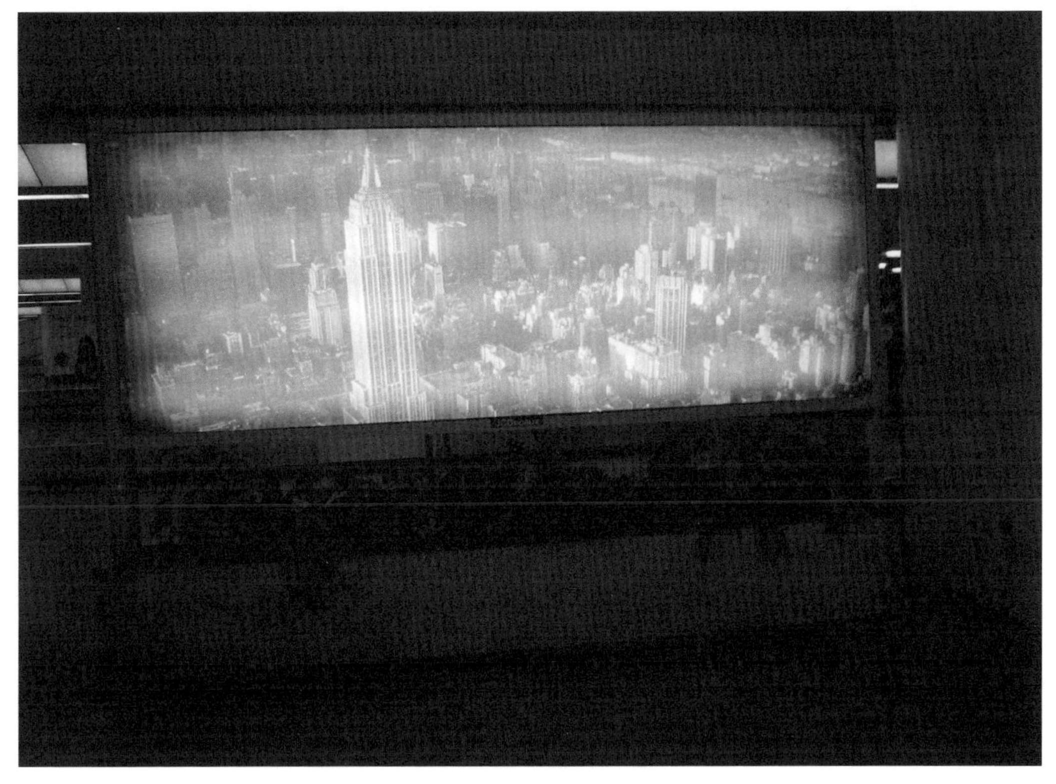

7. JFK Airport, New York. November 2009.

RECENT WORK

by Lizz Hickey

YETI: How long have you been making comics?

LIZZ HICKEY: I grew up drawing my own weird little comics, and then took a break and started making "real art" in school. After school I struggled between making comic prints from etchings and making regular ol' drawings. (Money definitely plays a huge role!) So it's been a lifetime, so far. Let's continue this life.

When and how did you start to work in other media—printmaking, etc.?

At school, for sure. Facilities at my school allowed for tons of experimentation. I was totally lucky! No strings attached! Plus, living in New York is totally awesome, too! There is sooo much printmaking here! And printmaking facilities! I bet you yourself know a printmaker and you don't even know it!

Do you see what you're doing as part of a tradition—if so, which one, and how?

Printmaking-wise, sort of. I try to follow the print processes to the "T." I am a pretty particular person in my own art—obsessive, but I definitely allow room for mistakes. When making prints, everyone should embrace strange smudges and mistakes that happen. Those are the things that make prints prints.

Did you EVER hear a good response/joke/comment to your last name, or have they all just been lame as all hell?

Lame as hell !!!!!!!!!!!!!!!!!!!!!!! Quit making fun of it, because I'm keeping it forever!!!

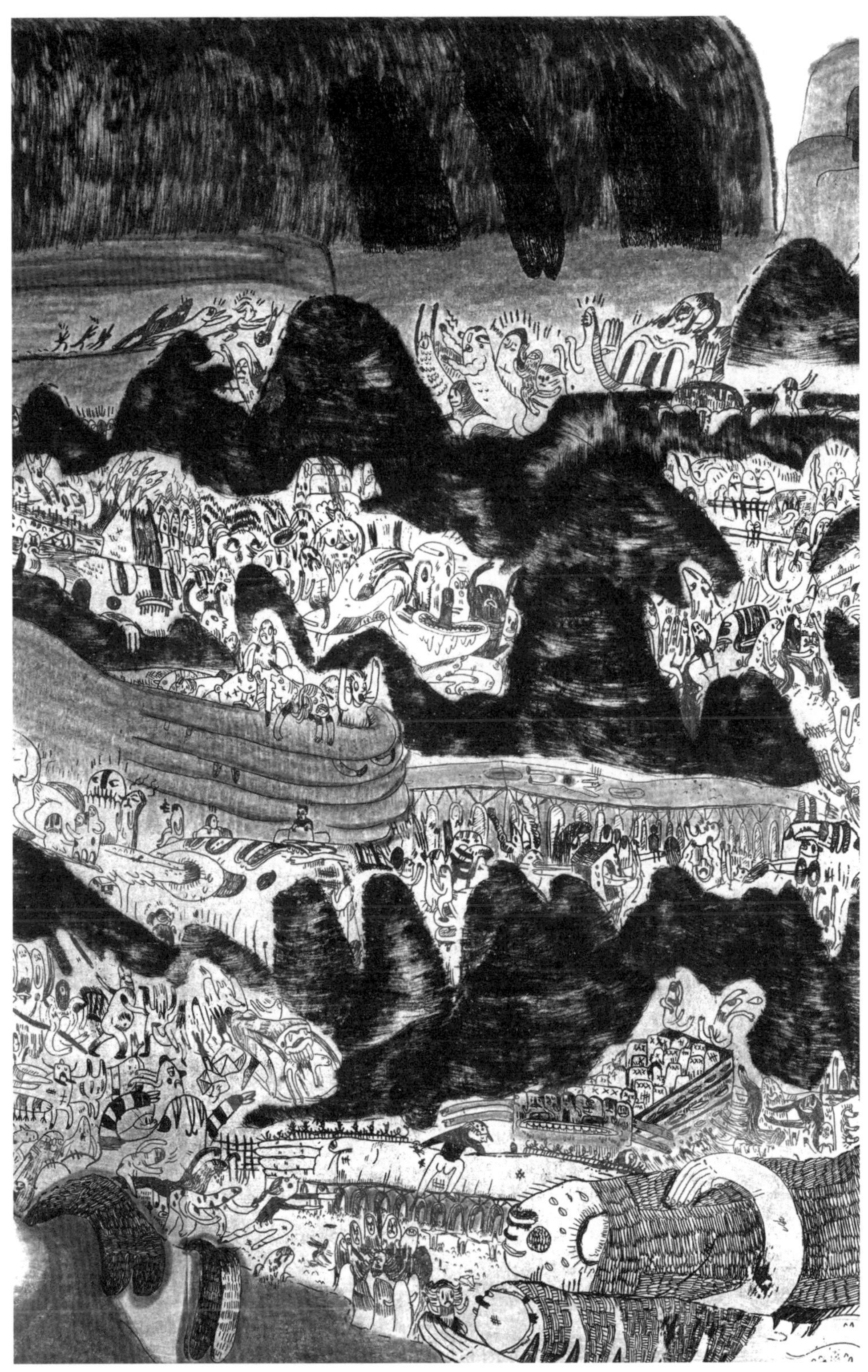

FER SHURE

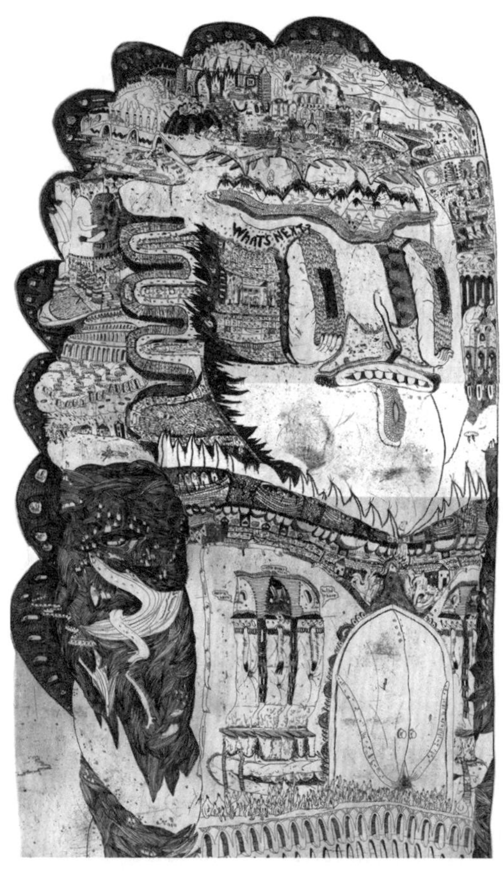

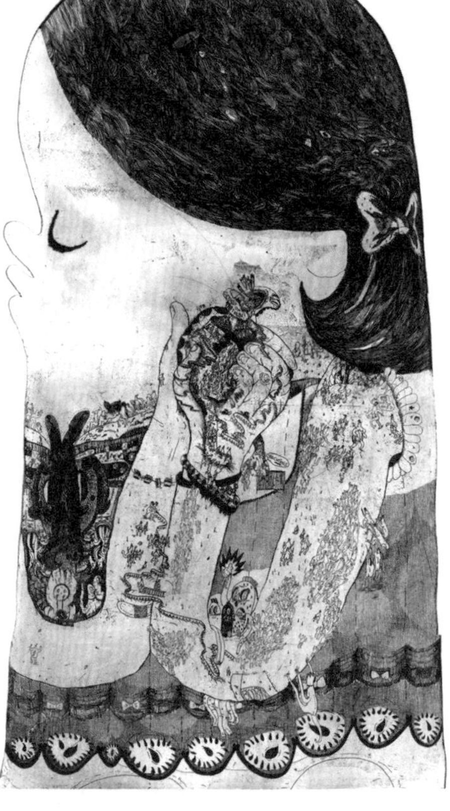

"chickenhead" "GIRL HEAD"

ETCHINGS ON COPPER
2008

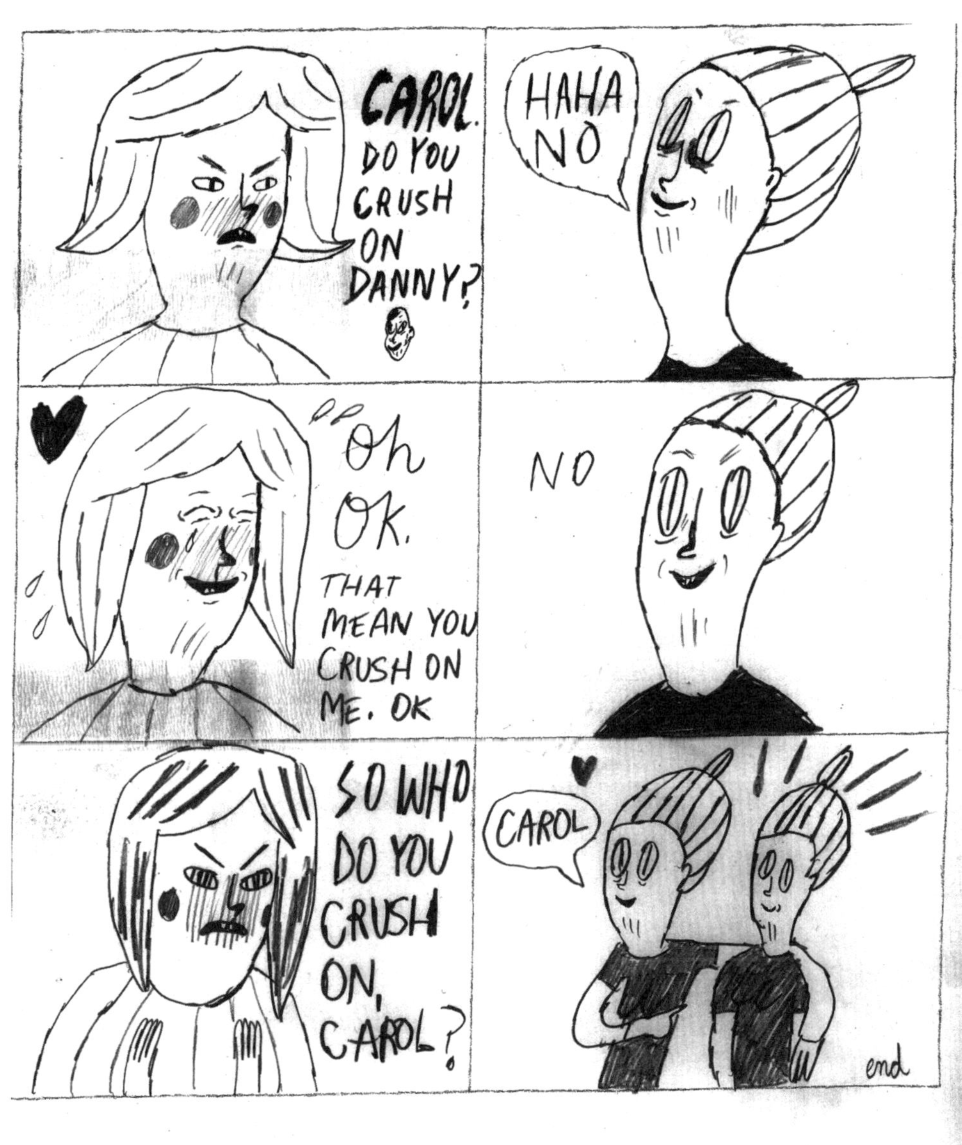

CAROL. DO YOU CRUSH ON DANNY?
HAHA NO
Oh OK. THAT MEAN YOU CRUSH ON ME. OK
NO
SO WHO DO YOU CRUSH ON, CAROL?
CAROL
end

-TWU WUB-

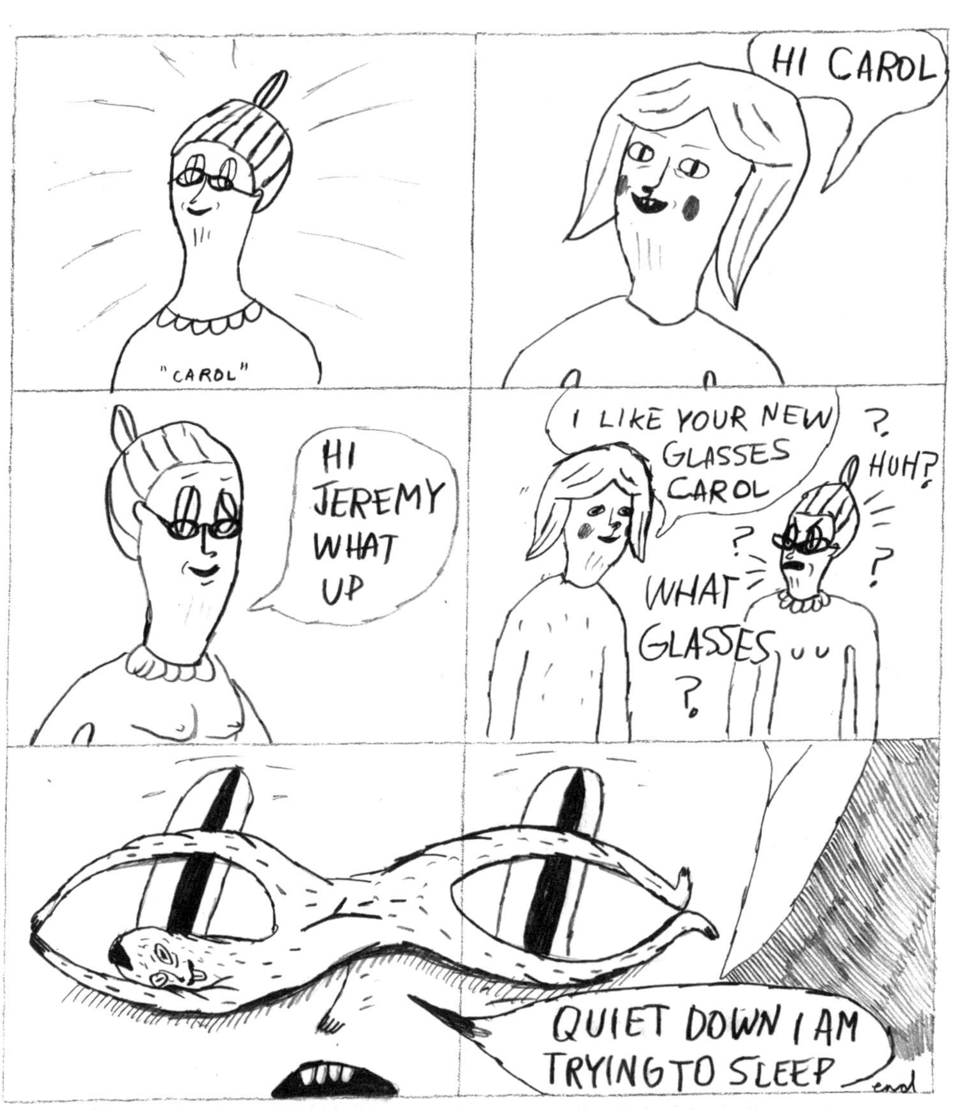

MARRIAGE MATCH

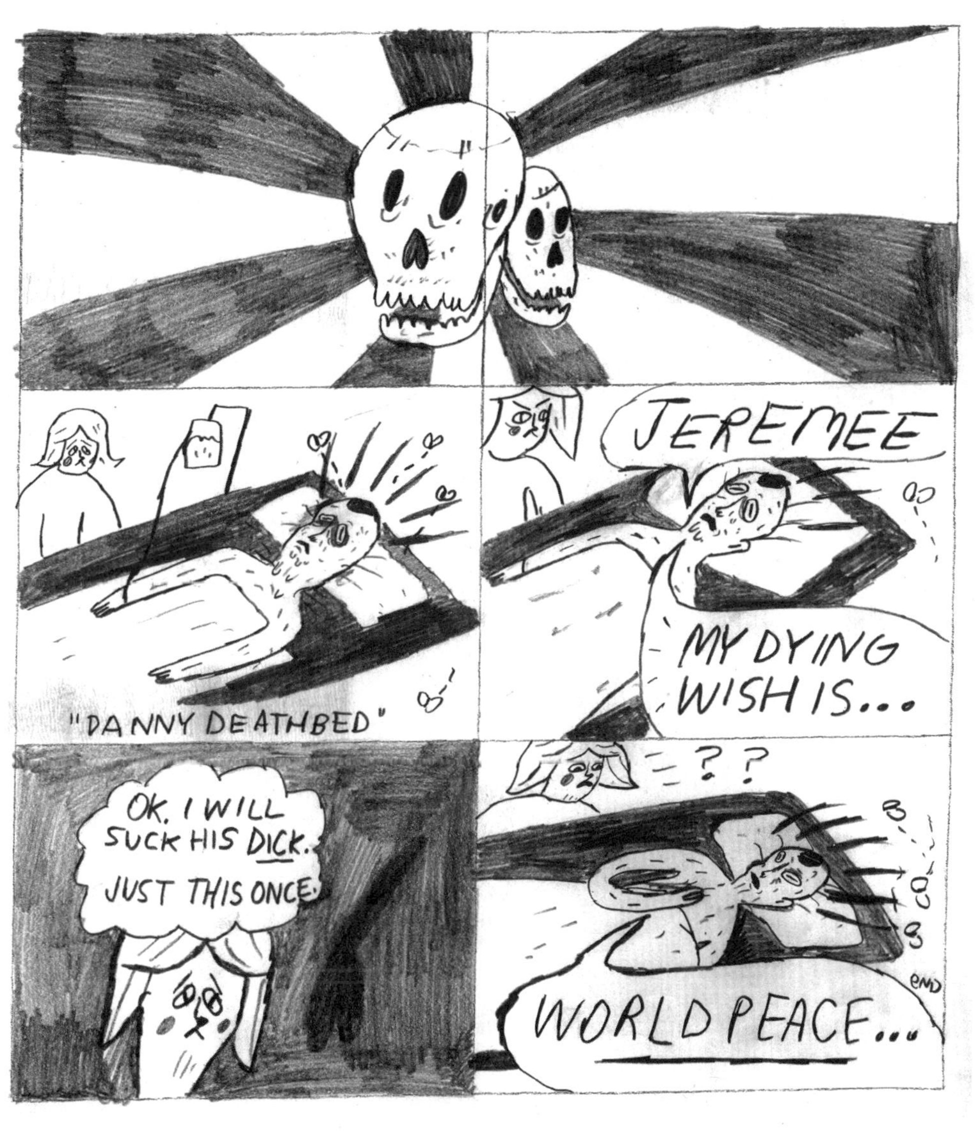

WHAT'S YER BLOOD TYPE?
I GOTTA KNOW,
DUD!!!

PRINTMAKING RULZ!

ETCH THAT SHIT!

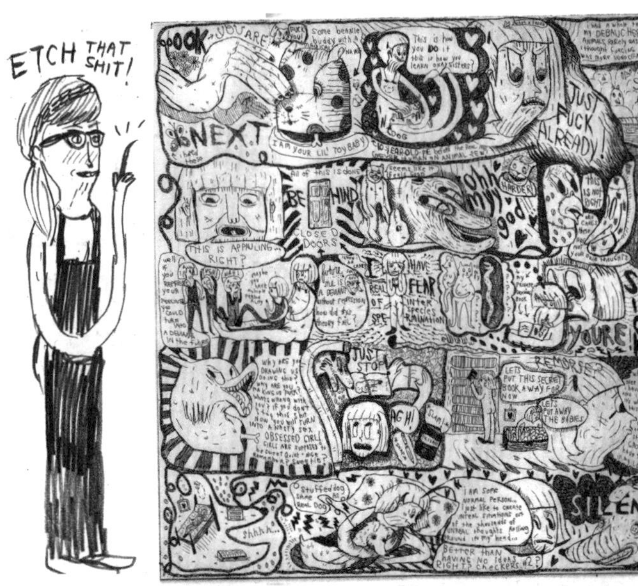

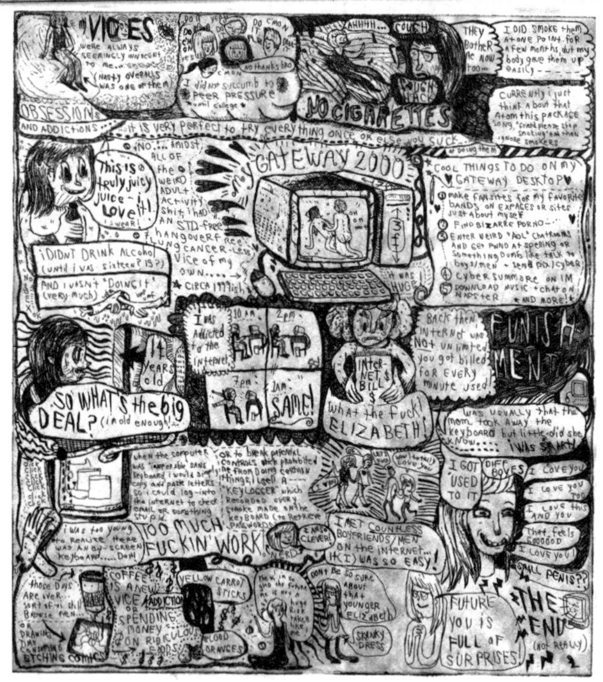

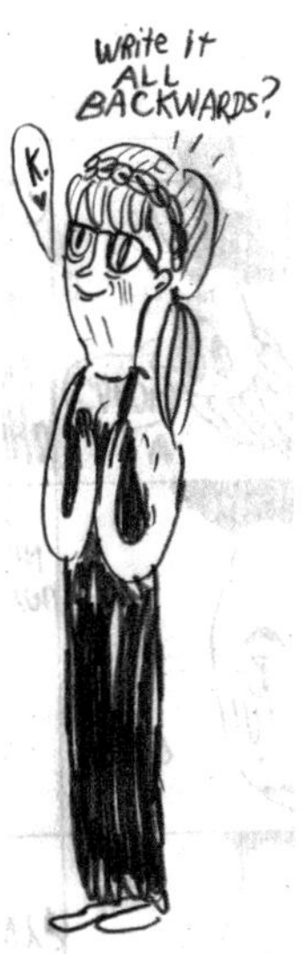

- ETCHING COMICS -

see more at LizzHickey.com

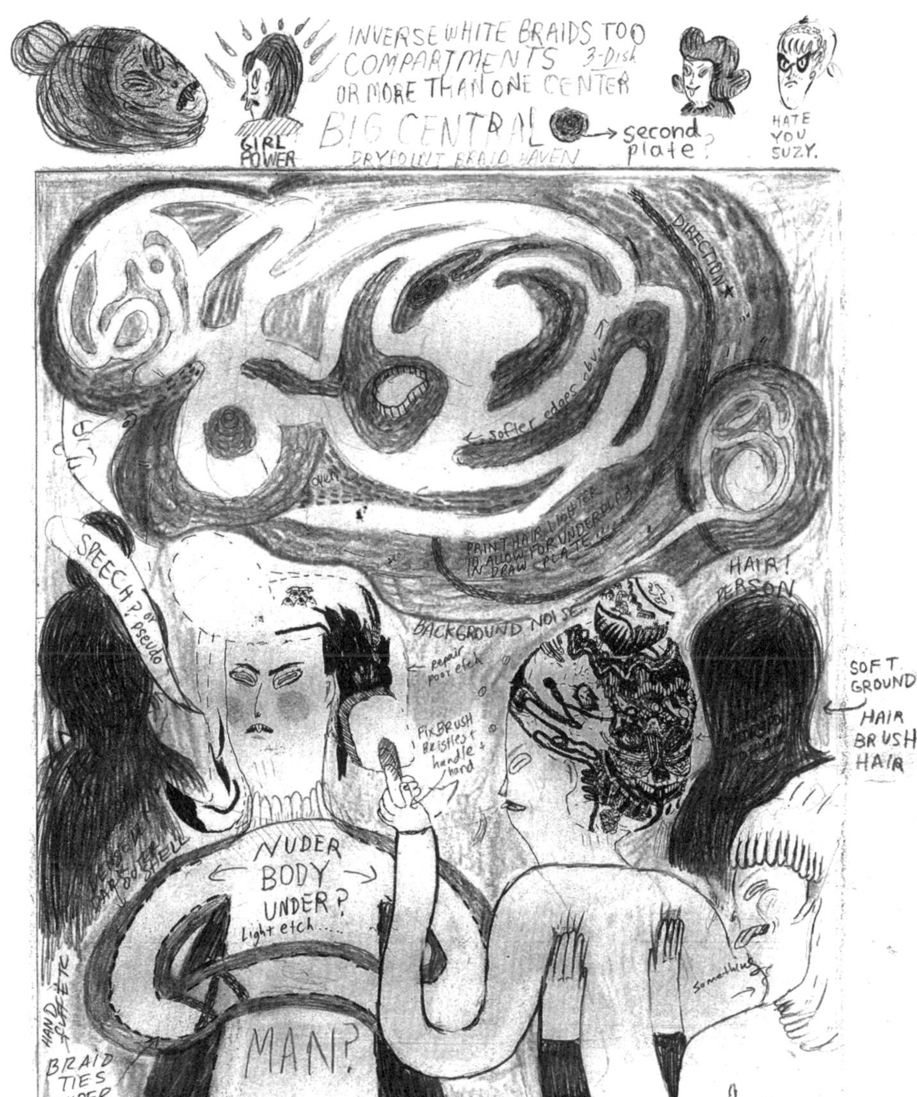

GIRL POWER
INVERSE WHITE BRAIDS TOO
COMPARTMENTS 3-Disk
OR MORE THAN ONE CENTER
BIG CENTRAL
second plate?
DRYPOINT BRAID HAVEN
HATE YOU SUZY.
DIRECTION
softer edges
PAINT HAIR LIGHTER TO ALLOW FOR UNDERPLATE
SPEECH? or pseudo
HAIR! PERSON
BACKGROUND NOISE
repair poor etch
FIX BRUSH Bristles + handle + hand
SOFT GROUND?
HAIR BRUSH HAIR
NUDER BODY UNDER?
Light etch.....
something
MAN?
BRAID TIES UNDER REVELATION
LIZZ HICKEY
QUEENBEEBRAID
AP 1/4

TOUCHED IN THE HEAD

An interview with Indian music scholar (and crazy record collector) VAK Ranga Rao

by Robert Millis

ILLUSTRATION BY PEDRO LOURENÇO

Bangalore Nagarathnamma [1878-1952] was among the last practitioners of the Devadasi tradition in India. The Devadasi were women who were "married" to Hindu temples and deities; the phrase means "handmaiden of God." They performed rituals and took care of shrines. They also studied classical Indian arts—dancing and singing—and were among the only educated women in traditional India. Many were extremely accomplished and performed regularly for their patrons, for royalty and for officials. It was a complex tradition, one that deteriorated rapidly at the beginning of the 20th century as a result of British colonial rule, Hindu fundamentalist politics, and a changing economy. Some wrongly confuse the term with courtesan.

Bangalore Nagarathnamma was a Devadasi of piety and learning, a renowned musician thought to be imbued with almost mystical powers. When the wife of the Zamindar of Chikkavaram became pregnant [the Zamindar was the younger brother of the Raj of Bobbili, a royal family from South India] she sought a blessing from Bangalore, hoping this child—her third—would be a son. Bangalore gave her a lime and told her to keep it as a blessing and said indeed the child would be a son. This was in roughly 1929.

> Bangalore Nagarathnamma was known to my mother; she would come and visit my mother's parents for auspicious occasions and sing. She had known my mother since she was a little girl. Mother's

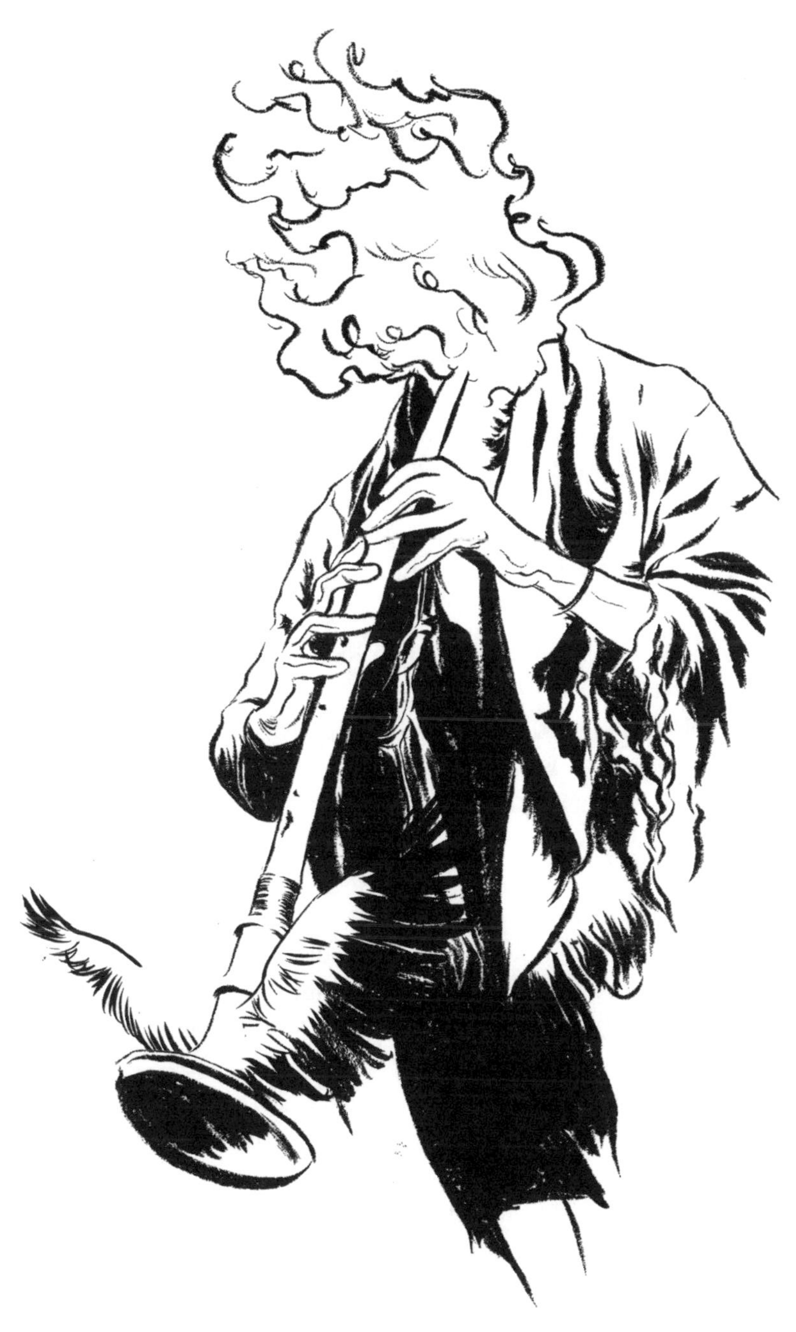

first two children were girls, and so she wanted a son. Bangalore said it would be a son, Mother then said, bless me, give me a blessing that my son will be a musician like you.

Bangalore was immediately uptight. There were strict guidelines in India at this time; Bangalore's class were the performers, my mother's class were the patrons. Bangalore did not want this balance upset, so she said angrily, 'If everyone gets on the palanquin, who will bear it along?' Mother was taken aback. Bangalore felt contrite—she had known my mother since she was a little girl—so she said, 'He will not be a musician, but he will make his name in music.' My mother had no idea what this might mean.

When I was 18, mother and I went to Nagarathnamma's shrine—she was dead by this point—and I was made to pay respects more completely than at any other temple or before any other holy man—which I did, without knowing why. By this time I was writing a column on gramophone records for a newspaper—the first such column in India, as far as I know— and the column had become quite popular. My mother then told me the story of Bangalore's blessing.

Venkata Anandakumara Krishna Ranga Rao still has the lime—now dry and shriveled—that Bangalore gave his mother. And, as she predicted, he has made a name for himself in music. He is a critic, essayist, film, dance, and music historian—and he has one of the largest record collections in India, with well over 45,000 78s. When I met him at his home in Chennai, his first words were: "I hope you do not frighten easily." He ushered me into his dining room. Memorabilia and bric-a-brac were everywhere. Rows of cabinets filled with 78 rpm records lined the walls. Bundles of records wrapped in newspaper and covered in cobwebs sat on top of them. Newspapers, books, and even more records were stacked everywhere. I was seated at a large table opposite him; the table was covered in junk. An old metal fan clunked slowly overhead, and birds sang in the hot dusty courtyard outside.

I cleared a little space for myself, and noticed the draft of a letter he had recently written to Dev Anand, a major Hindi film star. Dev Anand had just published an autobiography; Ranga Rao had noticed quite a few factual errors in it, so he had decided to write Dev with his observations. "He has not yet written me back." Ranga Rao's house may be cluttered but his mind is a steel trap, and I was reminded of the Charles Bukowski quote: "Show me a man who lives alone and has a perpetually clean kitchen, and 8 times out of 9 I'll show you a man with detestable spiritual qualities."

Ranga Rao is mostly self-taught, smart as a whip, erudite, opinionated, peculiar, funny, charming, and able to draw threads between the most dispa-

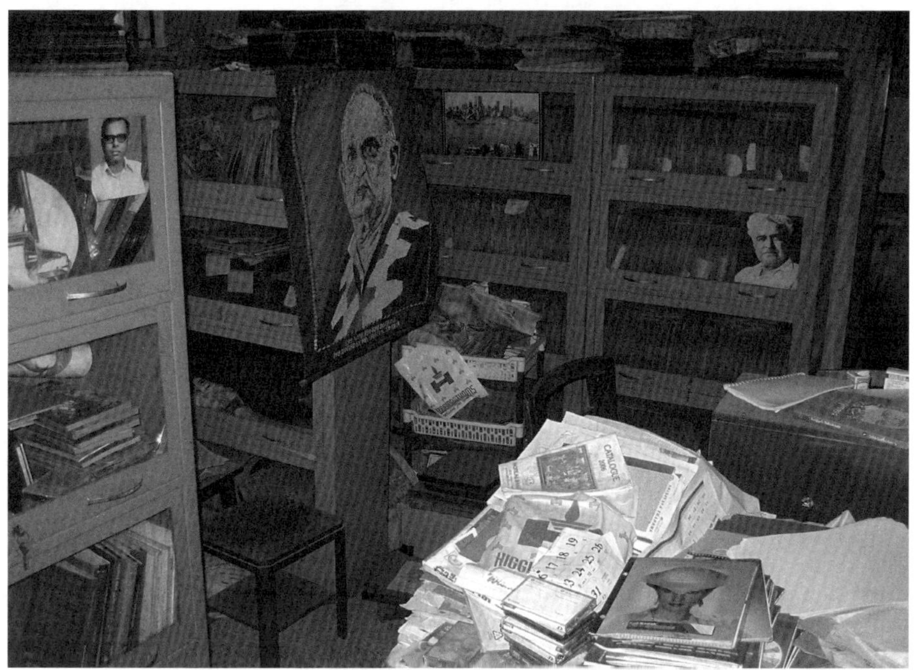

VAK Ranga Rao's dining room, 2008. (All photos by Robert Millis, 2008)

rate subjects, though music—thanks mostly to the influence of Bangalore Nagarathnamma—is always at the heart of it all. His English is excellent, and tinged with phrases from early Hollywood musicals. He spoke with a lovely Indian accent and seemed to be conveniently deaf when it suited his conversational needs. He was 78 years old at the time that we spoke.

45,000 records?

At the moment I can't play a 78 rpm record. All of the players are in repair and the people that repair them are dead and gone. But every record which I have in these cupboards and shelves is a record I have heard. Every one. And about many of them I have made notes.

What got you into record collecting?

What got you into speaking English? My family had collections of records, and I would listen to them, my sisters and I, we were living in a backwoods. There was no entertainment except a wind-up gramophone and records which we would play twice or thrice a week: different kinds of records, film music, classical records, religious records, comic skits.

Do you remember the first record that had an impact on you?

Do you remember the first word your mother said to you? When I was in a tantrum, they would play records so I would quiet down. I was two and half, maybe. As you know, there was a woman, Bangalore Nagarathnamma, who would come to our house on occasion and perform, as was the tradition at that time. Other Devadasi and musicians as well. Bangalore made several very early 78 rpm records and I used to laugh at them, they sounded so peculiar, totally unlike how she really sang. She told me how strange she found recording as well as recordings. How utterly different from her chamber performances. She had performed only before the elite, only before small groups in royal homes. I made fun of her recordings, I was young, she doted on me, I took her for granted. I have a 5-inch record of her on which she sings in a very peculiar manner. Not the way the piece should be sung. I used to make fun of it. This was the time of mechanical recording [pre-1927], when the sheer volume of the voice had to cut the groove. She said, "I was in a small room, I had to play the tambour and someone told me when to start and when to stop. I had to finish within one and a half minutes."

A little later, when she recorded longer ten-inch records, sometimes she would finish before they told her to stop so she would do a short alap at the end to fill out the time, but an alap comes always at the beginning of a song! [*An alap is an improvised section of a performance, occurring at the beginning, usually with no rhythm accompaniment*]. All her recordings were mechanical. Later on, the gramophone companies would appoint a professional music director, who was a man who could commandeer the song into neat sections and would teach musicians thirty times more accomplished than him to play the song in a certain way—alap length, refrain length, stanza length, order etc.—he would rehearse them as if it was a new song. This was a song these musicians might have been performing for twenty-five years.

How is this reflected in the recordings?

Well, if you know what you are listening to, the context, then they will be useful, but you must be schizophrenic . . . because the mind has to let go many of the qualities with which you normally judge musical recordings. It is not just pitch and language. Most people cannot or will not. I can make this schizophrenic leap but I don't make it consciously.

Was much Indian tribal or folk music recorded on 78?

Very, very rare. Now, there are some people who thought "Old Man River" was a folk song . . . Similarly, there might be less than one percent of authentic folk song recorded—mostly it was recreated in that style for the recording companies. The authentic folk music in Indian languages are maybe 10 to 20 records out of my 45,000 records.

When did you start actually collecting records?

In the '50s, almost till 1960, I was only buying the records that I liked. Then I realized there were people collecting stamps, people collecting books, people interested in refurbishing the houses of great men, but no one collecting records. Which is not true, I just didn't know about other people collecting records. So I thought, let me collect all the records I can, if I can afford it. So I went to various places—Bombay, Delhi, Bangalore—and I would stay four or five days and take out ads in the papers saying "Wanted: 78 rpm records in good condition." They would write to me at a particular address. My cousins were studying in Bangalore and would take me around on a motorbike to collect the records.

One time, my family, about 25 of us, booked a Pullman carriage, a whole train car, and went on a pilgrimage. We had a dhobi [*someone who washes clothes*] and two cooks, we took them along. We started in Visakhapatnam, went to Calcutta, and from there somewhere else, somewhere else, somewhere else. In each of the places we stopped, I made a beeline for the secondhand record seller. I collected over 600 records on that trip. I took ready-made wooden boxes, huge ones, I still have them. One person—in Lucknow, I think—said, "We don't have any here, they are in the 'go down'" [*a shed behind the main house*]. We went and got the records. He said: "You are taking them? Do you want any money?"

Well, not all our stories were so fortunate, but I managed to collect . . . I've got records on cardboard, on plastic, transparent records, puzzle records; apart from classical music, religious music, non-classical music, film music. I have recitations—speeches, for example, by Churchill, Mussolini, Ghandi. I have staged documentaries [*re-enactments*], actual documentaries, advertising, drama. I have birdcalls—I wish I could show you all of them, but I am not well enough to bend. The label says they were mechanical recordings, not electrical recordings [*which is astounding considering the difficulty involved*].

Did I tell you I am a great man? No, the point is, you are all educated. I am not. My mental circuit jumps the usual synapse. So I make connections which you normally would not. I put my common sense on the grid of what I have observed. The point is this: I have reared birds, not in a scientific manner, and made certain formulations: raise a nightingale with a crow and its songs get distorted.

Birds raised in the country, raised in the city, same species, different repertoires. Subtle differences. I just observed this casually, with no training, I heard a bird call recorded on a 78 rpm, and then the same bird call recorded 50 years later—it was different. Even the bird call has an evolution; it changes, like folk music. So what is authentic? Ornithologists with years of training are amazed at these almost unconscious observations of mine. See, I do not think that I am a genius; I am only uneducated, so new ways of logic strike me.

In Indian music, ninety percent of what people learn is by the note, but in some nagaswaram music [*the nagaswaram is a long reed instru-*

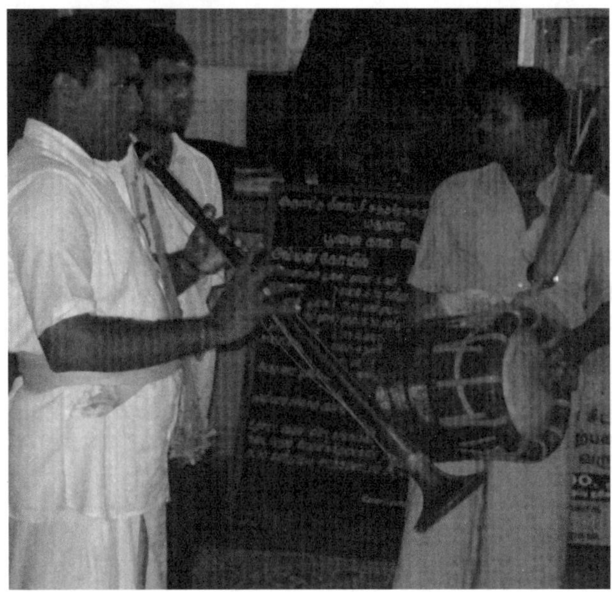

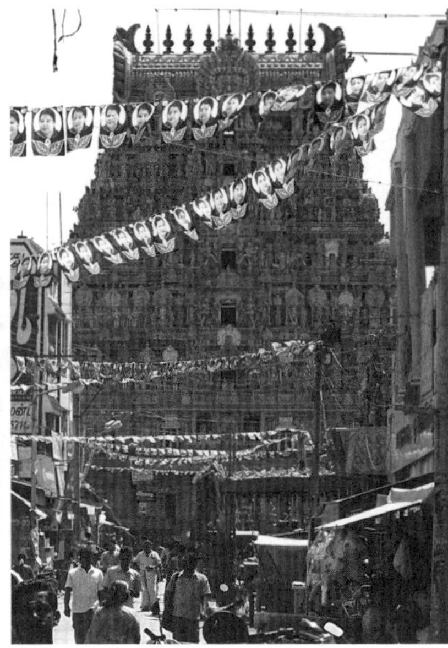

Left: Temple musicians playing nagaswaram, Madurai, Tamil Nadu, South India;
Right: Sri Ranganathaswamy Temple, Tiruchirappalli, Tamil Nadu, South India

ment, like a large shenai, used especially in South Indian temple ceremonies and processions], the student is not taught raga, he listens to his guru father and learns by the ear. I have learned that way; whatever I know. it has some basis in what I have read, but mostly in what I have observed . . . so, let me tell you, I am a great man, I am not a genius. I am great at making these connections.

I can tell you a hundred songs from Hollywood musicals; I can tell you who danced, the name of the film, the first line of the song, and I can go through the dance . . . Does this make me a better person than you? It is the way I am, my way of absorption.

I told you of the temple dancers who were also the court dancers of my uncle [*the Raja of Bobbili*]. We were all young children. These musicians would come and sing; some of the songs which would be sung at the temples would also be sung to us and some of the songs were also on the records, so this reinforced that, and that reinforced this, and I got a lock on it at a very young age. Then I would see some of the same songs in the cinema so in my mind there is no difference between what you sing on stage, what you dance on stage, what you see in a cinema . . . it is all one whole entirety for me. At three years old what is it you can understand? When I got older, I got into the literature of it, now I am the foremost interpreter of Telugu lyrics to dancers.

You've seen classical South Indian dance? We express the song through body language. There are three ways of expressing the meaning. First, word to word or word to meaning. The next is sentence to meaning, and the third is intent to meaning. [*He then enacts these three ways of expressing the meaning of "Twinkle Twinkle Little Star" as he might dance it . . . Sorry, you had to be there, it was great*].

You will get at the real meaning only if I go through the first two ways. In Indian dance, we repeat the refrain of a song many, many times to express the different meanings. I am no great dancer, but I have a way with dance, and it gives me a great high, for 43 years I have been doing this. Dancing in two temples at a particular time of the year. You see, for me, they are not all different—literature, film, music, dance—they are all interrelated, and I can see connections and I can make connections.

Music hall songs don't have intellectual content because—say, I am wining and whoring and I just want some background noise. I don't want intellectual stimulation, I don't want Mozart's symphony, I just want to carry on with my girlfriend and make eyes at her, pinch her bottom. You know classical Carnatic music, concert music? This material was also sung by traditional performers and temple dancers, Devadasi, whatever. But they make the entertainment quotient much more prominent.

If he sings it [*indicates his friend, who has joined us*] it will be like a chaste virgin singing . . He is a chaste virgin; except for his wife, he doesn't know anyone. I am sorry, maybe I shouldn't say such things about you? [*"Oh no, it is fine, I have warned him about you," his friend responds*], Okay, fine. I am not a chaste virgin [*that seems obvious*]; if I sing the same song you will think that I am making a play for you. I am not actually making a play for you; I am establishing before you my ability to make a play for you. He can sing it much better than me! But I am trying to establish that I can seduce you. I am not talking about the physical thing or whatever; I can win you to my way of thinking. This is because I have been exposed to traditional performers from a young age.

Many Indian dancers work their eyes in the most fantastic way, and when you catch the power of that on an audio recording it is amazing. They tell stories with their movement, abstracted yet seductive. I was lucky enough to see quite a few performances, especially in Thanjavur at the nearly 1,000-year-old Brihadishwara Temple, not far from Bangalore Nagarathnamma's shrine. Southern India has a deep respect for Nataraja, a depiction of Shiva as the cosmic dancer. There are sculptures, shrines, a seemingly endless array of processions, complete with nagaswarams blasting away in an endless improvisation. Watch Satyajit Ray's movie Jalsagar (The Music Room) *to get a sense of Indian dance and the intimacy of the old patron/performer paradigm.*

Meanwhile, back in Chennai, I am still trying to relate birds and kan-

garoos to Indian dance when someone arrives to deliver new cabinets. The cabinets are wrong and Ranga Rao gives the delivery person absolute hell. "You are a pain in the neck and lower down as well!," he exclaims. By the time he comes back he is onto a different subject, namely Jane Russell's films. Then the phone rings.

Yes, hello, yes. No. How are you? No no no I am talking about Jane Russell and Bob Hope. Yes. Well. I would rather come and have a joke with your wife about your gallivanting, and eat a wonderful dinner; she once promised me meatballs. But no, don't think dirty, she meant . . . Well, I have someone in front of me; we will talk soon . . . [*He hangs up*]

You are a grown-up so I can tell you, when you are making love to another person you have to stay attuned to the other person's needs. When you're making love to yourself—I am not talking about masturbation, I am talking about making love to myself—I can press the button I want, I can scratch myself here for ten minutes if I want to. If I am making love to you, I am sure you would not like me scratching your head for ten minutes . . . so in my life I have indulged myself. I had a very sybaritic life. For most of my life, in spite of parental pressures, my father's admonitions, I did what I liked.

I have never had a wife or husband or children, so my life is my own. The changes that come over me are dictated, happen, and are emulsified by me, not by other people. As far as art is concerned, there is nothing you can put in a balance and say, this is better than that. You can only say "I like this; I don't like this." I am a critic, and I think, I am not sure, that I can separate my personal emotional liking and critical acumen. It's a hard thing to do. If it is important to you to be a good, just, timely critic, you will make those adjustments. I admire people's commitment to whatever it is they are doing. If you are on the brink of madness with your work, obsessions, in danger of slipping in, that is what I like.

There follows a discussion on early American film and film musicals, as the birds chirp outside and the cars rattle by and the fan whirls: his absolute favorite is Fred Astaire. Other favorites include Betty Hutton, Carmen Miranda, Yma Sumac. He loves Hollywood musicals, he knows them all.

I was thrilled with *Annie Get your Gun*. Absolutely thrilled. Another favorite musical is *Easter Parade*. Why do I go to a musical? I want to be entertained, I want to ride a pink cloud, I want to feel as though a dozen people, wonderful, attractive, handsome, beautiful people are all making love to me at the same time.

He connects Hollywood musicals to Hindi film, points out influences in terms of music, ideas, sets, choreography, costumes... He recalls hearing a popular Greek song while traveling in Greece which led him to explore an

obscure but heavy influence of Bollywood on Greek film, circa 1960 . . .
Now these connections, you don't go searching for them, they just sit there. It is like a pearl growing, different layers—everything is connected; you just have to see it.
The phone rings again.
Hello . . . Yes, Bravin, hello! Getting old and getting bald. Not balled, b-a-l-l-e-d, but bald: b-a-l-d. Yes, sorry to disappoint you, but I am 78 years old. No no no. As far as you're concerned, no, as far as I am concerned, yes. It does. Yes. Tell me. Yes—which raga? Well, you won't be in danger of leaving your childhood behind. No, yes. I asked her to do a song once in a more enticing manner and she wouldn't do it.
But she will do it in a way which would be suitable for children like you, not grown-ups like me. You see, I don't judge by the size, you see, when you eat a mango, it is not by the size it is by the taste. Hahaha. Yes well maybe in my next life. Goodbye!
In America we judge mangoes by their size, not their taste.
You get mangoes but they are not tasty at all compared to the ones here . . . Here, there are orchards where the fruit smells like heaven and tastes like something beyond. Even after having a bath the flavor lingers. Like a good musical or even song.

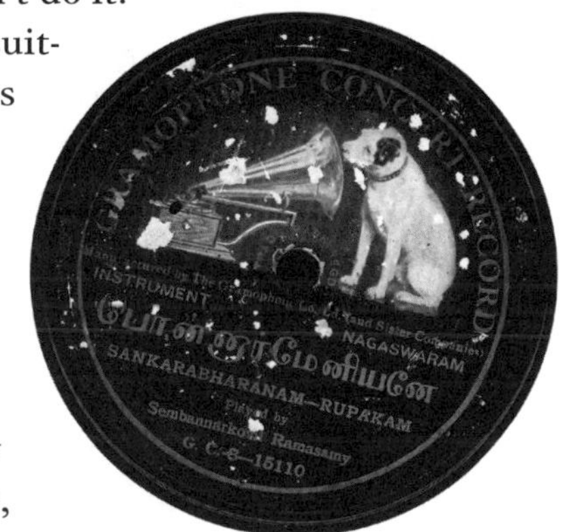

Gramophone concert record, HMV c. 1910 (the label of the nagaswaram recording included on this issue's CD)

I ask him about his library.
In one cabinet, one huge shelf is full of books about sex. They are not pornography, yes one or two books are *about* pornography. But, when I was very young I would visit my grandfather. He had books—Havelock Ellis, *Psychopathia Sexualis* by Krafft-Ebing, Margaret Mead's *Coming of Age in Samoa*—I would read them, I was six. My mother was horrified. "Why are you letting him read all this stuff?" My grandfather said, "He won't understand; they use Latin words for fuck or cock or words like this." I have my own copies of these books now. If you think it is my prurient interest in sex which made me read these books, you are right.

I am interested in case histories. If you are normal in every way, you will not be a case history and I will not be interested in you. These histories; these people must be as touched as I am. Next time you come, when I am convinced you're a little more grown up, I will show you these books. I have beautiful, beautiful books. That cabinet: the first shelf is all sex books, the next three shelves are about various aspects of show business, mostly films, and they are all coffee-table books. Then there are six shelves of paperbacks.

I eventually get the tour—-dusty rooms devoted to books and magazines, playbills, film posters, more broken record players, cassettes and 45s. Rows of historical reference works, biblical literature, books on dance and music, on art, literature, composers—some well cared for in locked cabinets, others crumbling away in boxes or on overburdened shelves. Essays in Telugu, Tamil, Hindi, English, books on architecture, travel.

This is my wealth. Generally I have found when foreigners write about these things they are more accurate, but more concerned with history than mythology.

Where are the shelves full of your work, your criticism, letters, essays?

To me, that is not important, that is for someone else.

What are you working on now?

I have a grant to do something about an early Telugu song composer, Sri Tallapaka Annamachary, who worked some 600 years ago. You have heard of the ten incarnations of Vishnu? These are his songs about the ten incarnations. I have located sculptural evidence and I am especially focusing on the last two incarnations [*the Buddha and Kalki*]. What the stories mean, where they come from, something else, something else.

And here again is the connection to the Devadasi from his youth, an interest in the intersection of art, music and religion.

He asks me about my work.

You have released records? Professionally? [*Then out of the blue*] Are there any calypsos among them?

Er . . . like Wilmouth Houdini?

Houdini? No. He was a magician.

The conversation then digresses on the name Houdini, on magicians, then mesmerism, and morphs into more digressions about ornithology, sex, film, and sweet liquor drinks, mythology, LSD and certain experiences he had in Bombay in the early '60s. Much of it is unprintable.

Will you tell your wife you met a totally touched man in India? But don't ever say that he is a nice person . . . because I would be offended.

This interview was synthesized from three long afternoon chats, along with research in various Indian newspapers [Ranga Rao has been interviewed many times in the local press]. I was left less with a deeper understanding of Indian musical traditions than with a sense that it is important to follow your callings, interests, and perversions no matter where they take you.

Sriram V's book *The Devadasi and the Saint* (East West Books) is invaluable for understanding the Devadasi tradition and Bangalore Nagarathnamma.

RECENT WORK ON PAPER

by Arrington de Dionyso

"I've given up completely on the idea of ever having a normal life. I'm here to *work*. I love touring and playing and painting and I have to keep going. I'm trying to figure out a way to bring my Indonesian translations of William Blake and the *Zohar* to Indonesia proper, sometime in the next year or so. I want to create larger installations with drawings that fill entire rooms, hanging from the ceiling and gently moving with the air to the sound of my music. I am also hoping to work on my writing a little more so that I can develop a critical theory for *Trance Punk*—it's a book, but it's all in my mind right now.

"Most children draw, some more than others. I always drew a lot. I stopped for a while and then started again. I am self-taught in the sense that I have never had any lessons. But I worked for years as an artists' model in various schools, so I've probably logged more than a thousand hours of *listening* to instructors talk about figure drawing while standing naked in front of college students. That ought to earn me an honorary degree for something . . .

"My music and drawings inhabit a world where sound and color are one—in the last couple years more than ever. It's all the same vocabulary—content, gesture, line, shape—improvisational elements engaging with compositional elements. More and more I'm embracing the synaesthetic dimensions in my work. I want to use my performances to create temples: an entranceway to a reality both non-ordinary and 'hyper-real.'

"My drawings and my music are both the cataloging of ecstatic states—in the tantric sense, using the physical gesture to attain a union with the spiritual, with the 'God Sound.' The reactions I get can be confusing sometimes. Is a depiction of nudity 'erotic' necessarily? Is a depiction of intercourse 'erotic'? If I want to think of myself as using erotic imagery to reach towards some kind of higher, transcendent poetic truth, then I feel some people get a little

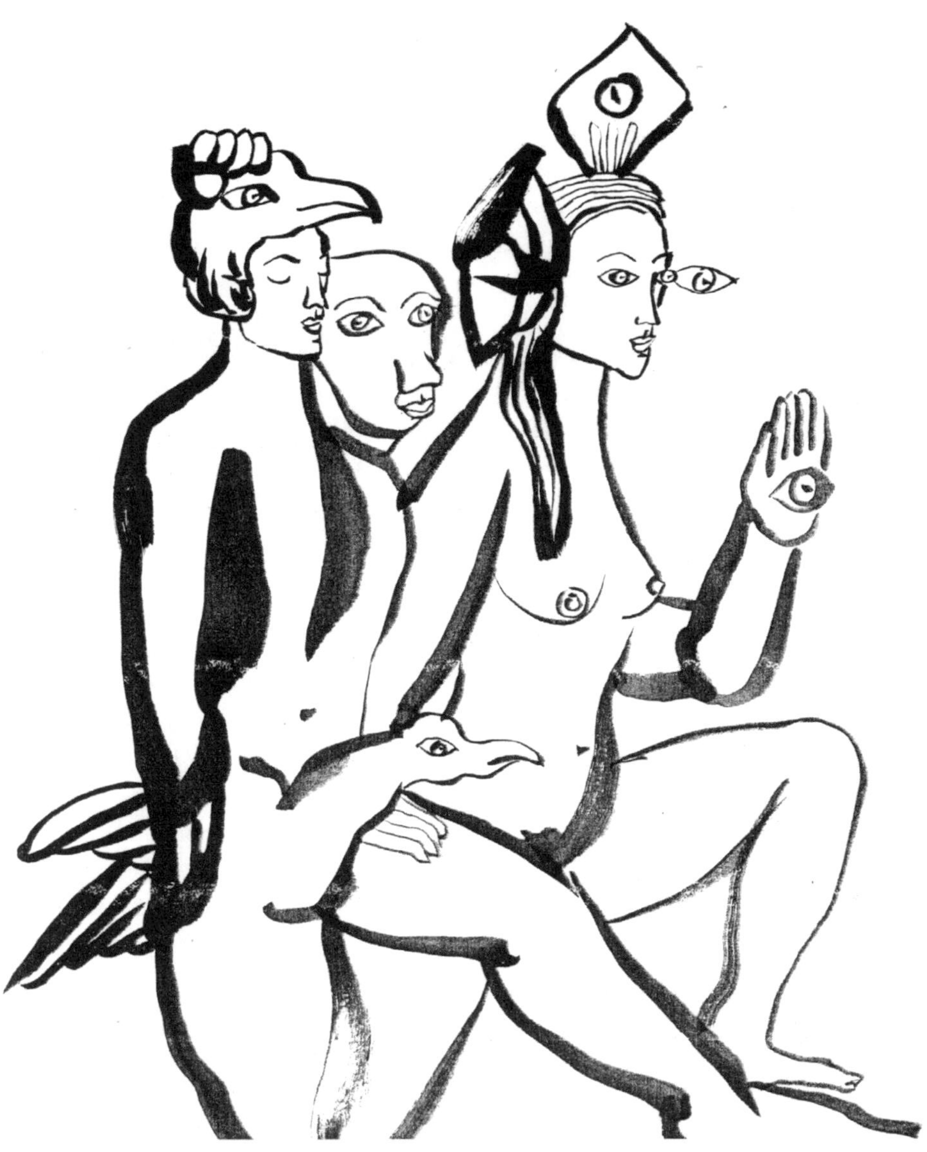

tripped up by only seeing cocks and pussies and titties and thinking it is only about that. Not that it's not about that, too—the experience of sex itself—but most of my drawings are far away from the literal. My 'erotic' drawings are just as much about microtones and raga and finding God and building temples in the body as they are about literal 'sex.'

"I embrace the trans-modernist addendum to post-modernist critique, by which I mean I believe in Truth and Beauty and I wage a war against those forces of the world that try to tell us that life is just to die, all just relative and meaningless."

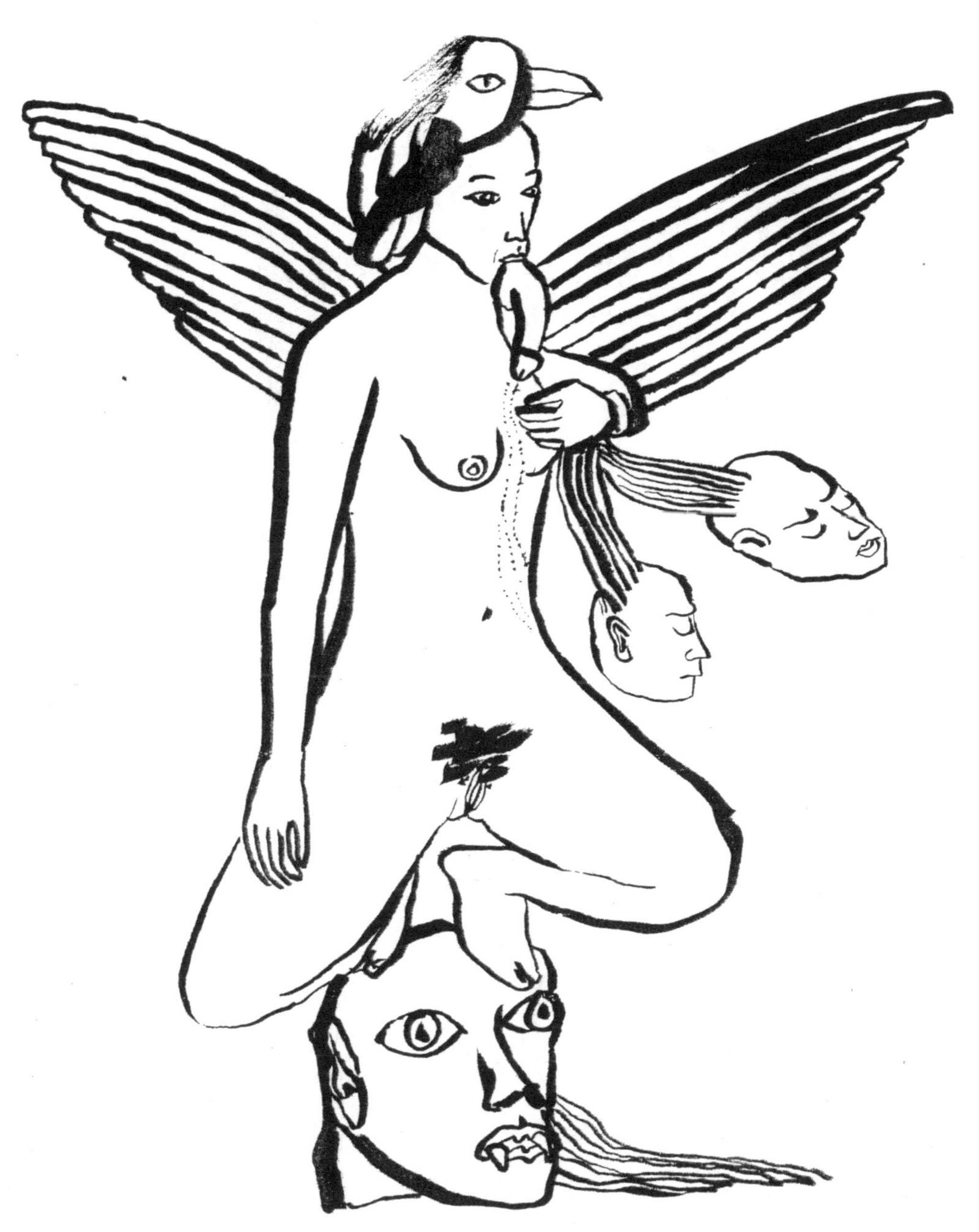

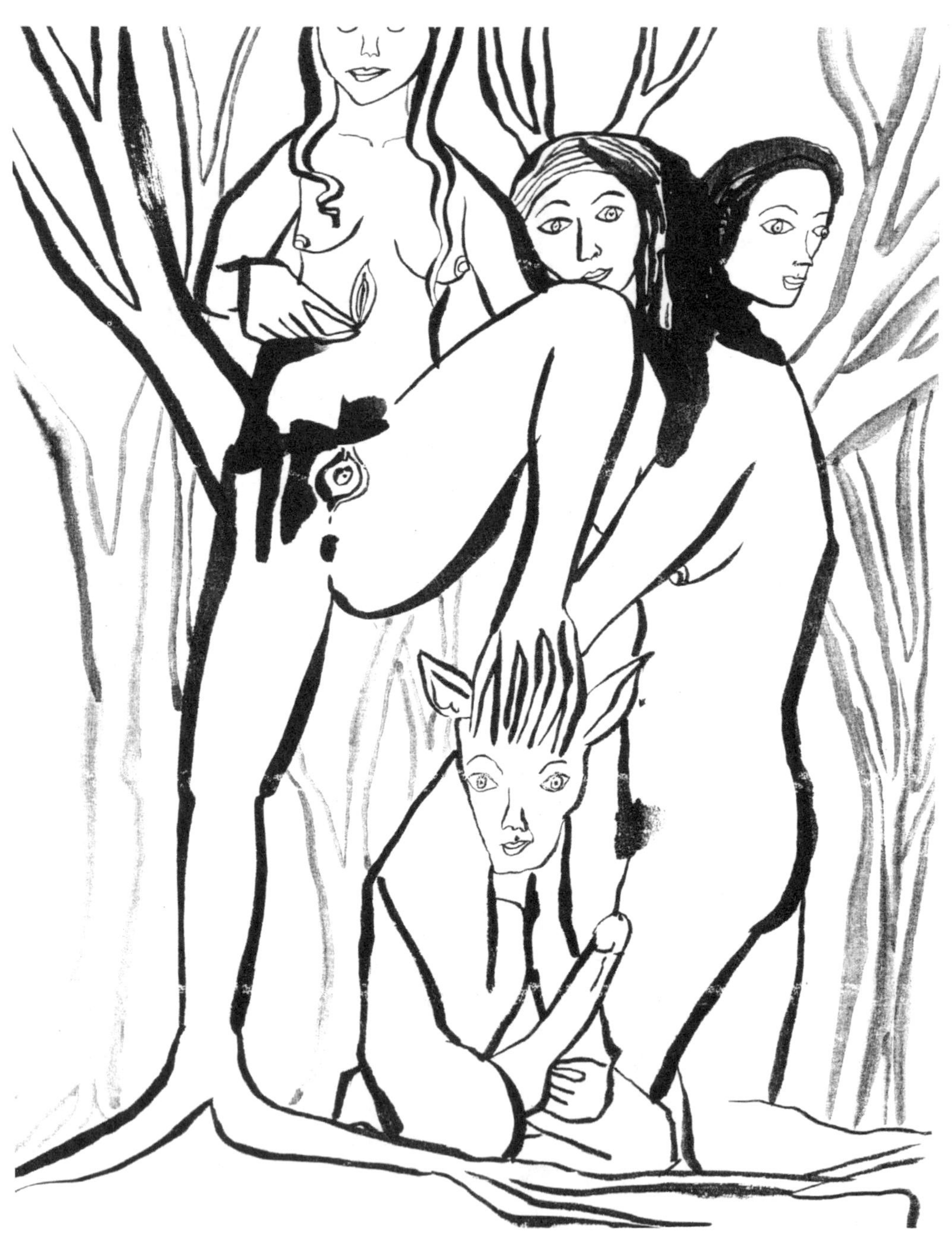

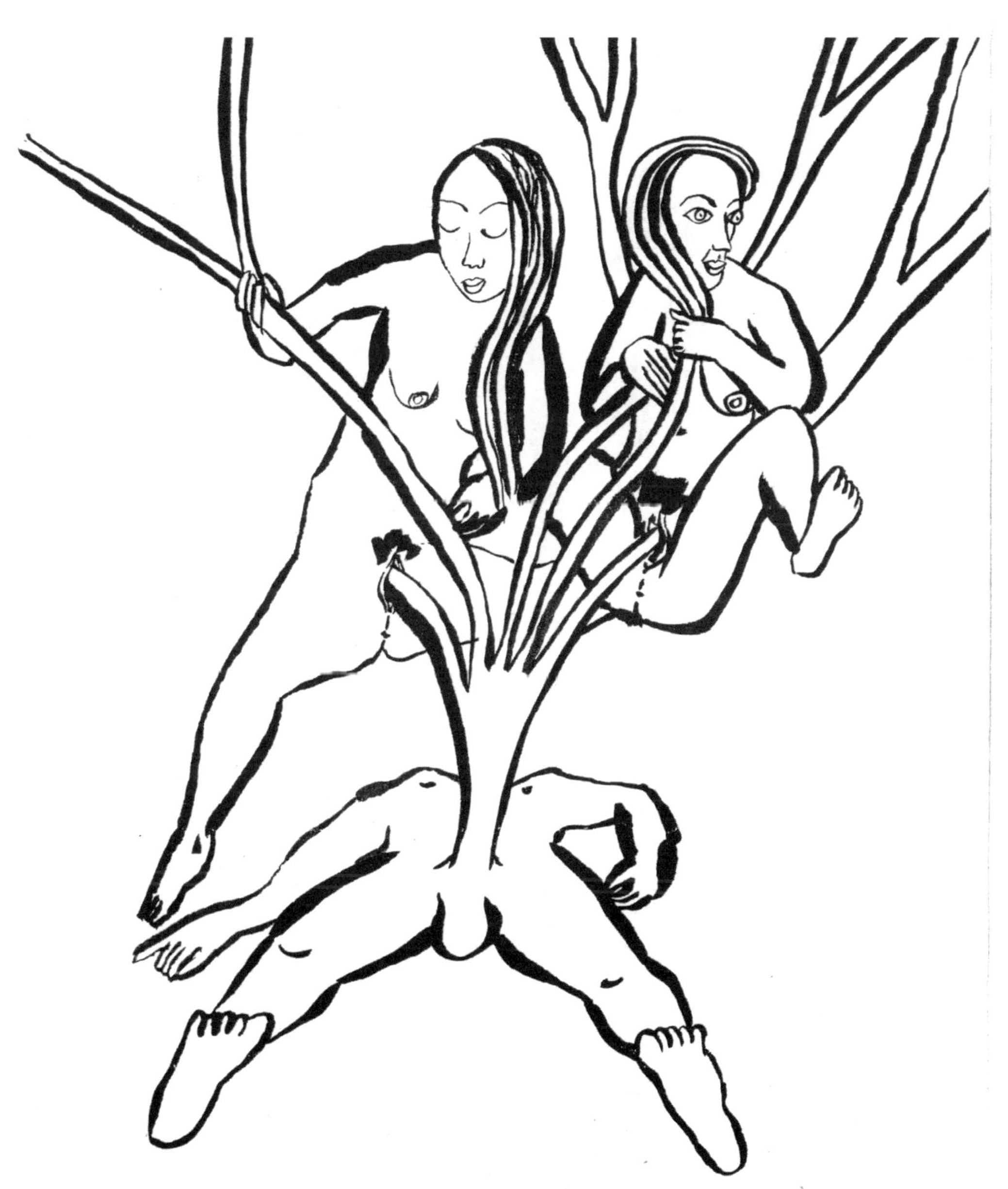

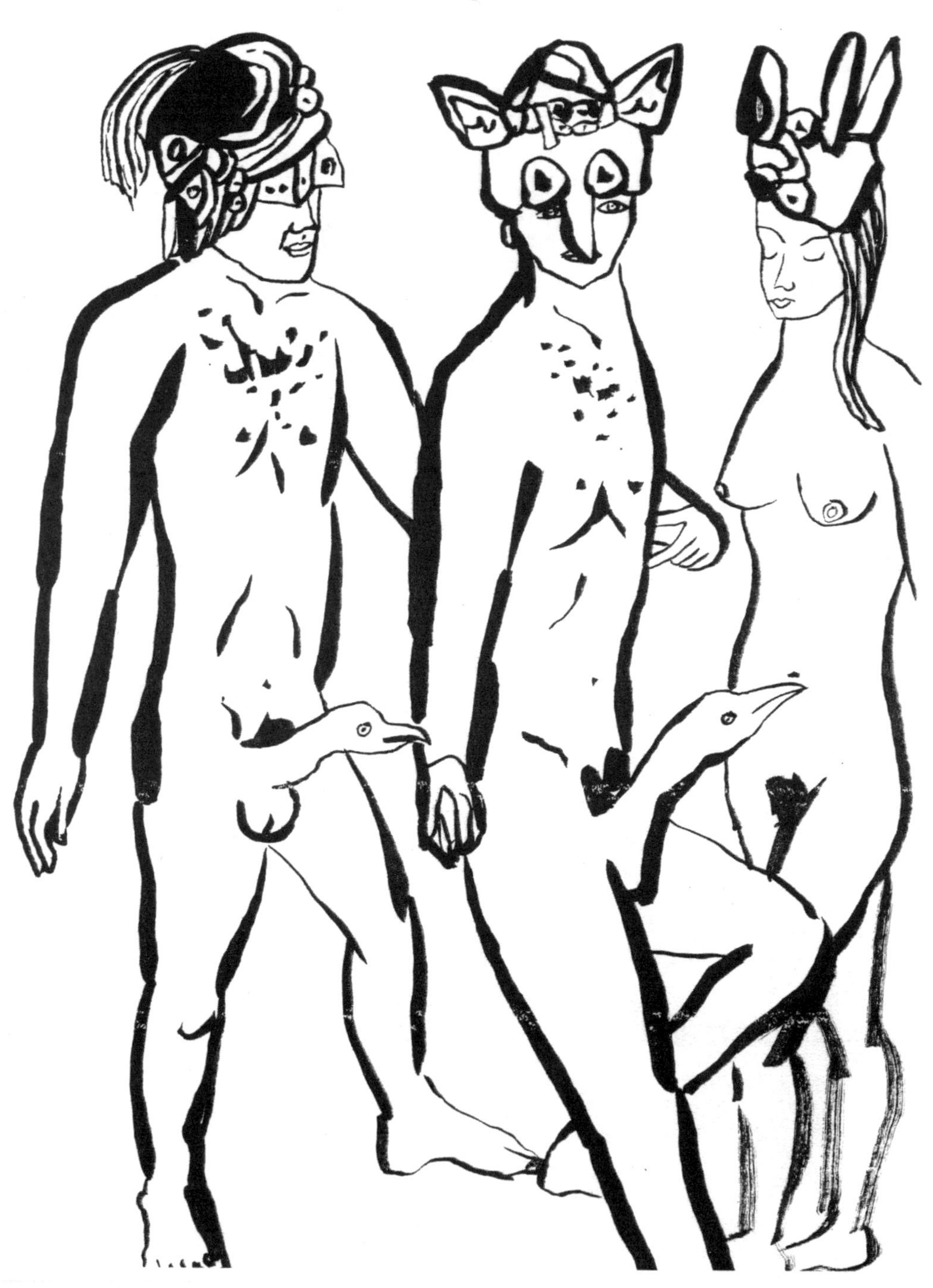

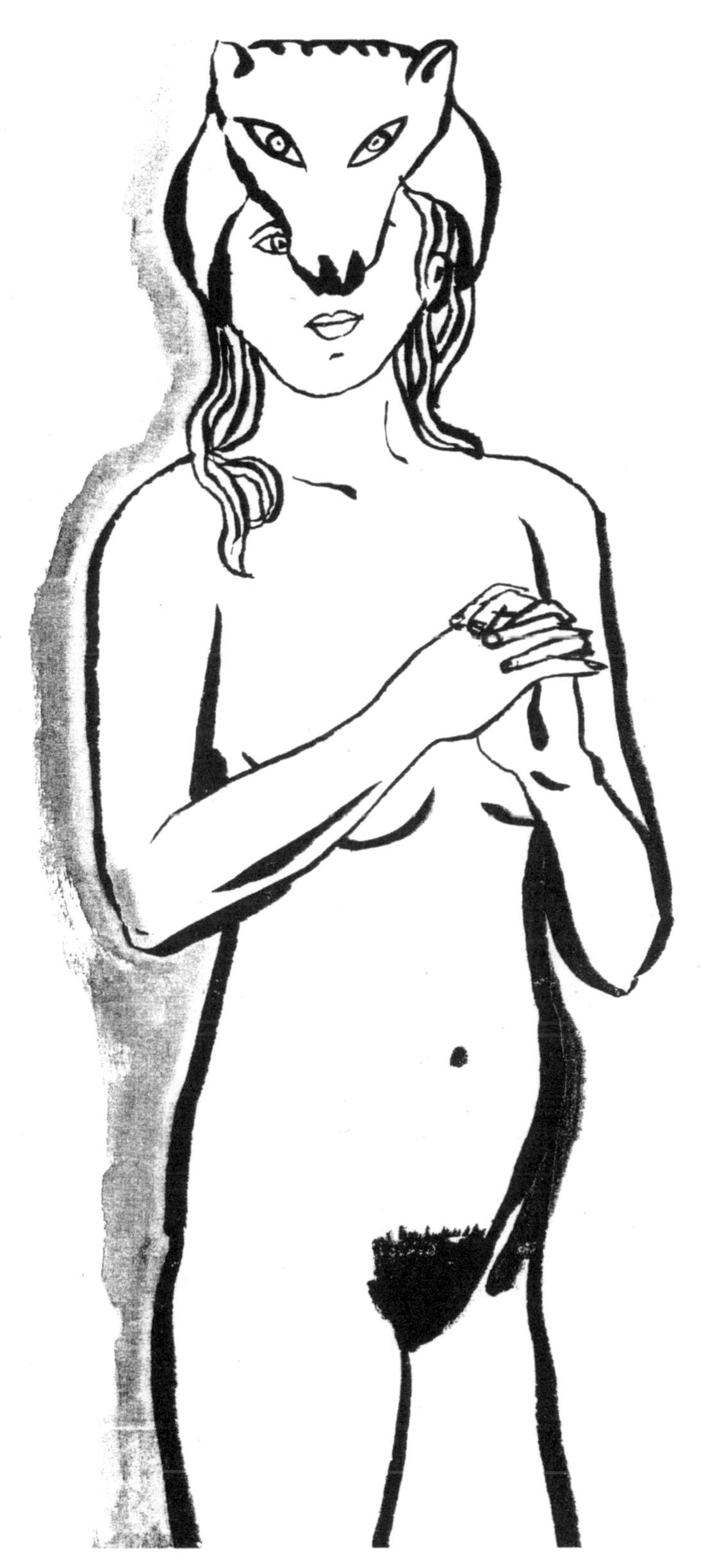

I HAVE A LOT OF STORIES TO TELL

A 1973 interview with artist/filmmaker/troublemaker Bruce Conner

by Paul Cummings

ILLUSTRATION BY PEDRO LOURENÇO

The following oral history transcript is the result of a tape-recorded interview with Bruce Conner on April 16, 1973. The interview took place at Charley Brown's Restaurant in New York City and was conducted by Paul Cummings for the Smithsonian Institution's Archives of American Art Oral History Project. It is reprinted here in a slightly edited form, with the permission of the Smithsonian—*your tax dollars at work!*

Bruce Conner passed away two years ago at the age of 74. His body of work is astonishing: creepy desiccated assemblage sculptures, gorgeous life-sized photograms, and what are generally assumed to be the first full-length collage films—movies made entirely from other movies (beginning with 1958's 12-minute *A MOVIE*—don't forget the caps). He helped create light shows given by the Family Dog at their productions in the Avalon Ballroom in the mid '60s, then a decade later helped to document the Bay Area's early punk scene with photos and as a contributor to the great 'zine *Search + Destroy*. Then there are the super delicate drawings, the often hilarious collages, intricately crafted mandala inkblots, and art-pranks that included running for mayor in the 1960s and then not attending an art opening, instead having two bowls of buttons for folks to wear—either "I

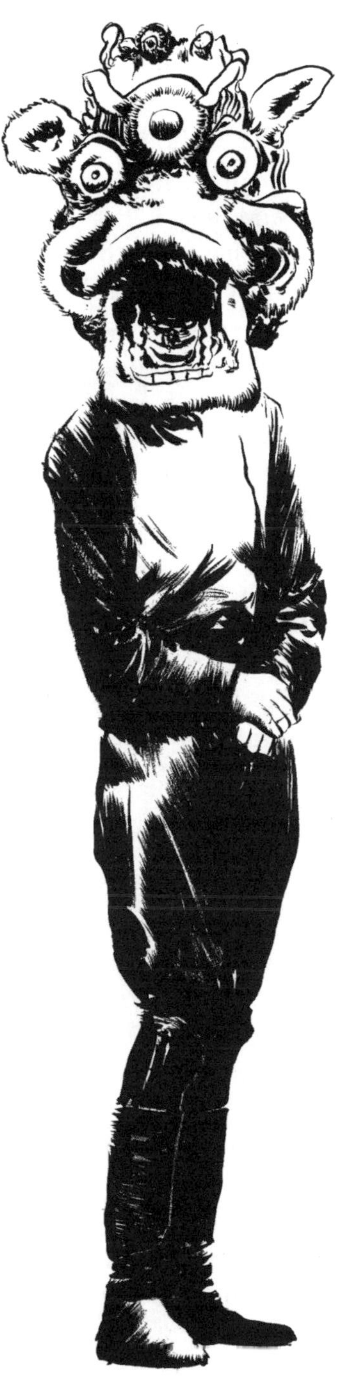

AM BRUCE CONNER" or "I AM NOT BRUCE CONNER."

I might have gotten the facts askew on that last bit, but it was something very similar. For a 1959 show, he made up these small, black-bordered cards that read "Works by the Late Bruce Conner." When required to be fingerprinted to work at a university in the 1970s, he had a set of his fingerprints made into an art object in a limited run, which the university then had to purchase. Clearly, he was stubborn as hell and maybe a bit nuts. I never met him, but I think about his work all the time, and I miss him. Conner collaborated with Terry Riley and Devo in his films; in the 1980s he had Half Japanese travel to New York to play one of his art openings. For years I was convinced that Bruce Conner was so incredibly cool—the work in so many different fields all so uniformly awesome—that he must himself be a hoax. Surely, half a dozen people were all pretending to be this one artist? The truth is out there.

PAUL CUMMINGS: You were born in McPherson, Kansas in 1933?
BRUCE CONNER: November 18.
Basically, you grew up in Kansas.
Yes. I was in Wichita, at Wichita University and then I graduated from the University of Nebraska. I don't remember the grade schools, but Robinson Junior High, East High School and Wichita University.
Did you read a lot? Were you interested in things, have books around, or in music? What kind of young life was there?
I don't know exactly where to start on my childhood sort of thing. I guess I will try to limit it to how it related to art education or whatever.
You must have had other interests before you fell into that, didn't you?
At grade school, art was one of the more popular class periods. I was in kindergarten, doing drawings of teepees which the teacher liked very much. She had me do teepees all around the board. I thought that was fine and I would stay there after school to do it and then would realize how much time it was taking, to do the whole board. We would have art classes and some of the other kids would come over and look at what I was doing. I would show them how to draw certain things. So I was there until probably the second or third grade, when everything changed drastically and my parents moved to another neighborhood which was economically more towards the middle class, upper middle class. The people in the neighborhood and in the school were totally disinterested in that characteristic of mine.
During junior or high school, did you have any instructors who you remember or who were important to you at that time?

The Wichita Art Association had drawing classes. All I can remember was getting dirty charcoal all over my fingers and not liking what they wanted us to draw and getting kicked out of the class for doing something wrong like throwing water at somebody. That was in grade school. I was maybe eight or nine years old. I was taking private lessons from a woman who lived just about three blocks from my house. She had me copying a picture of Abraham Lincoln's birthplace, a cabin, and she came over to show me how to draw a tree which she drew on the paper. I was watching her and was really disgusted with her tree. I did my tree on the other side and she came around and looked at it and admired it and told the other students that I had drawn a better tree than she had. My parents still have that some place.

Were your parents interested in this manifestation of yours?

Well, my mother was, but my father couldn't care less.

Has that attitude prevailed or is it different these days?

Oh, once I had people writing about me and shows appearing here and there and winning prizes and stuff, then things changed a little bit. Then I became a famous artist.

You went to quite a variety of schools. How did that come about? You went to the University of Nebraska and Kansas City and Brooklyn Museum.

Watson Bidwell was the head of the art department at East High School. There were a lot of people who came out at just about the same time. Corban LePell was in high school with me and he went to the University of Nebraska before I did; I went up there for art school, at the University of Wichita,

Were you an art major?

First of all, I wanted to go to an art school but my father would not let me do that. He told me I could not make a living being a commercial artist, which was what I was telling him I wanted to do then. Which was not what I wanted to do at all. I knew that if I told him I wanted to be an artist it would be impossible to do anything. So I told him I wanted to be a commercial artist and do advertising and stuff like that.

Where did you get the idea that you wanted to be an artist?

Well, when I figured I couldn't really cope with my environment except using that as a device to rationalize my behavior.

How was the university? Did it accomplish what you wanted from it or did it do things that you did not want?

I don't know. I always seemed to be more involved in just going through all the stuff that you had to do. Going to college kept you out of the army. While going to college, my father would support me. So I had to fulfill all the obligations of going to college and taking classes I did not want to take, whether they were art classes, or speech classes, or whatever it was. I had no idea how to make a living. If you went to art school you were not deferred. I had a tremendous horror of going into the army. That is probably why I went to college for so long.

I went to the University of Nebraska. Most of the people I knew were moving to places like New York, Arizona, or San Francisco. Most of the people I knew were not visual artists. They were writers or actors or theatre people or musicians. There were very few people in the art department that I had anything to do with except some of the teachers. I was an Art major and an English major. In high school I was going through a Modigliani period. I did a painting of fish which was a breakthrough; Bidwell said it was the best painting any of the students had ever done at that school. In college I was going through a Paul Klee period for the first year or so. Simultaneously, I was fascinated by Dada. We had a Dada show.

That was where?

University of Wichita.

In what year?

I don't know, 1952 or 1953.

Who organized the Dada show?

It was not organized.

Oh, it was just the students' Dada.

There had been a faculty show a couple of weeks before where they served tea and coffee and cookies. I asked for and got the hallway upstairs for the exhibit. It was supposed to be for two weeks. I put up signs announcing the opening of the exhibit, serving lukewarm tap water and soggy pretzels. The show had some gilded soup bones that Coleta Eck had made. She would take plain soup bones and paint them gold. Dave Haselwood had a toothbrush framed in an ornate frame; it was called "Professor Emeritus." Michael McClure had a sculpture he had started to do at one time.

I had a painting called "Old Nobodaddy," some of my recent drawings, and a collage I had done in high school. Michael, besides that, had several elephant drawings that he had done. He was showing how easy it was to do art. He would draw this sort of elephant with one line. Like a hand of fingers with an eye. He would show me how easy it was by closing his eyes to do it. He would draw several atop of one another. I would turn the pages and he would admire them and talk about how important they were and how aesthetic they were. The best one was "Elephant Graveyard," which had a black spot for a sun and, of course, the elephant was upside down with his feet sticking up in the air.

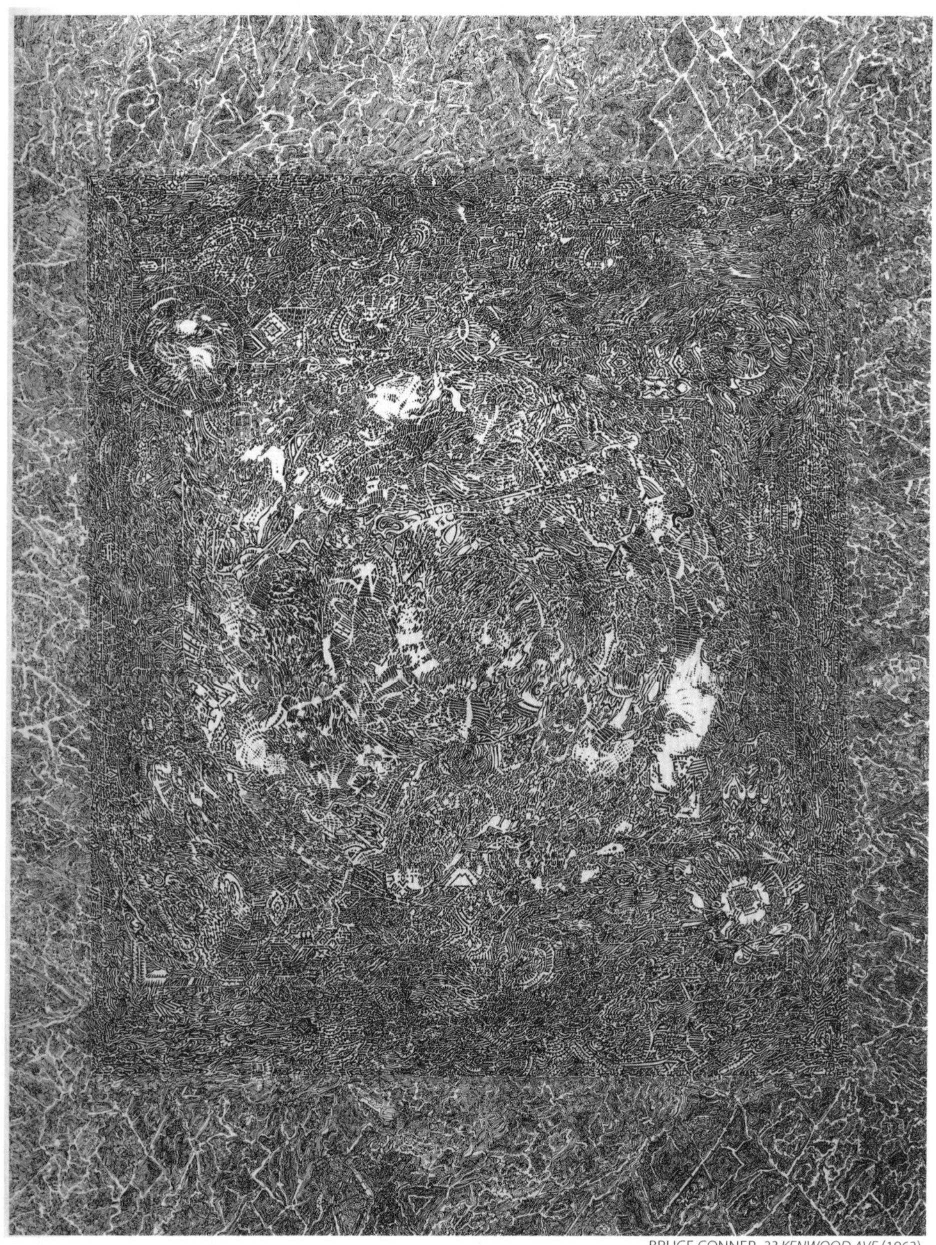

BRUCE CONNER, *23 KENWOOD AVE* (1963)

It was a good show. The head of the art department said that they had to use the hallway for something else about forty-eight hours after it opened, although nothing else went into the hallway immediately after that. I had a feeling that they did not have great sympathies for what we were doing.

What do you think provoked your interest in Dada originally? Was there also an interest in Surrealism?

I was interested in all sorts of things, Pre-Raphaelite paintings as well.

I was taking art history courses and being deluged with different attitudes and images. I could not really recreate what my interest at that time was.

You were going around trying a little bit of everything.

Fun and games.

Right, but yet I get the feeling that there is a certain serious attitude in your perseverance

Right. Do you think I have been persevering?

You have been continuing.

I am still getting older.

You went from there to . . . ?

The University of Nebraska.

University of Nebraska, and that was to pursue . . . ?

Get out of Wichita and go some place that was not too far away. It was supposed to have a very good art department, and I knew somebody. Corban LePell was there. I took painting there from Leroy Burkett, and watercolor from Gail Butt, and Rudy Pozzatti was printmaking. I did some prints there. I had done some prints before in high school. I did etchings, woodcuts and such. Oil paintings. The painting that I developed was like low relief in oil paint using white paint to build up areas and then painting glazes, etc., on top of it. It is like a relief of shapes like seashells, crustaceans, things that you might find in Permian Strata. I built up small details with oil paint and then oil washes on top of it. But then I also worked on paintings that were like Rembrandt, Goya.

These were of what? After paintings by those artists?

No, just paintings that would maybe look stylistically similar to those people. The paintings I was doing that were like relief were not like anybody else's paintings. I mean, they were my paintings. That was my first personal style of painting. When I was in Wichita there were not very many people that I could relate to. At the time, if you read a book you were a creep and a queer—generally someone that nobody wanted to relate to. There was not really any real artist group in Wichita. There was at the most twelve to fifteen people that I could identify with in the whole of Wichita, Kansas (who were under thirty years old) that would have similar interests. Compared to the kind of interest that people have now, you know, if you are in a town of 150,000 you are going to expect quite a few people to be interested in those things. I mean, absolutely nobody had heard of Dada in Wichita, Kansas.

You left Wichita to go where then?

I went to the University of Nebraska in Lincoln. I was there for two and one-half years. I met my wife there. She was taking a painting class. Her name was Jean Marilyn Sandstedt. After I graduated—a year after she did, because she went on to the University of Colorado—I had a scholarship to the Brooklyn Museum Art School for one year.

How did you like it in New York, or Brooklyn. Did you live in New York?

Yes, the Lower East Side—off East Broadway, on Division Street—where all the rag pickers of New York would bring their rags and clothes to sell. The store windows around there would be piled full. The glass windows would be piled with multicolored cloth. I thought about working this into assemblages, of using glass windows and putting things behind the glass, cloth and objects. It was a way of assembling objects within a limited space, and making it a two-dimensional surface. But the assemblage might go back into space or it may employ even more levels, like cross levels of Permian strata.

How did you find New York though, when you came, and what was the Brooklyn Museum School like?

Brooklyn Museum Art School was a surprise because I had a class where the head of the school would come by and say that he had noticed that most of the students did not have studios. Since they could not have space for studios right there, they were trying to make space in the building for them to have studios. He thought it was something that was a problem. Where I came from, the University of Nebraska, that attitude did not exist at all. It was the reverse as far as the administration was concerned. They did not approve of students sending to local, competitive shows because they were not professional artists. Also, sometimes the students would get into the shows and even win a prize when the head of the art department would be rejected.

I was not going to class because I would stay up at night listening to Jean Shepherd talking from 11:30 until maybe 5:00 in the morning.

He was on all night then, wasn't he?

Yes.

So this must have been what, 1955?

The beginning of 1956. So that generally wiped out my morning watercolor class. I don't think I hit that man more than about four or five times during the whole semester.

How did you find Jean Shepherd?

On the radio.

I mean, just dialing around or did somebody mention it?

I think somebody said, you know, "You ought to listen to him. He talks just like 'ya, ya, ya, ya." It was kind of a bunch of crap because he would just ramble for a long, long time but then, every once in a while

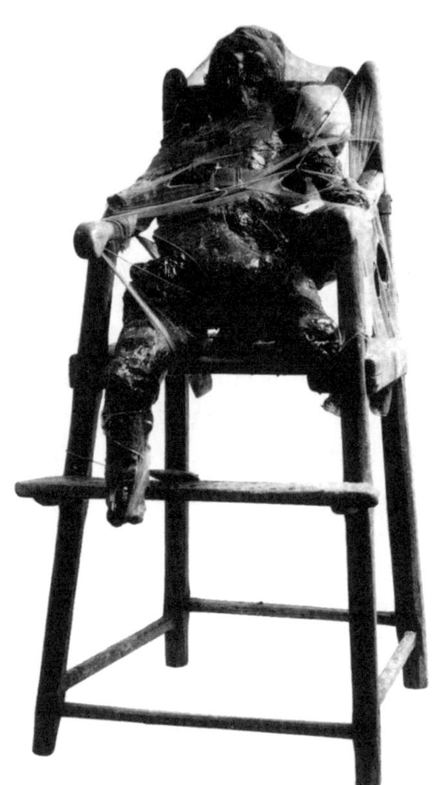

BRUCE CONNER, *CHILD* (1959)

he would do something. He would say something that he had not said before. He kept running through a lot of the same things. Structures of his stories were very similar. It was obviously something you could not listen to if you were not doing anything. I was painting all the time he was talking. I went to Reuben's class and worked on painting there but mostly I would bring paintings that I had done at home. By that time I was showing at the Alan Gallery and he was also showing at the Alan Gallery.

Right.

He was in the position of being my instructor and I was his student. But we were also exhibiting in the same gallery. So there was a problem with him criticizing my work. Towards the end of the semester he finally got through that and criticized my work and told me what was wrong with it which was exactly what I knew. But it was good to hear it from him.

When did you start showing with Alan then?

It must have been 1955.

Because the first show I read was 1960 with him.

Well, no. I mean, I was in group shows.

Oh, I see.

I went around with slides, photographs and paintings, portfolio. I was walking down the street with four framed oil paintings and a big portfolio and my slides, and photographs. It must have been sixty pounds of stuff I was walking tall. The guy would say, "I can't see anybody. I am making money. Can't you see I am making money. Get out of here!" It certainly was not a very friendly reception.

I went to twenty galleries, being rejected one right after another. Nobody was really interested except that there were a few places where the people who ran the gallery would sit down and look at my work. There was a woman who had a gallery on 57th Street, Bertha Schaeffer; I showed her the slides. She said, "Well, this is interesting work but I can't handle it here in my gallery. It doesn't fit what I have, but why don't you go to Charles Alan."

He had just opened his gallery and had people I considered to be really conservative, and I was doing abstract work. I went in with the stuff and he was really interested in it. "Do you have more work?" I said, "Yes." He said, "Why don't you bring it down because I would like to buy one of these and maybe I will buy something else." So I got the other stuff and came back and he bought three pieces. That was absolutely amazing to me after all this rejection. That is why I never got another gallery in New York. I figured that anybody that would do that, not withstanding whatever kind of economic advantages, that was the person to stay with. People would tell me when I was showing at the Alan Gallery, "You know, he is an honest dealer." I had this impression that a lot of dealers in New York were not exceptionally honest and that for somebody to find an exceptional phrase to say about Charles Alan, that he was an honest dealer, meant a lot.

Honesty has many definitions on Madison Avenue.

Well, my feeling is that Charles has been one of the most honest, dependable people I have ever worked with.

He carried you then for ten years?

I was in group shows until my first one-man show. He was there waiting and watching to see what happened. He had a certain kind of Catholic taste in what artists made and what he would show. That first show was made up of my collages. I figured I would not be able to show them, that Charles would not like them. Previously he had talked about somebody whose collages he did not like. So somehow I felt that he did not like collages.

In any case, I stopped painting. I had gone through some other stages. I had started larger paintings and figurative paintings, which were actually kind of oversized drawings, using black paint, white paint.

Sort of like washes. But then, at the same period I started getting very much involved in collages and assemblages.

I did a big collage at the University of Nebraska in 1954, which I showed in San Francisco and it won the main prize in the San Francisco Art Association Annual in 1958 when Thomas Hess juried the show. I had been working in collages for some time, since high school. In high school, when I was taking a crafts class, the teacher assigned us to do mosaics using pieces of colored paper and cardboard, various textures and stuff. I was totally bored with the mosaic concept and began laying things on top of one another and making different shapes. It was much more interesting. I did a collage.

I knew it was not mosaic, but I took it in and she was really pissed off. She said, "That isn't a mosaic; that is a collage." She took it to show to Watson Bidwell who was head of the art department and said, "This boy was assigned to do a mosaic and look what he did," and Watson looked at it and said, "Yes, very good, isn't it?" What was the point of doing a bad mosaic when you were working with something and it turned out to be a good collage?

Right, right.

I was at Brooklyn Museum Art School in 1956 and then in the fall I had a scholarship at the University of Colorado, where my wife was going to school. I was not married to her then. I was there for one year. She graduated with an M.F.A. and I got a D and a C Minus from Mr. Wendell Mack in Life Drawing and Graphics. He did not like my attitude. It was very clear that I was not going to get a master's degree after I had gotten those grades; if you made less than a "C" you were flunked.

Flunked, right.

Especially in two classes. He just wiped me out. It was basically jealousy. He had been working with intaglio engraving and pushing all this stuff for years and years and he had never had a show in New York. He had never even had a gallery in New York. I was a student who had had that sort of thing. He considered me intolerable in my attitude. After that, I left there. I got a job in Wichita, Kansas that summer, saved up some money, married my wife on September 30, 1957 and, immediately after the ceremony, we flew to San Francisco.

Why San Francisco?

Where the hell else would I go?

Well, you know, New York.

New York. I hated New York. I couldn't stand it. I was hungry and I did not know very many people. It did not seem to be a friendly place and I felt claustrophobic after living in Kansas where you can look out the window and see the horizon line.

Right.

When I was in New York it was like a maze, a rat maze, going from one little box to another little box and passing through passageways to get from one safe haven to another. If I would try to get out and try to go out and see the horizon, I couldn't see it. It certainly was not where my mind was at that time.

Did you know people there in San Francisco?

Yes, well, Michael had moved there several years before and I had visited him there in 1956, one summer. He had married Joanne and they had had a baby and we had had a correspondence going. I moved to San Francisco and practically the first week we were there we found an apartment for rent a block and a half from Michael on Jackson Street. Michael lived in a building with Wally Hedrick and Jay De Feo. They were both painters. Next to them were Bill Brown and Joan Brown. And above them was, I think, Craig Kaufman and Jim Newman, the guy who had the Dilexi gallery.

About six months later, Wally Berman moved in half a block from me, down the street. George Herms came in about a year after I got there. It was a group right in that area. Most of the other artists were over in North Beach. That was the "bohemian" area where the fabled degeneration was supposed to be mythically existing. I got to see the whole beatnik phenomenon: how the media related to it, how the neighborhood changed, how it was exploited and how it degenerated, decayed and turned into boutiques.

Right, right.

So, when the phenomenon of Haight-Ashbury happened, I predicted how the changes would take place. I was over there on Jackson Street for one year and then I moved to the Haight-Ashbury. At that time it was a lower middle class area with low rents near the park. Nobody bothered anybody. In 1958 I was painting my windows and creating collages, assemblages, theatre events and parades through North Beach. Things were happening there that people later were calling "Happenings" in New York. We never called them "Happenings" because if you announced a "Happening," it did not happen. I mean, how could something happen if you announced that everybody is going to assemble at 8:30 and there is going to be a "Happening." Hell, we had street theatre. That is what it was.

One thing that is interesting is all these people living in such close proximity. Did that come about because you knew each other or was it kind of by chance that you all lived next door or down the street or a block or two

24-Hour a Day Art Show

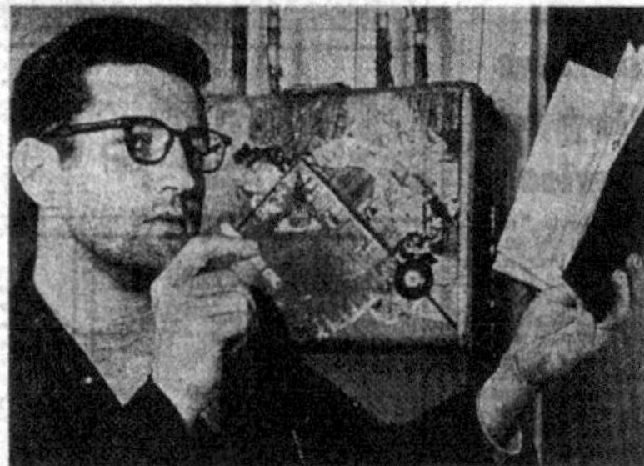

THE 24-HOUR ARTIST
Bruce Conner at the Batman Gallery

Bruce Conner, sometime San Francisco sculptor and sometimes of other regions, is back in town with a characteristically fanciful surrealistic exhibit, lasting only three days and only through tomorrow, at the avant-garde Batman Gallery, 2222 Fillmore St.

Always good for a novelty, along the fantastic line, Conner is producing two major novelties in his current show.

"It will be open 24 hours a day," he said.

"Why that?" he was asked.

"Because there are only 24 hours in a day," he explained.

Novel also will be the fact that in a group of 13 brand new paintings, 12 will be untouched by Conner's own hand.

"They're big canvases that I bought prestretched, primed and white," he said. "I never handled them at any time even when the gallery hung them. Someone else printed onto them the words that I supplied: 'Do not touch!'

"But the 13th canvas, bought and delivered in the same way, I did handle. I myself printed on it the word, 'Touch!' Then I covered it with glass."

Conner will remain in attendance at his exhibit as many hours as possible, with a bit of sleeping time only in the afternoon.

Among his "sculptures" on display are his familiar "Valise, Marbles, Old Shoes, Pillow," the brilliantly colored assemblage of a strange brain. It recently was in an exhibit at the San Francisco Museum of Art.

"Whenever a girl comes to the exhibit," went on Conner, "she may get into the case among the marbles if she likes. Susan Darby, the actress in the local run of Wedekind's 'Lulu,' was in there for a while. And Sunday night at the preview we had a white rat running around in the case. It was a very nice effect."

Conner, nationally known, spent last year in Brookline, Mass., where a Ford Foundation grant helped him make experimental movies. Before that he and his wife were a year in Mexico, where a son was born to them.

Does his wife approve of his art?

"She must be interested in it," Conner mused. "She spent a couple of hours at the show when we were setting it up."

away?

Well, of course I always wanted to go someplace where I knew someone. I knew Michael but I did not know Jay or Wally or any of these other people. I guess the artists had found this building which had inexpensive rent, huge flats with high ceilings. Because he knew artists in San Francisco, Michael had found out about the space and moved in there.

How did you find the cultural life at that time?

The cultural life in San Francisco? You mean the art world?

Yes.

The art world was absurd. There was the Six Gallery which you definitely have heard of because of the poetry readings.

Right, right.

It was a place where Mark Rothko and all those people who were at the Art Institute . . .

At the school.

. . . had exhibited. Wally Hedrick and Jay De Feo had shows there. There was no market for art. The galleries were absurd because the galleries that were showing the things by San Francisco artists were run by artists themselves.

Were they co-ops or . . . ?

They were co-ops or several artists wanted to put something together. The Six Gallery was that sort of thing. The Six Galley would have an opening and everybody would have a lot of beer and wine and get drunk and maybe Wally Hedrick and Dixieland friends would play music. The only way it was opened afterwards was that one of those artists who ran the place would have to go and open it up. It was never open. They were sick and tired of it when nobody came, so it was never opened.

Oh, I see.
You could see the shows if Wally would take you down and unlock it and give you a private tour of Fred Martin's show, something like that. The idea of having shows was silly. Most of the other people that I knew that were artists just figured it was absurd. Why have a show? Just have a party. If you are going to have a show, why bother to take on all the trimmings and expectations of what art should be as a permanent work of art? Why spend your money on that if nobody is going to buy it? You really are doing it for yourself. I guess it is like a spontaneity—outside the values limited to a rectangle in oil painting.
Right.
Artists were using oil paint which I felt was a pretty limited medium for spontaneity; for using what was around for you. We figured you would use anything you wanted to. The main thing was to make it, to make the image. To make the thing that you were trying to do, and whether it fell apart or not was of secondary importance. In fact, for me it became of primary importance. It became a dialogue of how you relate to objects. You have a choice of how you want to relate. If you want to you can take assemblage or collage and seal it in a solid block of plastic.
Right.
Or you don't. Time is working on it. Manuel Neri would make his sculptures of plaster on cardboard, corrugated cardboard. The first time they were shown at the San Francisco Museum a couple or three years later, they had to sweep up the floor underneath every day because the plaster would keep popping off. Joan Brown was doing things like little wooden triangles made into fake sandwiches, and glass milk bottles filled with plaster and doing that whole art food concept before that was happening in New York.
When was she doing those?
1957 or 1958. I went to the Art Institute and there would be this card table with this indelible stuff they had done. Maybe somebody would bump into it and it would fall down. Things would get broken and people would pick them up. But by then it was gone and it was really not very important. The importance of things is who is going to pay attention to it. Nobody was there with the eyes, ears, nose, and throat of the media. They all lived in New York.

New York is the center of that kind of communication. All the magazines come from there. All the information comes from there. If it is not in New York it is "not seen." It is not taken seriously unless it has come to New York. Whatever was happening in New York did not seem to apply to what we were doing at all.

Where does the mandala image come from?
Where does the mandala image come from?
Yeah, but where did you pick it up?
Where did I pick it up? Well, the windows of Chartres and everyplace else that I can think of. Jung says where you pick it up. I read this whole book about it. He says it's a meditative, contemplative kind of thing. It has a purpose. It relates to centering yourself or focusing your attention, your consciousness.
But when did you start using it?
When I was at the University of Wichita, and the University of Nebraska, I was doing drawings which would have a large central circular image. When I was in high school I was borrowing books out of the Wichita Public Library on witchcraft, alchemy, with all those drawings that were used as illustrations in the alchemical works. I thought the illustrations were just fascinating. Most of the things that I do have their basis in my interests in high school and before that.
Did you see the Cryptoligian book on magic?
Yeah. That was one that I was very much aware of. When I came here to New York in '51 or '52 I met Lionel and Joan Ziprin. I designed some greeting cards for them. At that time they were making what we call "studio" cards. The only greeting cards that weren't imitations of that monopoly of greetings from that Kansas City greeting card company. Harry Smith was designing three dimensional Christmas cards. They were satirical with a little bit of black humor and totally unpopular. They were called Ink Weed Studios.

They were totally disorganized as business people. They were not a business. They were very much involved in kabala and magic theory, Tibetan mysticism as well. Harry Smith was very much involved in that. They would tell me stories, fantasies. Lionel gave me a book of kabala that was all in Hebrew. I could not read it, but he said it was good for me and it was good luck to have. And it has mandala images in it.
Where did the Cambridge, Massachusetts period come in? That was what, late in the fifties that you were up there?
I left San Francisco in 1961 and went to Mexico. In 1958 I got very involved in all kinds of chemical transformations. Besides changing my environment in a lot of different ways, I was involved in theatre, dance and music. I was working on concerts with Terry Riley. We were doing parades through North Beach. I was creating paintings, drawings, assemblages and collages. I was making sculptures and I was doing movies. I was a factory—working on my total environment.
The movies started early then too.

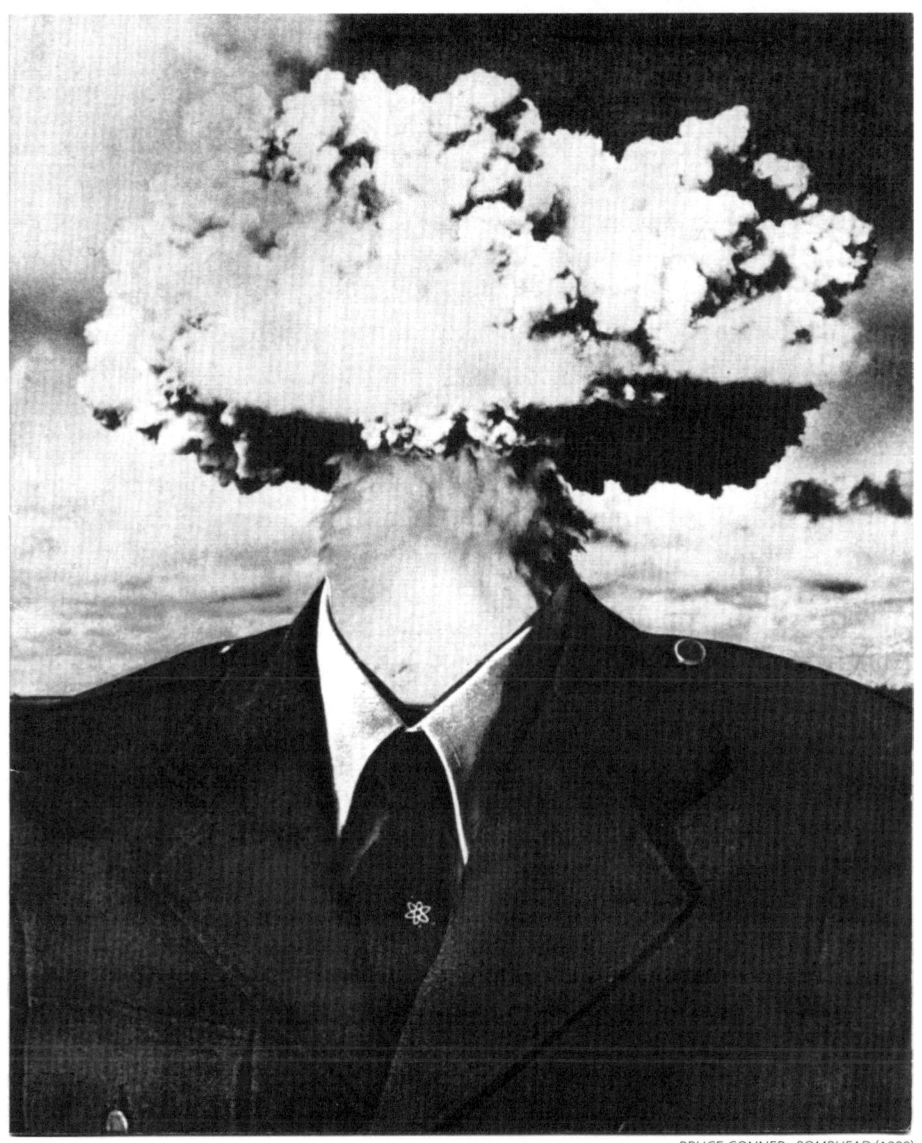

BRUCE CONNER, *BOMBHEAD* (1989)

1958 was *A MOVIE*. I went to Mexico for a year, in 1962. Ferus gallery had bought some collages. I made $7,000 that year. Everybody told me you could live cheap in Mexico. I planned to go to Mexico and live cheap and produce all these great productions. I'd show them in the United States and sell them. I went to Mexico and found out that all in all it cost me more to live there than it did in San Francisco. It cost a lot traveling to and from the border and everything else that I had to contend with.

Nobody bought my work when I wasn't in the neighborhood anymore. At the end of that 12 months I came back to the United States.

We had a child. My son, Robert, has born in Mexico in 1963. I was totally penniless. Didn't have any money at all. I went to Wichita and lived there. My parents helped me furnish an apartment, gave me some money. I was there for five or six months. I had met Leary in New York before I went to Mexico. We'd gone around looking for mushrooms in Mexico. I made a movie called *Looking for Mushrooms.* Leary kept telling me I should come to Massachusetts and live. I went there at Christmas time for a week and a half. I liked all the people. I liked the place. Later that spring I drove there. When I arrived I found out that everybody had gone to Mexico and that everything was closing up. I was still practically penniless.

The only income was from whatever had sold at the Alan Gallery. It was really hard scraping. So I got stuck in Massachusetts; I couldn't get out. I got a Ford Foundation grant the next year. That managed it pretty well for us for a year or so. Mainly I got stuck there because of the work I had. I had a whole station wagon full of stuff when I got there—a lot of it was collages and things I was still working on. Couldn't afford to ship the stuff to California. I couldn't move to California. I couldn't afford to move my family and me and this stuff also. I got involved in doing a movie about Kennedy's assassination, which more or less meant living in Brookline. He was born eight or nine blocks from where I was living. I moved back to San Francisco in 1965. I've been there since '65.

Well, how did you find life in Massachusetts at that point, with Timothy Leary and the other people, were they "gone" pretty much by the time you were settled there?

I don't know whether I want to talk about them too much because it doesn't really have anything to do much with my art. I did my art in spite of them. They didn't help. They were something that I had to contend with. I lived in this house with Tim Leary, his daughter and son, and Richard Alpert was with them there and about nine other people. It was a very destructive kind of conspicuous consumption of all spiritual and physical materials. It wasn't very positive at all.

So, but eventually ending up back in San Francisco.

Finally.

You say it like it was a great . . . .

I couldn't show my stuff in Boston. There wasn't any audience there for me.

Well, you had some shows with Swetzoff.

Yeah, but nobody bought anything. I mean the only person that bought anything was Hyman Swetzoff. He sold a couple of drawings, but I don't remember any collages at all, assemblages. I did like him. He gave me the shows despite the fact that he wasn't going to make money from them. Reviews were horrid if there were any.

What about the art world around. Did you get involved with ....

It's all teachers and professors. The art world revolves around spectator sports. People who don't perform. People who don't create. They sit and watch musicians play somebody else's written music. They watch somebody on the stage performing a play.

But they aren't very much interested—as far as I could tell—in a poet talking to them. They weren't very much interested in any living artist. They were much more interested in dead artists. It's a great place for the spectator arts. There's lots of good plays. Lots of theatre, and dance, and music, and that seems to be what it is. They sit down and watch. Oh, they don't want to get involved. Not at all.

Did you know any artists around there?

Hyman Bloom. He lived in Brookline about as far away as Kennedy's birthplace. I would see him once in a while. I had always respected him and thought of him as a very fine artist. He doesn't seem to be very much noticed at all nowadays. He's picky; he won't let anybody see what his paintings look like.

Nobody has seen his paintings for years and years. He invited some people to his studio to see my movie, *A MOVIE*. He thought it was a great movie. There were all these canvases there in the racks. Canvases up against the wall. Whatever he had been doing, he didn't want anybody to see it.

There just weren't any artists for me to associate with. People who had any dynamism. They either adapted to the educational complex, the area, or they had gone to New York. They just get siphoned into New York and that's no reason to return to Boston at all. I went to a surrealist art exhibit at the Museum of Fine Arts. It was the tamest, blandest surrealist exhibition that I can imagine. Like the tamest Magritte that we can think of. The most sane Salvador Dali. The place was filled with these people you see cartoons of in the New Yorker. The dowagers with all their pearls. The short mafia at guy with the cigar in his mouth. And the reaction of these people was "outrage." They were outraged at the world's tamest surrealist exhibit. "What's going wrong with our museum?"

What would they do with a real one?

Well, they never have to be concerned with one. They obviously are being protective. I went to the opening and there were three people that I knew. In that whole crowd there didn't seem to be more than four or five people that could be identified as artists. Mostly the people I

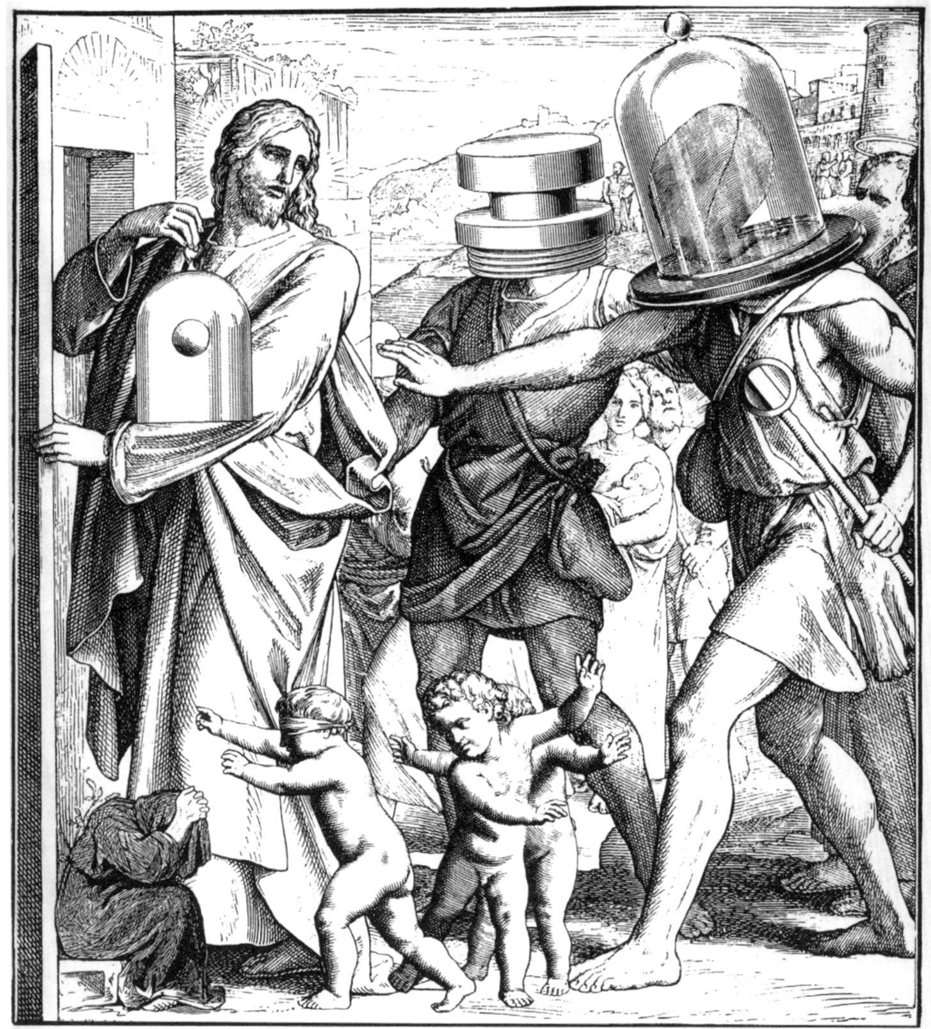

BRUCE CONNER, *BLINDMANS BLUFF* (1987)

knew were musicians, George Crevoshay and Larry Leitch. People who are involved in electronic music and performing Richard Maxfield's compositions. I performed in some concerts at Harvard, and at Boston University. Even wrote some.

You did some drawings once that were sort of like music.

Yeah. That's my music. They look like music. They are music. These musicians can perform it just as well as they can perform John Cage. So it seemed to be musicians and people that I met through musicians. Artists or students. There was a design student at Harvard who had seen my work and he tried to do something like it. He was more like somebody who could talk rather than do things. That's the way people were at Harvard anyway.

Talking.

Talkers.

Who was that?

You know, if I could remember right off hand, it would be worthwhile. Most of the time prior to 1965 I'd never allowed a photograph of myself to be printed. It would be of the back of my head or something.

At the University of Illinois there used to be a biennial show. They asked me for a photograph and I sent them a picture of a volcano erupting. When the catalogue came out there was a photo opposite the page with my wax sculpture, "The Crucifixion." There was this very sensitive kind young man, large dark eyes and black hair. I had no idea how that had happened. I found out four years later that Thomas Garver was responsible. He had been in charge of putting together the catalogue. When I sent in the volcano, he had decided to pick a picture out of his collection of photographs that he had [taken]. He put the picture in.

I see. Why did you do that about the photograph?

I've got to tell you about the musicians too. The other musicians that I was interested in were people around Jim Kweskin, such as Geoff Muldaur and Mel Lyman. People that were involved in folk music or popular music.

What interested you in music?

I always liked music.

Yeah?

I like music a whole bunch. Probably more than any of the visuals. I'm learning to play the piano. It's difficult. I've always had a block against little black dots, written music. Most of the things that I have done I've done backwards. Not the way that you are trained to do it. Most people don't do things intuitively. People who can't relate except in a superimposed structure. I generally find those structures constricting. I know it isn't the way.

I got involved in music when I had a show at the University of Chicago in 1963. At that time there was a band playing once every week on campus. It was called The Twist Band, and the man who was running it was Paul Butterfield, played amplified harmonica. I had never heard anything like that before. Playing harmonica was something you didn't have to tune. You wouldn't have to learn notes. You could carry it around in your pocket.

What about the amplifiers?

You could decide whether you wanted to or not. I learned how to play the harmonica. Now I'm playing organ or piano that sounds like music. But I've never learned formal music training.

Well, what kind of music? I mean whose music?

Whose music? My music.

Well, you say it as if what you've been doing before wasn't music or was leading to music or was something else.

I was not learning music. I didn't learn music structure and form. The situation where you don't learn to play your music, you don't learn to improvise music, you don't learn to make music. You learn other people's music. After years and years of having those aspects of your consciousness atrophy, and be distorted then you supposedly are going to be—if you're a real exceptional person—somebody that can write music. My experience is that the more you get involved in that formula end the way they require you to think that the more difficult it becomes. I've only found things that work. If it works I want something to be glued down and stay on the wall more than thirty minutes.

It works.

And if it falls off an hour later and makes a mess on the floor then I've got to find out something else to do with it. It's that kind of practicality that I'm speaking of. A lot of things that I've been involved in I've done because nobody else was doing them. I would make a certain kind of movie because nobody else had done it. Not because it's brand new, but because it was a movie that I wanted to see. I kept wondering why nobody had done it. When *Last Year at Marienbad* came out, I read reviews of it and I thought somebody had made the movie that I wanted to make. Time, space, breakup, past, future, bits and parts of concepts and still photographs. Everything coming together into one concept. Thinking. Total consciousness of all you're involved in. Future expectations and past memories. Building on top of them. Things, of their own accord, start breaking in on top of it. None of the arts are totally separate.

Well, you know, that's interesting because I was going to ask you if you see an interrelationship between music, collage, films, drawings?

They are different forms to use.

Do you see them, you know, as different aspects of the same ideas expressed through, say, music in this instance, or films or are they kind of equal but parallel patterns that you follow, and move from one to the other. Or do they blend together at certain points?

I'm sure that's all true. What you said is all part of it. The same things appear in different places. Parallel. Merging one into another. Opportune things. The time that it happens and where the situation is. Producing something at a certain moment in time has a lot to do with what it means. At the time it's made it has that time and subsequently it's going to continue to change. Things that I've worked on I expected or even pushed them to make them change. Layers of paint that I know are going to crack. I know in a period of time, sometime in the distant future, the paint will come loose revealing what is underneath it. My collages are things built on top of other things. A lot of different surfaces that aren't just patterns and such.

You mean underneath.

Underneath. There is also the potentiality of how somebody is going to relate to it. I never put frames around the collages. That's one reason why they didn't sell so well. Potential buyers thought something was wrong with them because they weren't framed and "finished." If they're a part of your environment they should be able to sit there in the middle of it .

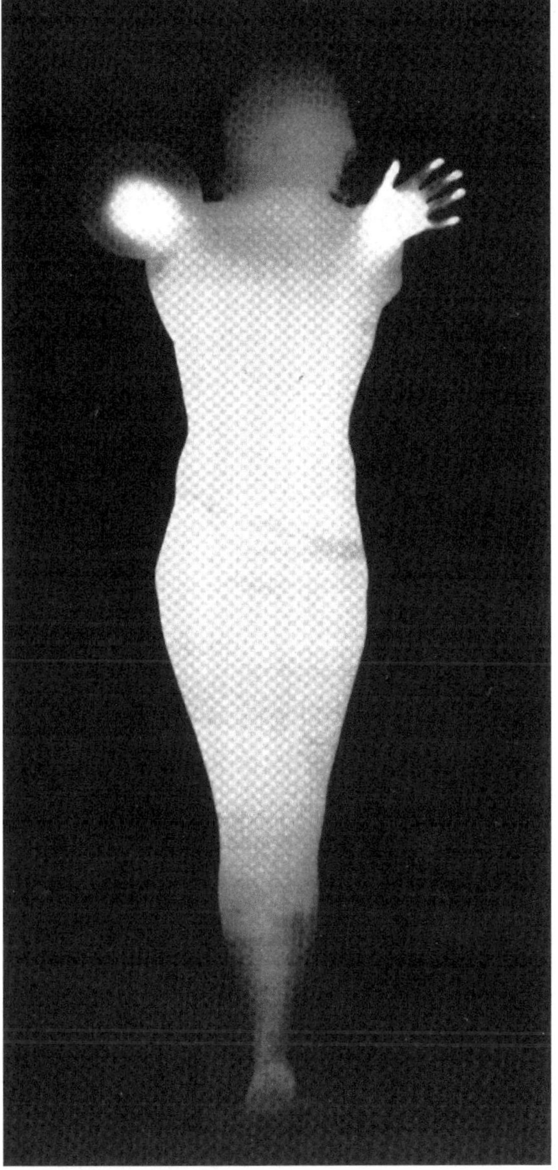

BRUCE CONNER, *ANGEL* (1975)

I have a collage of yours which is about so square and little pieces keep falling off of it, little sort of black things, fuzzy things and it was sold to me by Dioz and it was really in good condition except that these things are falling off of it. And if you would look at it now there are a lot more things that are falling off of it. And I'm sure he'd be terribly nervous about that. Ultimately, a great chunk will fall off revealing ....

How long is any of it going to last anyway? We come back here in another six months and you'll find the menus changed.

Or the whole decor will be gone and it will ....

How do you relate those things to the museum concept? It's an obvious part of the environment. You're not going to limit anything by putting a frame around it. It's limited or it expands because of the context it's in.

Well, you know, it's interesting because before we started this we were saying that you hadn't talked about the art, your art activities and talking about the films recently. And Amy Baker last night said to me that when she had the print show on a couple of months ago at the gallery, that so many people came in saying, "Yeah, Bruce Conner films needed, too" ....

Or they came in looking for Bruce Conner collages.

Yeah.

Or sculptures.

Yeah. What about these different things, is that a problem for you to cope with that people see you as ....

Yeah, because there's an audience that expects a certain thing. They're not there looking for what Bruce Conner is doing. They haven't had the opportunity to dig that much into what Bruce Conner's doing. They come with the assumption that I'm like other artists who only do one thing or variations of that one thing forever and ever.

The watercolor in six sizes with six different prices.

Or the, you know, the dot pattern, reproduction technique, Lichtenstein, or ....

Handy silk screens, whatever.

Some artist is going to make his sculptures out of wrought iron forever and ever. He almost invariably does because that's what everybody expects from him.

How do you cope with that external pressure and that sort of vague image that film people have, art people have, music people have?

I can't do much about it except tell them that there's something else. I haven't got the energy to tell them what all the other things are.

Right, right. But do you find that it's a kind of hand on your shoulder, or ....

I'm crazy about this silverware.

Yeah, well they want a good stainless steel. But the whole business, their similarities, does that give you problems or does it tie together from your point of view that it's just another manifestation of the activity?

I don't want to have to explain to people or sell what it is that I'm doing. There ought to be somebody out there who's going to do my biography while it's happening. Theoretically ....

It's still happening.

Yeah, but I mean Andy Warhol had his biography. And Lichtenstein. All these people get their biography coming out as often as possible.

Somebody's talking about what Rauschenberg did last month. My situation is that nobody knows what the shit I've done the last nine years until it comes out in this show at the Martha Jackson Gallery. Nobody's prepared them for it. Nobody has any idea how it relates to anything else. I mean how it relates to anything in the past.

I got a Ford Foundation grant for filmmaking. I got an application blank which I tore up and threw away because I decided it was a waste of time. That was '63. I talked to somebody else later who said, "Why don't you do it. I work at the Ford Foundation. Why don't you fill the thing out because it's sort of like a game?" I decided I would play it as a game. I would play it like a dialogue between me and an invisible audience. I'm exposing myself telling them all of my history.

My vaccinations. Explaining my whole theory of art and life and what I intend to do in the future. How I'm to use whatever alms they will give me. I started drawing parallels of this kind of activity with religious rituals. Confessionals, and ringing of bells, and doing penance in the streets. Fantasies of movies that I would make. It offered me a chance to fantasize. It was my opportunity to write in an entirely different context. I've never been able to write in the context of publication. I knew all the crap that you have to go through. You write it. You type it out. You make a bunch of copies. You send them out to all the magazines.

Over the next two years you'll get the copies back. It's most disastrous. I've never been able to do that. This was a way for me to have an audience. I would write letters. Well, they loved it. Somebody loved it. They gave me a film grant and all I had made was sixteen minutes of movies. I didn't expect to get it because there were a lot of other filmmakers who were more qualified and should have gotten it. Like, Stan Brakhage was the man who had most to do with me getting into filmmaking, and he didn't get one. He really should have.

How did you do that?

Do what?

Get into filmmaking, in that way?

Well, I was involved in film societies and he was the first filmmaker I had ever met. When I was at the University of Colorado I started a group called the Experimental Cinema Group. We had ten film programs. Four hundred and fifty people joined the group for three dollars. The films were experimental film, old avant-garde films, historical films, silent films, foreign films, etc. There were a couple of his friends in the group. Brakhage would come from Denver and advise us. He brought his films and showed them. He told me I ought to make movies.

But I didn't want to.

When I got to San Francisco I knew Larry Jordan, who was sort of a student of his. He was a friend of Stan's and the films that he was making were very similar to Stan's. We started a film society and I ended up using his film equipment. I was able to get into a position where I would be encouraged and actually have the equipment and learn how to splice film. It depended on me and Stan Brakhage and Larry Jordan. At that time there were no film classes anywhere in the United States. There was one at NYU that Hans Richter was teaching. But you had to have two years of undergraduate study in something like sociology before you could take his class. The other one was at UCLA. It was a technical course for film technicians.

For the Hollywood business, yeah.

And now there's a hundred and fifty thousand film students in this country.

True.

Well, it wasn't easy to do it, and the kind of movies that I made weren't like anybody else's movies. With the Ford Foundation grant all of a sudden instead of being an artist that had made a couple of short films, I became a filmmaker who dabbled in the arts.

The first major demonstration of what had happened was when I had a ten-year retrospective at the Alan Gallery—a selection of collages from over ten years in '64. Brian O'Doherty from the *New York Times* came and saw the show. Charles told me he wanted to write about the show and he'd like to see my two movies. I showed him the movies. The review came out and it was spectacular. It was like one-third of a page, on Sunday. Three-quarters of it was about the movies.

People came to the gallery and said, "Where are the movies? What's this junk on the walls?" I was very proud of the show. I wanted people to see what I had done. This kind of notice was something that I had always wanted. It meant some attention was going to be paid. But it was totally diverted and twisted around. The gallery sold two things out of the show—didn't make enough to pay for the announcements. I decided to make a movie to ruin my reputation as a filmmaker.

Which one was that?

It's—nobody has seen it outside of the one time it was shown. It's called *Leader*, and was designed to drive the audience out of the theatre. They could say, "He used to be a good filmmaker before he got the Ford grant and that ruined him." That was the purpose. But it was shown in Boston at the Swetzoff Gallery; Bob Brown had got *Flaming Creatures*, which had an underground reputation as a dirty artistic movie.

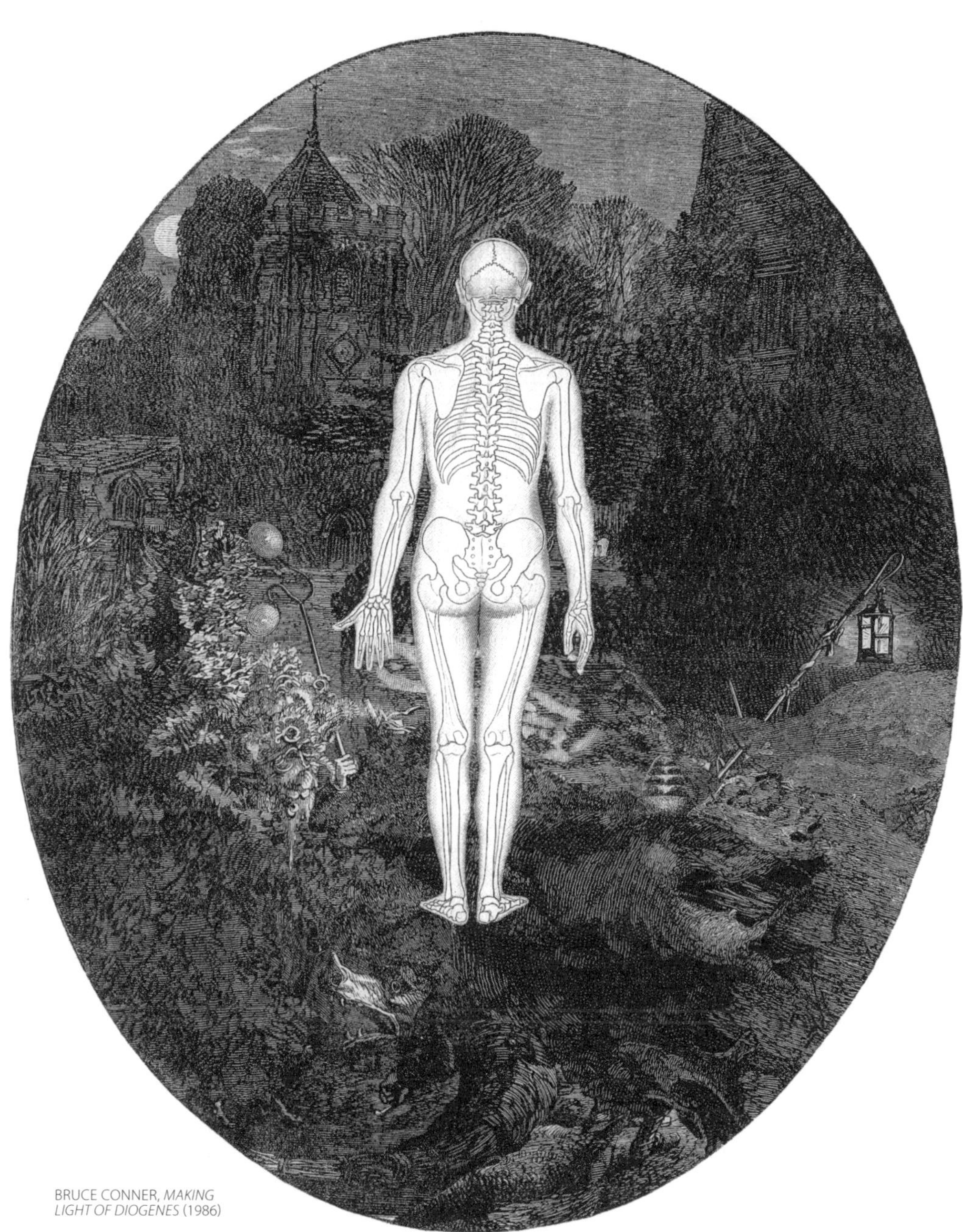

BRUCE CONNER, *MAKING LIGHT OF DIOGENES* (1986)

The "aesthetic people" of Boston were arriving to see this dirty movie. They might get raided by the police, but it's really not a dirty movie. It's artistic, right, but maybe we'll see something. And instead of showing my movie at the end of the program, he showed it before *Flaming Creatures*. Of course they hated it. And it became a scandal. They unplugged the projector, they yelled and screamed, and honked the car horns outside. They unplugged the projector again. Took away the movie screen. It became a celebrated cause. My attempt to ruin my reputation as a filmmaker failed immediately. They heard about it in New York. Jonas Mekas wanted to buy it and show it at the Cinematheque and to put in the . . . .

What was it made of? A series of leaders?

It was just leader. Ten, nine, eight, seven, six, five, four, down to three. That's all it was for thirty-five minutes. So the only other thing that was happening was the soundtrack.

Which was?

Which was recorded off of a television dramatization of American soldiers captured by the Nazis. It came through a television set (which had some distortion) onto a tape machine. It was then rerecorded over and over and transferred onto another tape. That tape was transferred onto sound negative and then transferred onto the film. So it had all these generations. It ended up like a third of the sound was inaudible. It was difficult to understand. You had to pay attention. And since it obviously wasn't visual; it had to be aural and it took a lot of effort. There were whole dramatic sections that I repeated.

Basically it was dialogue between the filmmaker and the audience. The filmmaker was the Nazis that had captured the Americans. "You Americans are embarrassed you have been captured. Well, you won't get away." "We've got to get out of here. We got to get out of here." I'd repeat phrases like that over and over and over. "We can't stay here. We got to get out of here. If we get the gate open we can get out of here." By the end of a program and by the end of the movie everybody would have left. They would have gone out the exits. I mean, I was making it for myself as an audience, but it was also a dramatization which would eventually be told as a story to you through this microphone.

In a way you were dramatizing the audience, too.

Yeah, they were part of my work.

You haven't shown it since?

Well, I sent it to the co-op. I wanted them to sell it by the foot. I should have said, don't sell more than ten feet. People could buy a Bruce Conner film at thirty cents a foot. But then Jonas wanted to buy the whole reel. That meant it was going to go out as a film. I told them to send it back. When I was in San Francisco there was a funk art show. Sheldon Renan put on a show which was supposed to be funk film.

Afterwards there was supposed to be a panel discussion. I had that roll of film loose without any reel on it. I handed one end of it to same people in the first row and held it up. It went zigging and zagging through the whole audience. They wrapped it around their heads.

They tore off parts. They threw it. It was a good audience. Berkeley audiences are good participatory audiences. And that's where the film went. That was the end of it. Well, it exists. It did what I wanted it to. It went into pieces and parts and went into other. I've seen parts of things appear in other people's work. I think that is entirely a part of the process.

There are marvelous things that we haven't gotten into, such as your adventures at Tamarind.

Oh. You know, all of these should be broken up into, you know, the subject of discussion. That's sort of why I wanted to start out getting a general structure. Like, I never mentioned Tamarind. But, there are other things, you know, that would be, could be, used as pivotal points to talk about.

Well, there are a lot of things I don't know about you.

I have a lot of stories to tell.

About the world. You mean people.

No, it's another art form. I might project or assume the character of a personality. Like the person that's producing this is the Black Dahlia, and it's also the person that killed the Black Dahlia. Instead of there being individual actors before me, I'm using objects and characters that aren't defined as separate performing characters. Mental attitudes. The relationship of victim to assassin. Positive to negative. But they're both lovers.

I mean, the Black Dahlia is loose within the structure of the attack of the man who had destroyed her. It's all basically love or passion that's been distorted and altered. Changed because of social or cultural imposition. But what I would get back from the culture of this society would be hate. Which, you know, isn't it at all. Or, you know, things which might be critical of the falsity of . . .

What did they say because of the nylon stockings and all . . . .

Yeah, yeah. I mean all that sort of thing that might be attacked as male chauvinism now. It's a cliché, and it's something somebody doesn't want to get into. Very superficial, but that's more or less what the attitude was. Such an identification with all this sort of high heel shoes, long fingernails, costume jewelry, and all the disguises of women. Which are like some kind of theatrics that may disguise really a horrible creature.

They are theatrics. Not a kind of. They are.

Well, sometimes. ✪

YOU MUSES ASSIST

Alasdair Roberts interviewed by Erik Davis via Skype in the fall of 2009

ILLUSTRATION BY TARA SINN

ERIK DAVIS: Do you have video?
ALASDAIR ROBERTS: Mmm, no. Why? So we can look at each other?
You haven't done that?
No; I don't have a camera on my computer.
No problem. So, where are you located right now?
My home is in Glasgow.
You live in the city?
Yeah. And you're in San Franscisco?
I'm in San Francisco, in the city. I think I saw you the last time you were here, at the Hemlock.
I played there a couple times—once with a band, as well.
I wanted to start off with a little thought experiment. Before I launch in and talk about folk and acoustic music, I wanted to give you a chance to characterize your music. But rather than talking to me, I kind of imagined like you're on an airplane and you meet, like, this Sufi musician. He's a totally cool guy and you connect and he doesn't know anything about pop music or folk or Brit folk or whatever and you wanted to explain to him what your music is. What would you say?
I would say . . . [*laughs*] . . . I would say to him that I make music which draws on Scottish and, more widely, British and European traditions—song-based traditional songs. And my own compositions come out of the world of traditional song.
They come out of the world of it. One of the things I really want to talk

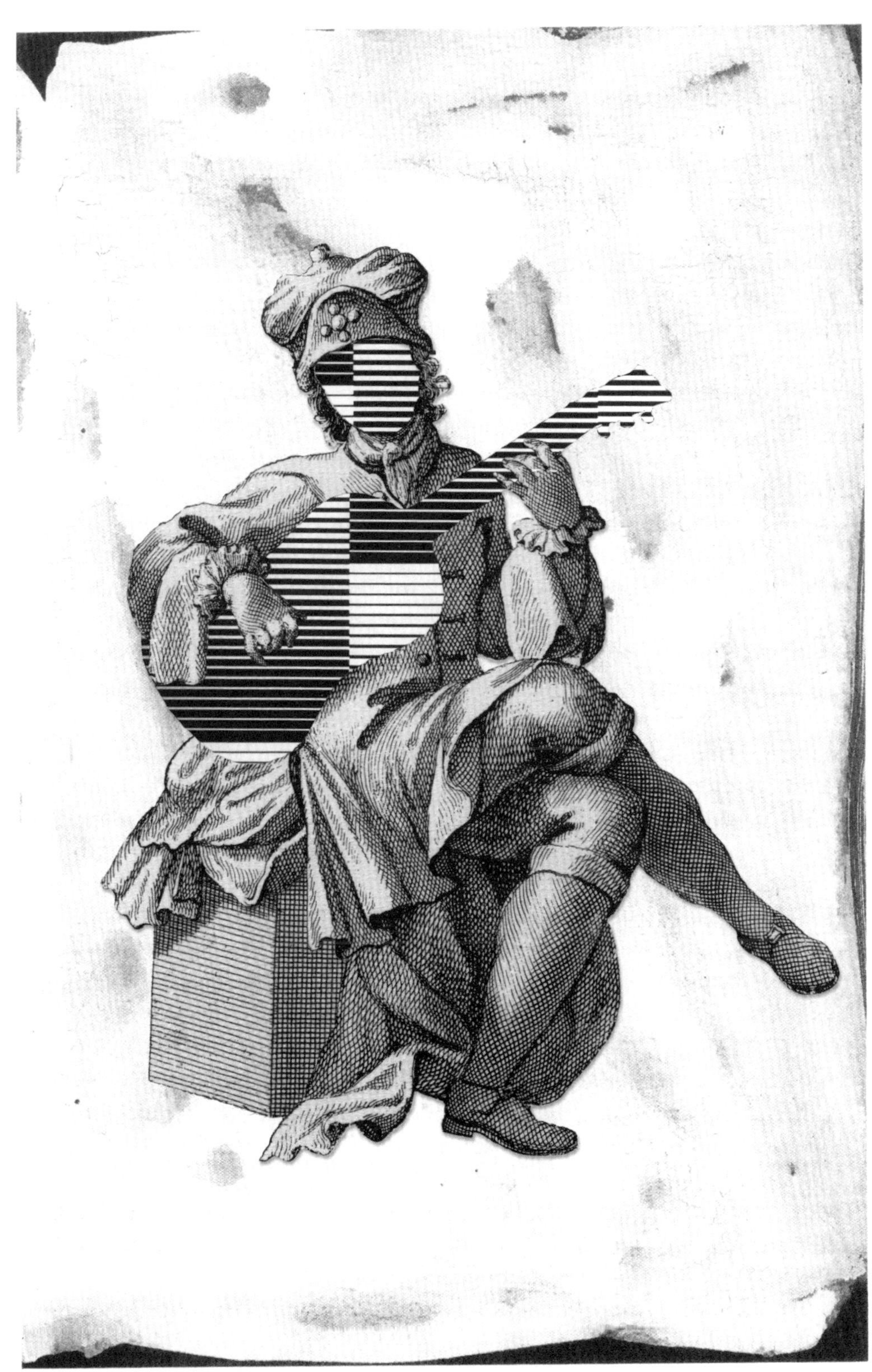

about is just how you relate to the idea or the practice of tradition. You come from a world . . . and yet there's transformation in the music. And how you carry that—how you feel about that relationship. So, our hypothetical Sufi asks, "Are you a traditional player, or are you changing things, are you adapting . . . ?"

I'd probably explain to him what my latest project is. I just finished making a record of traditional ballads, and I play guitar and sing. And then I have a great group of other musicians playing on it. I've got a bass player, a guitar player and a great English traditional singer. The songs are traditional, drawing from all over the English-speaking world. To me it sounds like a straightforward traditional folk record, pretty much.

I like the sense that you move between a more experimental vein and then a more straight-up vein. Is that something you do consciously, or is it just that your desire for the kind of music you're making shifts and moves back and forth, in a way?

In terms of these traditional ballads that we just recorded, a lot of them have been in my brain and repertoire for the past couple years . . . I've been itching to record them. Sometimes it feels like doing that material is really important to me and when I'm doing it, it seems like the most important thing to be doing. It also feels in some ways like a blockage or an obstacle to be got through in order to be able to work on my own material. The one informs the other; they exist in a kind of nexus.

Here's another way. Let's say you were in a psychedelic rock band, and were deeply into psychedelic garage music. At this point in time, that's a tradition. I could look at your record collection and find a bunch of Nuggets *records, and the Seeds, and the Elevators, and some of the players have died. And you're using their music and playing it, so it's already a tradition. In some sense, Brit folk is like that—records from the '60s and '70s that have a great richness to them. In some sense, you could do a version of your career just knowing and playing music from the styles of that period. And yet it's more than that. It's something else. And I'm trying to figure out, what is that something else? What is the something more than just relating to an earlier generation of contemporary folk players? What else comes through the music that seems to need its own voice?*

I'm trying to look beyond the generational thing—trying to look further back to all the other singers. I don't necessarily listen to a lot of the folk revival stuff. I love the folk I've listened to recently, it's just unaccompanied singers; I'm exploring Gaelic song a lot more.

Do you feel like you're a carrier of some of this music? When you listen to it and absorb it and try to bring forward some of that sense of the past, do you feel a responsibility for presenting this material to people who would otherwise not hear it? Or, is it just music for you?

That's something I've been thinking about recently, whether I have some kind of responsibility for the songs. For whatever reason, I'm attracted to those old songs and enjoy singing them. For instance, a ballad we recorded, "The Twa Sisters," which I learned from an old singer named Jock Duncan, a traditional singer who's from Gelliebrae and lives in Port Lockery. When I sing that song, I think about Jock Duncan and imagine him listening to it, and then me passing that song on, from Jock to the world, or from Jock to whoever I'm playing for. When I'm singing it, I'm thinking about all the people who have sung it before, trying to somehow locate my voice within theirs or vice versa—their voice within me.

How do you experience the tension between a more contemporary rock environment and its rules for listening versus the sense of carrying something from the past?

One thing I've noticed: when I say to people I'm doing this record of traditional songs, people will say, "Oh, so it's like covers—cover versions!" And to me, it doesn't feel like that at all. They're not cover versions; they're interpretations of ancient material. It's not like a band covering songs which were written ten years ago. Some of the songs could be hundreds of years old.

It's a funny balance, because when they're older, they're actually more alive. If you cover "Satisfaction," your version will always be in some echoing relationship with the "original," which is on a disk that everybody can access. But if you're going to sing "Pretty Polly," an Appalachian mutation of a Scottish ballad that goes back hundreds of years, it's way too old for that. It's much more from the world of the dead and yet, paradoxically, it's more alive, so that your version has as much, sort of, presence as any other one.

One song that we recorded is this ballad, "Little Sir Hugh," you know that one? Or, "The Jew's Daughter"? It's, really . . . quite an offensive song. It's supposed to relate to a specific historical event that happened in the twelfth century, where a Jewish girl murders a Christian boy—throws him in a well.

I'd been wondering whether it was morally, ethically, or politically appropriate to sing such a song. We did end up recording it, but we're still debating whether it's appropriate to air. You know, if I put that song out, I'd have to explain that I'm not an anti-Semite. The views of the characters in the song are not my own. But on some level I think it's important to memorialize things, that those kind of things were rumored to have happened. It's like a historical excavation of a certain time. Human relations have little to do with this kind of bucolic fantasy of the pastoral ideal. It's more about the kind of visceral weirdness from the time.

Almost like your EP The Wyrd Meme.

Oh, have you heard that? [*chuckles*] I thought that the songs were kind of weird, and I was thinking of this idea of meme, a nugget of cultural information which somehow gains currency at a certain time, somehow becomes fashionable. I suppose it crosses over from some sort of sociological field, the idea of a meme. And it seemed to me that there was a time when this kind of weirdness had become fashionable. You know, like, everyone was all of sudden trying to be weird. People were talking about "weird folk," that kind of thing.

I was not prepared for Spoils, *my friend. It's a real breakthrough, both musically and lyrically, a visionary incandescence different from your other work. I'm curious whether you feel that?*

One reason I chose the title *Spoils* is because I was at some level disappointed with the record. I didn't feel that the songs had been presented in the best way possible, but I'm glad you like it.

Was your concern more that the performances were not what you wanted, or that the songs themselves were not quite doing what you wanted?

It's more to do with the manner in which they were recorded. I initially went to the studio and thought, just me and the sound engineers could do this. I wanted more people to play on it, and it ended up with a lot of people playing on it. But I would rather have assembled a really shit-hot band beforehand, and then we'd gone into the studio and done it live and got more spontaneous performances.

There's something, not unfinished exactly, but open-ended, even off the cuff about it. It also seemed like you were stretching and exploring different ways of coming from a folk framework, but opening it up, making the songs longer, putting in parts that are in a different key—that sort of stuff. Were you consciously exploring the form?

Yes! I mean, I could talk you through every song, you know? [*laughs*] The first song is "The Flyting of Grief & Joy (Eternal Return)"; it's based on this . . . you know William Henderson?

No.

He's a Scottish folklorist, song collector, and songwriter. He wrote a song called "The Fight of Life and Death," about this eternal struggle between the forces of life and death. At the end of the song, it's like, death digs a grave but then life comes along as a flower, as a plant seed. It's this idea that death and life are the same thing. So my song came out of that William Henderson song, but instead of life and death, it's grief and joy. And the eternal return thing was a lot of stuff I've been reading. This idea of eternal recurrence was coming up—and kept coming up into my brain, and what to do with it—this idea of history, repeat-

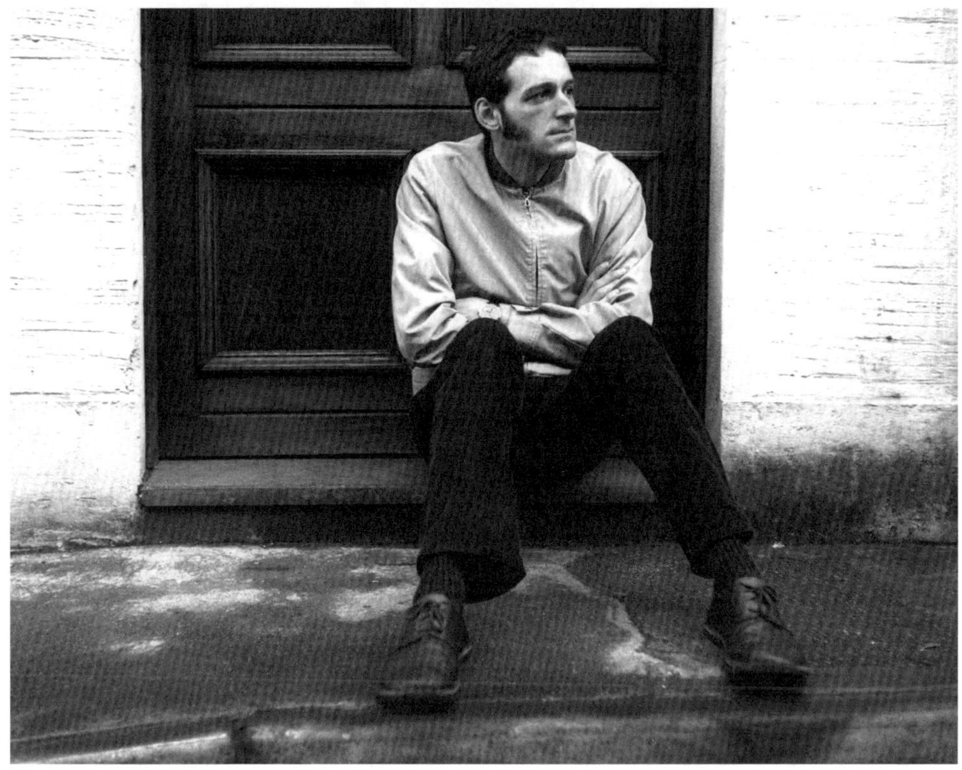

ing, cyclical time—the cyclical nature of time, as well.

Does it feel sometimes that there's an aspect of our moment that has a quality of return to it?

I suppose one way that I figured it was thinking about this idea of progress, that when we think about the classic symbol of the idea of eternal recurrence, separately you can tell it's progressing. But it's also destroying itself at the same time. So, essentially the idea is that what seems like progress is actually destructive. You can apply that to technological process as well: some technological breakthrough may be great for some reason, but really destructive for other reasons. So I was trying to get at that kind of idea philosophically.

That was another interesting thing about the record, the strain of—I don't want to call it neo-Luddism—but the strain of probing and wrestling with technology. That was partly what gave it, for me, a kind of prophetic feel, that you were using imagery and a certain way of organizing images and meanings that were very traditional. But you were looking at some of these contemporary issues, most obviously with "Ned Ludd's Rant (For a World Rebarbarised)." Is this something you've been wrestling with more in general, in your life and how you think about the world as you see it?

I was trying to confront what I perceived as my own kind of Luddism.

Why do I still find it an appropriate way of making music, to be playing guitar and singing songs? Writing songs and singing traditional songs—like, how could that be appropriate anymore? Like, the fact that I don't make laptop pop music or never really embraced technology in that way.

Do you feel hampered by that in some ways, or proud?

Neither. I mean, that's the path I chose. Or have chosen so far. I feel neither hampered nor proud.

It seems like the folk musician has this extra role to play in our time because the music can be for many people a path, their own way of being a Luddite, their own step away from digital technology or the idea of the networked society that we're in right now. I'm just wondering if you feel that at all, if you experience that in terms of the way that people relate to you and your music?

Yeah. Maybe not me, but certainly the idea of traditional music seems to be for some people about escapism, fantasy—almost like a grown-up Dungeons & Dragons kind of world, you know? It's an escape from the real world rather than an engagement with it. But I've always hoped that what I was doing was engaging with reality. And that's not supposed to be about sword and sorcery or, like I was saying, the bucolic and the pastoral. It's supposed to be more about people's relations to each other and the real world and things that are actually happening.

I want to talk a little about the ouroboros image, which is a great image of the eternal return. You have a lot of Gnostic words and images in your songs. When I think about the serpent swallowing its tail, it reminds me of one of my favorite lines from the whole record: "Now the age has come to rust, we've seen the death of wonder / Now we rob graverobber's graves and redisplay the plunder."

[*Chuckles*] Oh yeah.

And it's the sense of feedback, of something consuming itself, like our culture is doing that. That's how I read that line. I don't know if that's what

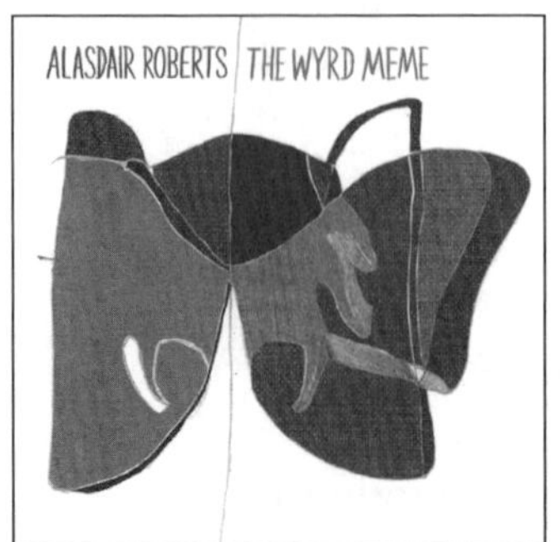

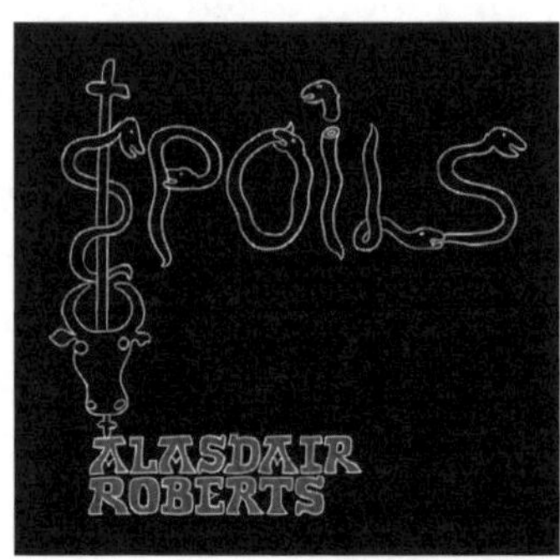

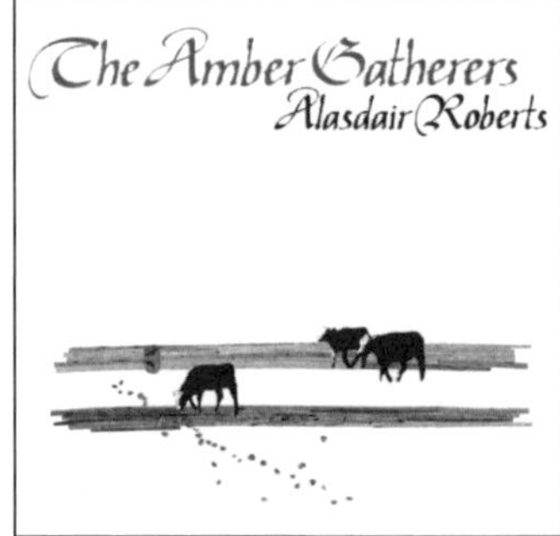

you meant, but for me it was about like, Oh yeah, this is sort of what we do online. Somebody posts some reference to something and someone else refers to it and it becomes this thing that's referred to over here, blah blah blah blah. It's this sense of endless circulation, of old bits that have been sampled from another time. Is that all that you were talking about?
Yeah, I think that it might be something to do with it. [*laughs*] Yeah, I think so. I don't really think about it that much, but it's also a pun and a reference to the poet and writer Robert Graves. Robbing graves, Robert Graves—I was kind of thinking about Robert Graves. I've been really into *The White Goddess* for a long time. I suppose it's something to do with that.
Are you interested in the ways that people try to recreate the kind of tradition that Graves talks about in The White Goddess, *whether through poetry or ritual or music?*
I suppose I'm interested in the idea of Bardism and how that can talk to the . . . I was going to say something, but I can't remember what it was.
What, about the Bard?
I've got it here, actually, a picture of a guy who died, a Welsh poet who just died. His name was Dick Jones. Apparently, he died at age 75. He was the arch druid of Wales—the presiding official of the annual national day. So he was a farmer, and a poet as well, and he wrote in a traditional Welsh meter, which Robert Graves talks about, as well—it's kind of like an ancient sort of Bardic form of poetry.

Whatever I do, whatever one does, comes out of what one's consuming. I was just reading a lot of this stuff, and processing it and then filtering it into the stuff that I was writing.
Do you feel it's relevant?
That what's relevant?
This kind of, you know: references to Zoroaster and . . .
[*laughs*]
. . . and Abraxis and . . .
[*laughs*]
. . . and the use of, you know, even mentioning Ned Ludd. Nobody knows who Ned Ludd is . . .
They do now that I've mentioned him.
Well, that's what I mean! Do you feel like an antiquarian, or is there something more pressing about some of these arcane allusions?
I suppose it's more the idea of the eternal recurrence—that what happened in the ancient past is repeating now, so there's not really a distinction between then and now. So it's equally valid to reference Mithras, or Zoroaster, as it is to mention Elvis Presley or Michael Jackson.

Do you ever hesitate to use obscure, twenty-dollar words? So many musicians are like—well, you know, that's a little bit too arcane, that's too many syllables, it goes a little bit against the grain.

When I was listening to the mixes of the record I was thinking, God, these songs have too many words in them . . . It did cross my mind, and it reminded me of when I was in school—people used to say that I'd swallowed a dictionary. And I really got the impression that it was kind of a labor thing, because I wanted the words to flow naturally, but I love words, too. Maybe if I wasn't doing music I would be a linguist or an etymologist or something. I think that different languages are my way into music.

Yeah. The musicality of language is a real key element of traditional poetry and I don't think it sounds belabored to my ears. The love of the sound of the words, and especially the historical heft of a lot of these words also comes through—the way you feel the history of the words inside them, that's true of a lot of Anglo-Saxon words—when you really play with them it starts to feel like another time is being called up.

Yes.

Did you have a sense at a certain point, like—oh, wow, this music is really calling me more deeply than I had expected?

I started kind of writing songs when I was young, so it just seemed like the natural thing to do. But the traditional songs and ballads, I started exploring those more when I was in my early twenties. Have you heard of *Tocher*? There's a school of Scottish studies in Edinburgh and *Tocher* is [its] journal . . . so it's like, folkloric stuff, transcriptions of songs and the like. Recently I've gone and looked at back issues of this magazine and it kind of made me realize that that kind of terrain, that kind of historical, musical terrain of Scotland is going to always be my work. I will always be engaging with it in song.

How else do you feel close to that tradition, or to Scottish history, or toward the sense of a nation, of a people?

I know a lot of other musicians here that have a similar relation to tradition—some who are doing a lot more traditional music than I am, and some who completely reject the idea of traditional folk music. I know people that I've learned the songs from, such as the song on the new record called "The Lover's Ghost," from a couple called Allison Moreland and Jody McIntyre. Have you heard of them? They're traditional ballad singers. Jody's a songwriter, as well, but Allison's originally from Glasgow and Jody's an Argyle man. Allison has this song called "The Lover's Ghost," a ballad from Newfoundland. It's really beautiful, one of those revenant ballads—ghost ballads. We recorded it for this new record.

The ghost, as a metaphor, the revenant, is a lot of what is appealing and weird about traditional music. It's not just melodies, it's not just words, it's not even just traces of history—there's a certain kind of haunting that comes through, with the darker and more melancholic things, for sure. Do you have that sense at all, that by being in love with this kind of music, opening yourself to a transition through time, that there's a connection with the spirits of those who were in the past? Or is that too romantic?

I wouldn't say romantic. I mean, I've dismissed that as fanciful, but there have been certain times when I've been playing and felt a certain presence, or something, you know, something else in the room. Something behind me urging me on—some kind of ancestral spirits, in that sense. I felt that at certain times, when I'm on stage and it's going really well, it's there's something presiding over me.

No, I appreciate you saying that. It's nerve-wracking to say things like that because it can sound pretentious or stupid. I think it's also something a lot of people actually do touch in various ways. And it's important to stand up for it—to me that's partly about honoring where these things come from, that there is a kind of transmission in music through time. It isn't in any kind of supernatural way, necessarily; it's part of the way we relate to others and to the others in the past . . . Are you content with the world of music-making that you exist in now?

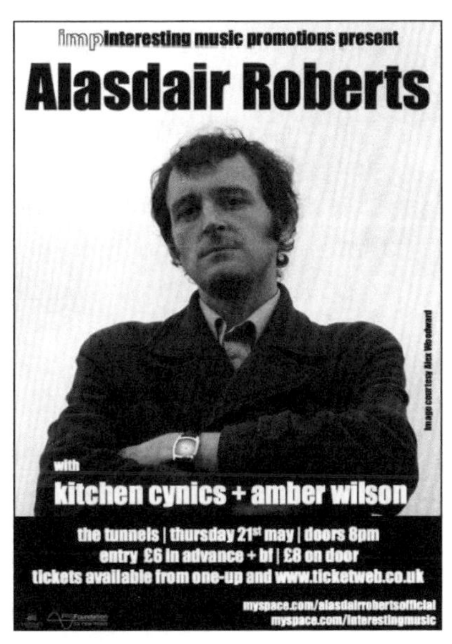

I would like to be touring a lot more.

What is it about touring that you like?

I just like playing for people. Anybody, anywhere.

So, why don't you do it more? [laughs]

There's some . . . it's, eh, complicated.

Right, your next tour, was it delayed?

I was supposed to be opening for Bert Jansch. He had to cancel his tour in August in the States, so that didn't happen.

It was a shame he had to cancel that. It would have been quite a fine bill. Does he play a particular role in your sort of pantheon of influences?

Well, certainly as a guitarist I listen to him a fair bit. I wouldn't say he was the main . . . in terms of guitar style, I was really influenced by guys like Dick Gaughan, Martin Carthy, and Nic Jones. That would probably be my triumvirate of British folk guitarists. ✪

VERY NEW DRAWINGS

by Alissa Wessler

For as long as I can remember I've had an insatiable thirst to make things in one form or another. I often think about how the things we create when we are children are the most unaffected and imaginative, so sometimes I get a little jealous of my childhood self and wish I could steal back all those good ideas I once had!

I am interested in creating installations and otherworldly environments that engulf you and invite you to explore. Last summer I had the opportunity to build a walk-through cave installation at Johansson Projects, a gallery in Oakland, California. I had read about a man who spent years of his life trying to build a "stalacpipe" organ inside the Luray Caverns of Virginia and how he finally succeeded. This lithophone really does produce music by tapping the ancient stalactites with rubber mallets and the effect is eerie, sounding like a bone church far underground. The recordings I've heard are made complete with little cave drips here and there. I am fascinated by man-made spaces that attempt to replicate natural wonders, and I am equally amazed by natural spaces, inherently full of wonder, which man attempts to improve upon.

Lately, I've been working with a local print shop called Container Corps on a new version of this funny old book. The original *Struwwelpeter* was published in 1845 by a German psychiatrist, Heinrich Hoffmann,* who, the story goes, wanted to give his son a moralistic picture book as a Christmas present. Disapproving of the books available, he decided to write and illustrate his own, the result being a humorous (and often macabre) collection of poems about naughty children coming to inevitably bad ends. My favorite one is about a bespectacled hunter who falls asleep under a tree, only to awake to see a hare wearing his specs and holding his gun!

* Translated variously into English as *Shock-Headed Peter* and (in Mark Twain's version) *Slovenly Peter*.

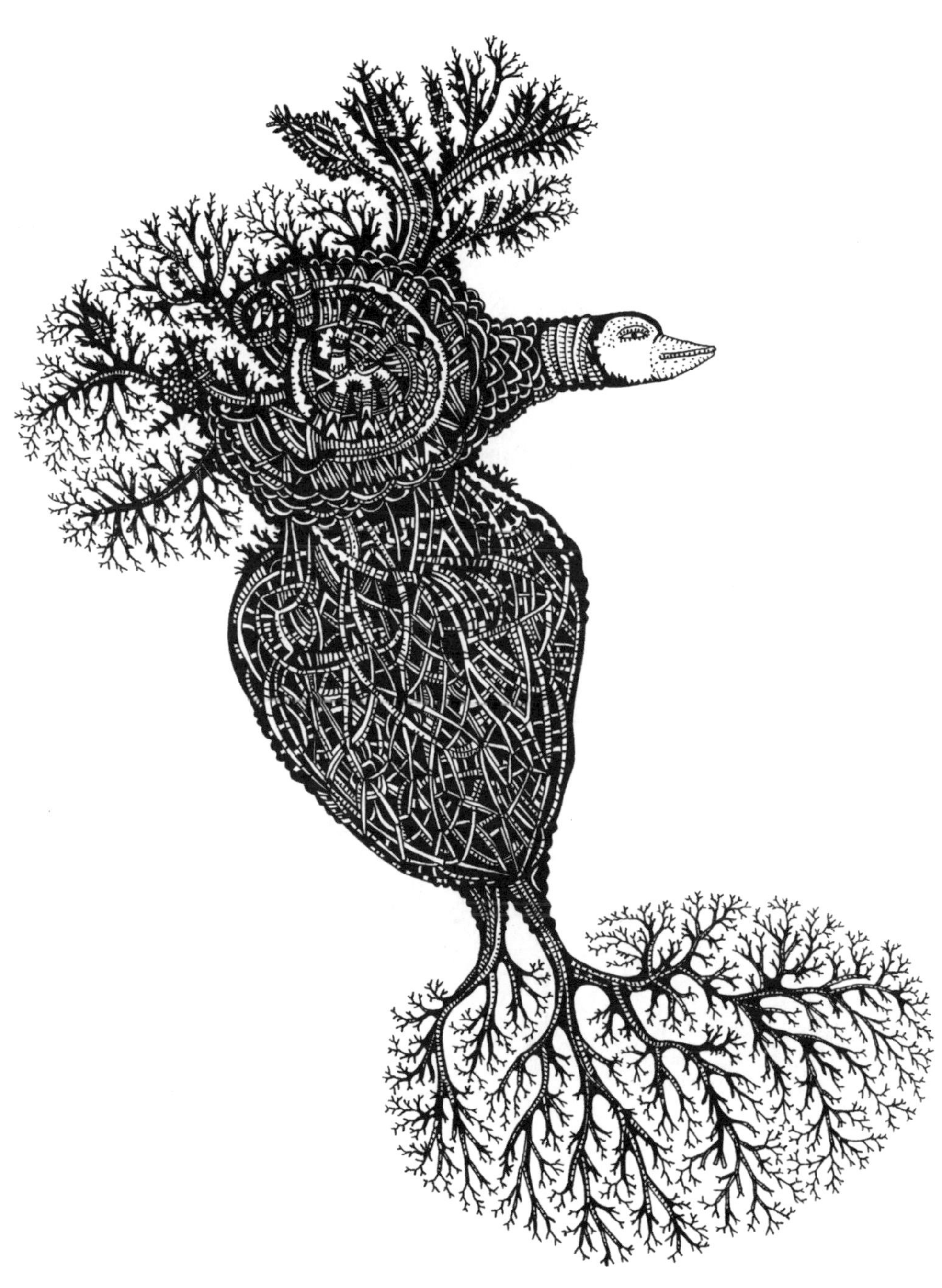

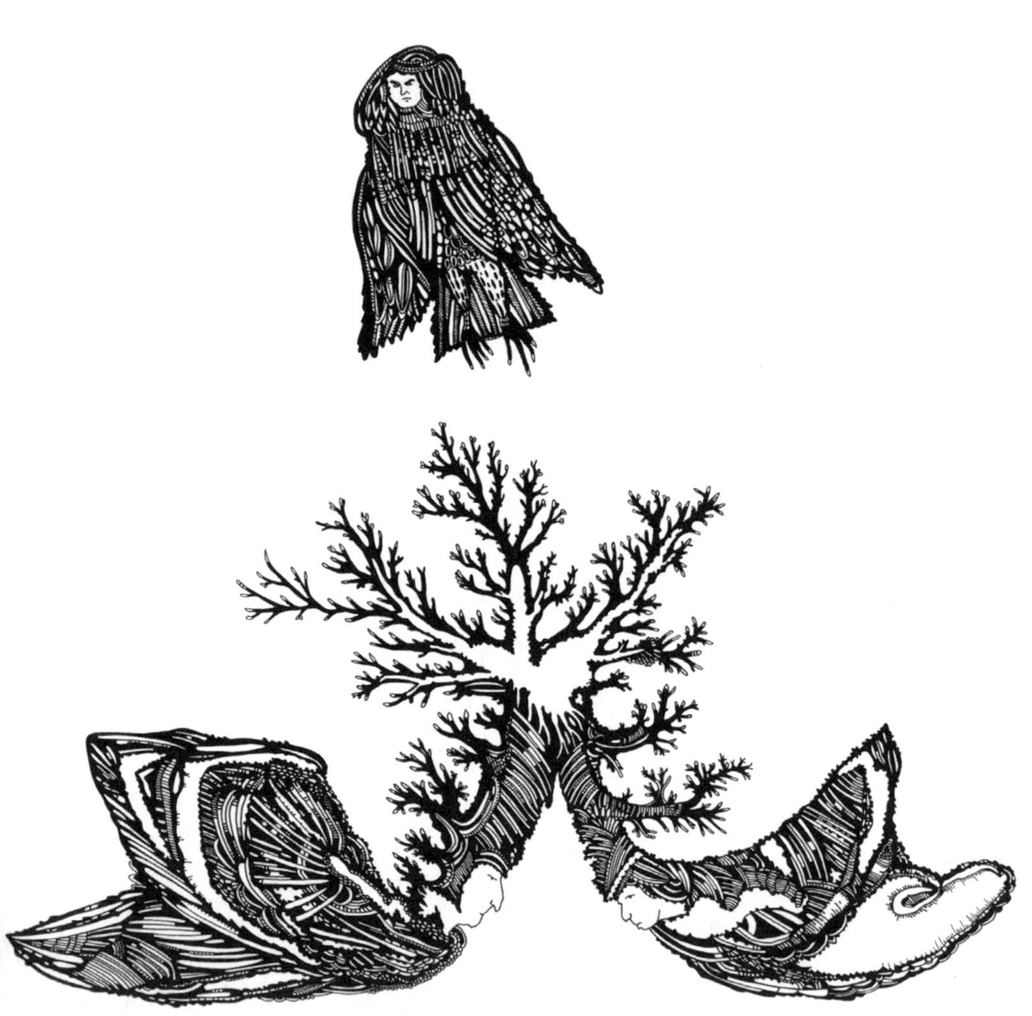

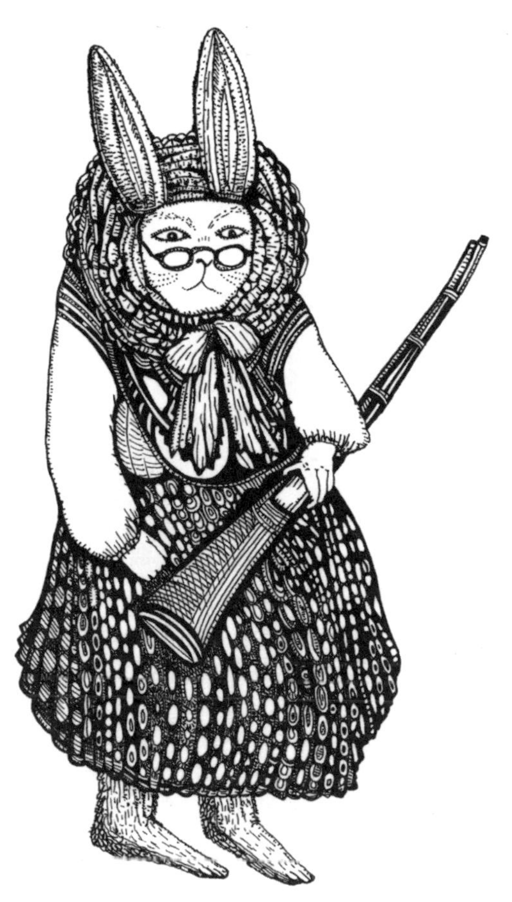

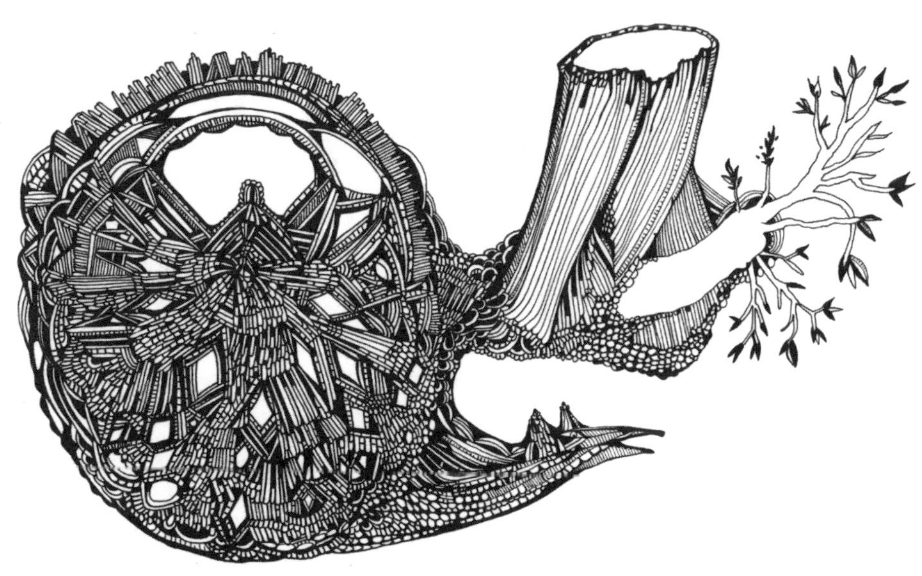

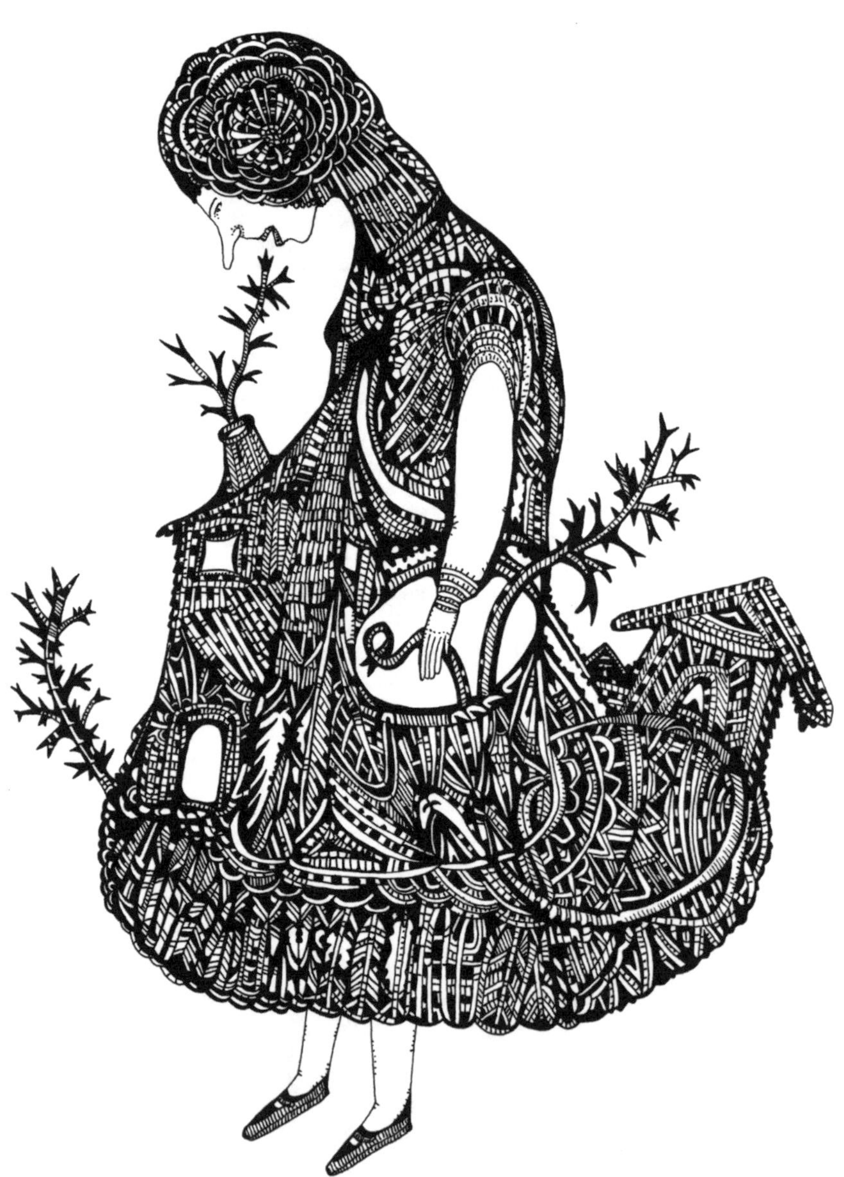

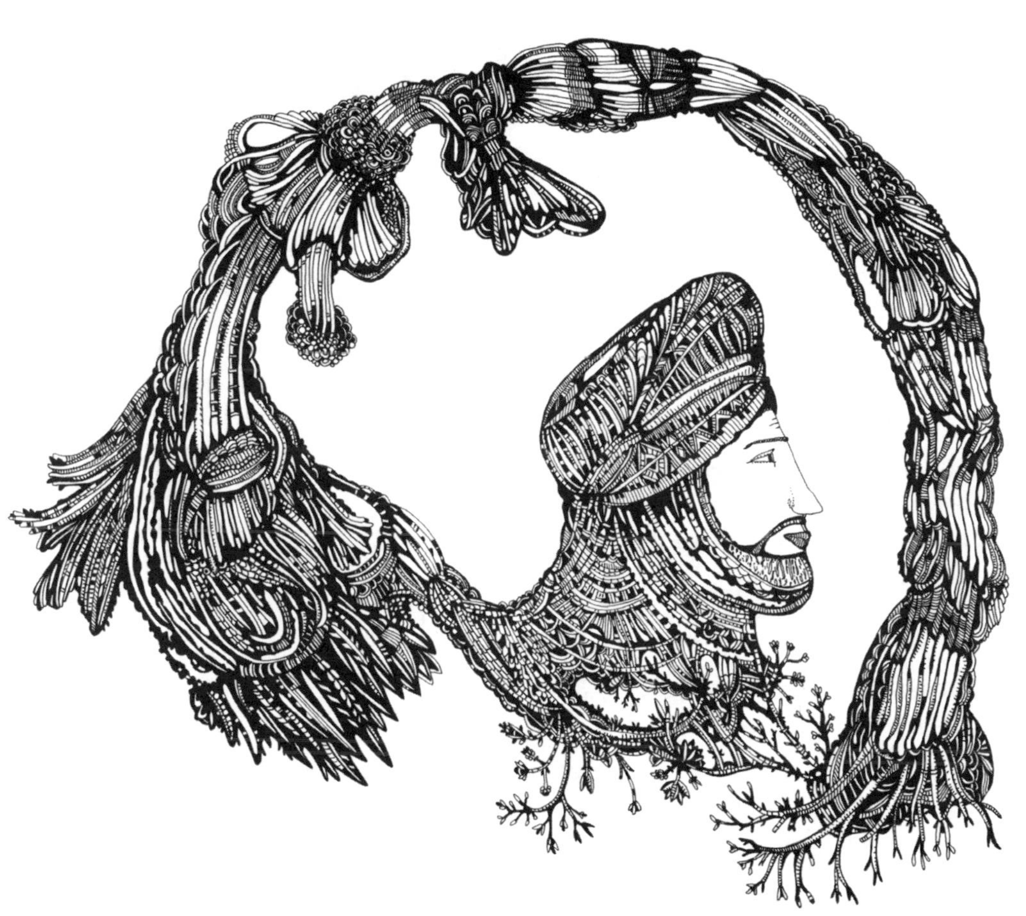

REPTILIAN GROVE

by Joaquín V. González

Translated by Gilbert Alter-Gilbert

ILLUSTRATION BY PEDRO LOURENÇO

Writer, statesman, educator, jurist, and bibliophile from a family settled in northern Argentina since the days of colonization, Joaquín V. González (1863-1923) was one of the architects of the modern Argentine nation. Over the course of a distinguished political career, he was elected to the Chamber of Deputies, and served as senator, governor of his province, Minister of the Interior, Minister of Foreign Relations, Minister of Public Instruction, and Minister of Justice under various administrations. In 1905, he authored the Argentine Labor Code, notably advanced for its time and, when anarchist and socialist immigrants threatened insurrection, González instituted the Law of Residence to keep them in check. He founded the University of La Plata, to which he donated his spectacular personal library. Beginning his literary career as a belated romantic poet, González was not caught up in the concerns of his "modernista" contemporaries. He was not so much an assimilationist of international literary trends as he was a latter-day encyclopedist; he authored fifty books in a variety of genres covering a wide spectrum of subjects. His works include *Canvas and Bronze*, *Sentinel of the Andes*, *Native Fables*, and *The Fires of San Juan and Other Stories*. The following might well be González's first appearance in English; the text was originally published on the excellent blog *A Journey Round My Skull*.

***

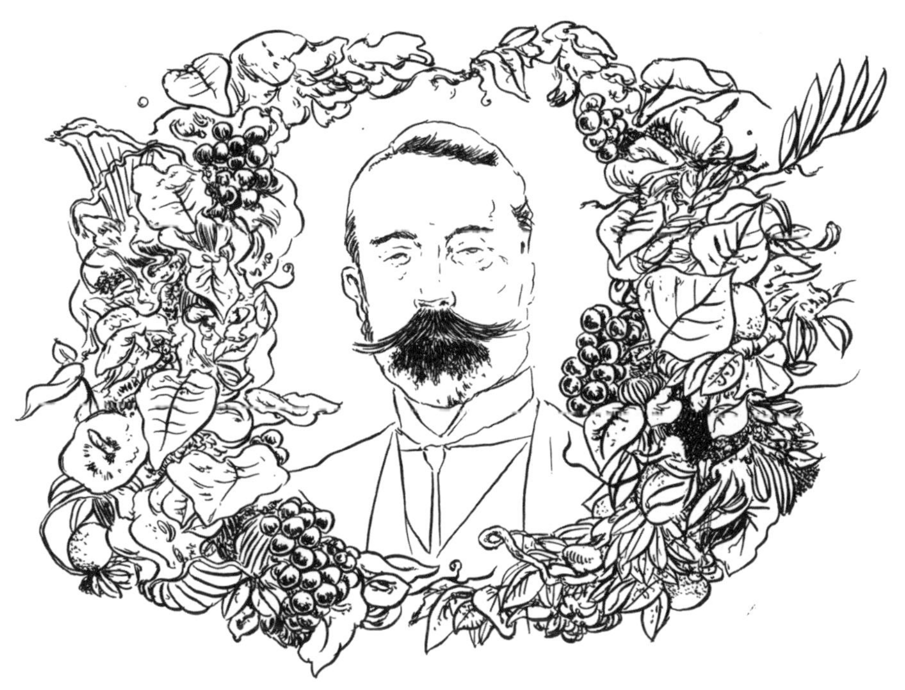

Pedro, the high pastures shepherd, was well-skilled in carving crude reed flutes. Obliged to go alone through the wilderness, among desolate forests rank and overgrown with a havoc of toppled hardwoods, slimy, hooked vines, greasily oozing carob trees, briar thickets, and nettle-torn glades, eternal hours behind his flock, with no other company than his dog, he developed the habit of entertaining himself with native melodies, which gushed from a hollowed reed, coaxed by gusts of his breath and by the agile movements of his dancing fingers.

His canine companion was completely entrusted with the flock for long periods of time; his frequent barks were consensual signals to make known site and distance, and the news that might crop up in the lonely valleys, and on the thorn-tangled hillslopes.

It was true that since childhood, they had lived together, fed on the same milk sipped from the same clay saucers; and from the time they took their first steps, both learned to trek with the sheep, skittering up and down the most intimate paths of the earth, negotiating with equal nonchalance the jagged passes of the loftiest peaks, the sticky silt of the bogs and mires, and the slippery banks of the torrents, whose finely-pebbled sands were smoother and softer than the rugs of Smyrna.

When they came upon one of those brilliant and limpid clearings where the sun gleamed like the surface of a diamond, Pedro would be knocked down by his frisky companion, and would bowl over the dog in turn, and they would roll and tumble in the clover, Pedro hugging his frolicsome playmate, who howled happily and wildly from joy, not without throwing, from time to time, intently serious glances toward the mossy and flower-carpeted hillsides, where the cotton-white flock denuded the tenderest meadows.

It didn't seem strange to either of them that they could read one another's thoughts, that they communicated from afar their watchwords and their fears, the one conversing with his polychromatic barks, and the other with whistles or with shouts, or with the rustic melodies of his handmade flute.

For them, the loneliness of the mountains was not lonely. Although they knew that there was no other living soul within leagues of their surroundings, they gave no thought to the matter: valleys succeeded other valleys, separated by the intervening hills, which reproduced to infinity, in tones ever more diverse though each time softer and more nebulous, the innumerable echoes of nature, of the flute, of the birds, of the wind, of the arroyos.

The repercussions of the dog's barks, sharp and penetrating, lasted a long time, and it seemed as if some other dogs and shepherds answered them from remote mountaintops and distant valleys, or beckoned them to mingle their sheep, to share their cares, and to accompany them on their migrations.

In this way, the loneliness of the mountains wasn't so lonely Here, all song had its reply, every shout had its echo, and every difficulty was proclaimed by invisible waves throughout the land.

Peaceful and happy were their excursions during the spring and fall.

Wintertime froze the dew on the grass and the flowers of the fields, arrested and congealed the torrents in their courses, and the poor shepherds were barely able to stand the sunlight hours, even when condensing clouds did not conceal them for days on end . . .

They had everything, on the other hand, in the spring: enough sun to get drunk on, and to cozily warm them, together with their flocks and their pastures tapestried with clover, green, and gold like newly-budded fennel, because in these Andean regions, nature was exacting and honest to the point of severity: snow, frost, and the mist in the winter; flames and wildfires in the festival months. They looked forward to autumn and spring as if starved for loving kisses and raptures of delicious pleasure.

II

Shepherds suffered most when the summer sun scorched the boulders, seared the pastures, converted sand into smoldering embers, and dried up the springs and fountains. And Pedro, he of the rustic melodies, rising at sunup, and returning at dusk, spent countless hours wilting during the blazing afternoons, when all life in the valleys, forests, and hills seemed to consume itself, and his bedraggled flock came limping back exhausted, huddling under the trees and the rocky overhangs of the cliffs, while his inseparable friend droopily circled him, panting and suffocating, tongue lolling, eyes moist and supplicating.

Then, even if the loneliness of the mountains didn't seem lonely, his weariness and abjection transmitted itself to all the objects which at other times repaid his moods with happy echoes and harmonious resonances. And his juvenile imagination, excited by the perennial caress of nature, reeled and swooned and, as during a feverish delirium, dreamed the most extraordinary things, and saw in the trees, and among the distant pinnacles, and in the mirrory surfaces of the wavering air, a welter of weird and rarefied images, frantic, superhuman, diabolical, ominous.

Only at these moments was he frightened, and wished that his companion had words with which to speak. But he contented himself with watching his eyes, reading in them the heartfelt expression of fraternal affection and, turning to scan the horizon, searched the snarled screens of the forests for scenes of familiar reality. Then the reverberations of the atmosphere would stir up his thoughts and scatter his impressions, and he would succumb all over again to the febrile disorientation of solar asphyxiation.

On one of these most stringent of days, he drove his flock up the narrow throat of a mountain pass, so as not to miss out on the shade and the refreshing breezes; and before noon the bordering ridges were dotted with sheep, like the folds of Lebanon, in the Canticles. At the bottom of the gorge, a torrent burbled among enormous stones; gigantic trees followed the fissure, gradually thinning out as they climbed the mountainside until the leaves of the last of them brushed the summit; there, aloof and immune, some condors wheeled in their forbidding cerulean fastnesses, and the January sun began to foment a swelter among the currents of the air.

Soon enough, afternoon arrived, and with it the hour of the oppressive and deadly siesta. Poor Pedro took refuge under the limbs of an ancient oak which had become uprooted and fallen on its side. His lambs, sheltered in secure asylum, needed no care: keeping vigil over them were their mothers and the loyal dog, who never slept on his watch. But if the heated air weren't agitation enough, some indefinable fear lurked in the lonely woods, some mysterious, loathsome threat abided in the caves and in the deserted nests and forsaken dens, while the shepherd dozed on the baking sand. Siestas are friends of midnight, and in them appear rapacious goblins, menacing insects, fantastic and terrifying visions of suffocation and silence... Then again, the brain of an adolescent is rich in strange ramifications, aberrant memories, and the stinging fears engendered by tales heard on fog-shrouded nights.

He was fearful of everything around him; in spite of the intense heat, a freezing twinge of apprehension contracted his tanned and weather-beaten skin; he glanced behind him left and right, determined to defend himself against attacks by beasts, demons, or witches, and climbed the trunk of a corpulent tree where, at a goodly height above the ground, he seated himself on a massive bough, screened off by spiky foliage.

His dog, brother in upbringing, and lifelong friend, busied himself by keeping his post and, a true sentinel, was inviolable. Just at this moment the boy might have begun to believe that the solitude of the mountains was solitude indeed, if he hadn't remembered his flute, whose little mouthpiece made from tree resin was peeping from one of his pockets. Ah, no! the loneliness of the mountains was not so lonely, after all, despite the subtly fleeting phantoms of the January afternoon, which dissipated like puffs of dust in the candent air, with the echoing birds and beloved songs.

When the sacred and sepulchral silence of the steep granite bluffs, with which the somber noises of night had been lulled into desultory accord, was disturbed by the flute's first notes, the narrow canyon widened into a smile which the shepherd, though terrified, could not confine to his face. He summoned up, one by one, and dispersed amongst the infinite sinuosities of the mountains all the melodies he had gathered from the ancient valleys, without knowing where they came from; for him, they were like the rushing torrents, gushing up from the earth, and flowing through the mournful flute from forgotten times and distant lands and, as all the world of memories, generations, and races, moaned and dreamed in the pastoral musician's mellifluous tunes, the sun retreated briefly between two neighboring crests, warming the earth down to its entrails, drilling into the hollow, scooped-out world of caves, dens, and burrows, and expelling, with its radiant pokers, the mysterious and infected world of reptiles.

And the reed and resin flute continued to elicit from the silence of the solemn siesta all its dormant echoes; it was as if their soft and plaintive confidences, surging from the heavy foliage which hid the artist, were the invisible tones of the forests, modulated by this wandering soul of the mountains, never revealed in their true forms, but in the harmonious vibrations of space, in the songs of the birds and the melodies that the shepherds executed on their rustic flutes, without knowing what or whom they might be luring . . .

Half put to sleep by the somnolence of the atmosphere, by the ecstatic rapture of his music, and by a vague fear beyond all control, Pedro kept his eyes squeezed shut and, in this way, found himself more confident and relaxed. But it was necessary, at some point, to rest from playing and, when he suddenly broke off his song and its inebriating spell, he surprised, as if during the course of a delectable dream, three monstrous serpents with flecked, varicolored skin and fascinating stares which writhed in violent, entranced contortions above his head, encircling him with their shiny elastic loops, and slithering in spirals along the rugose and enormous trunk of the tree which served as his refuge . . .

It was at the shock of this unexpected and horrendous vision, that the poor shepherd boy let loose a strident scream that sent a shudder a thousand times, then a thousand times again, through the slumbering hills and ridges, the relentless mountain spires, the dense forest canopy; he plunged into alarm the nests, the grottoes, the flock, and the bands of wandering guanacos which responded with loud, startled whinnyings. In the branches of the tree, blocking immediate exit, twisted and twined in an impossibly prolific confusion before the shepherd's bulging eyes, hundreds of vipers and lizards which, gripping him with terror, clambered, jostled, darted, and dangled, emitting sparks of blood from their rancorous eyes, gnashing fangs of ivory fineness, agitatedly coiling themselves into indissoluble clusters, and dropping in knotted clumps onto the ground. On all sides the sand was alive; moving, crawling, as if each of its innumerable grains were covered by undulating, oscillating, reptilian life, in spontaneous and marvelous generation. The tree's ponderous trunk, its leaves, its stems, its red roots with their parasitic plants, its cracks and crevices, its gashed and hidden places, acquired in Pedro's horrified eyes the sinuous curves and restless wrigglings of a viper, and were colored with its inimitable tints, blazing around him like light and fire.

The hideousness of the situation reached its climax when he saw that they threatened to imprison him in their scaly hoops and frigid folds, to clamp onto his flesh their ivory hooks and the forked filaments of the scarlet tongues which flicked furiously from their gaping gullets; wreathing, winding, intertwining, the snakes viciously bit one another's twitching, resonating, rattle-tipped tails and, irritated by their own poison, sank their dripping teeth into the peeling bark of the tree, or lashed out at their own flesh in delirious and suicidal frenzy . . .

To the horrific scream of fright, the faithful dog responded with a dolorous, flebile yowl which sowed panic in the resting flock, and by the time the poor animal had reached his unfortunate friend, the latter had arrived at the supreme resolution of leaping to the ground to try to make a desperate run to save himself from the ophidians, which he could hear everywhere around him, hissing, sibilating, crepitating in his ears, rubbing, grazing, scraping his cheeks with their cold, scaly skin, and boring into his neck with the points of their mortiferous lancets. Every few yards, he swiveled his bewildered, horror-stricken face, mesmerized by the same nightmarish spectacle, and saw that the reptiles crept faster and faster in a hungry, hissing horde, struggling to reach the fugitive prize, in order to wallow in his youthful blood.

Aghast, the poor shepherd frantically tore off his hat, his poncho, and the rest of his clothes, so as to fling them to the voracity and avidity of the diabolical swarm of persecutors. These, in a gasping, writhing heap, squirmed in blind fury over the heated earth, to molest him, to torment him, to pierce him with holes like a sieve. As they fastened onto his cast-off garments, puncturing them again and again with their needle-keen teeth until all that was left was a handful of pulverized shreds, the luckless boy managed to hobble quite a distance in his demented flight before he lost all awareness of the whereabouts of his pursuers, and of the canine comrade who trailed him whining, and of the cloud of dust raised by his panicked flock retreating towards the far-off corrals . . . ✪

TERROR TEAM

by Beatriz Monteavaro

1. I have been making drawings and things my whole life. I just didn't call it art until later. I'm going back to calling it drawings and things. I started playing drums when I was twelve. I have been playing in bands since I was eighteen.

2. People have been making stuff and making noise since the beginning of people. I do consider that I am part of both traditions. Although birds were surely singing songs and spiders making webs long before there were humans. I am following in the tradition of birds and spiders.

3. I have been part of the music scene in South Florida from 1991 to 1998 (Human Oddities, Methadone Actors, Funyons, Floor, Cavity) and from 2009 to now (Beings). I have been part of the art scene in South Florida from 1999 to now.

4. I have a solo show coming up in June in Los Angeles at Las Cienegas Projects. In July, Amnesian Records will be putting out a 12-inch EP of my band Beings. We plan on touring in July.

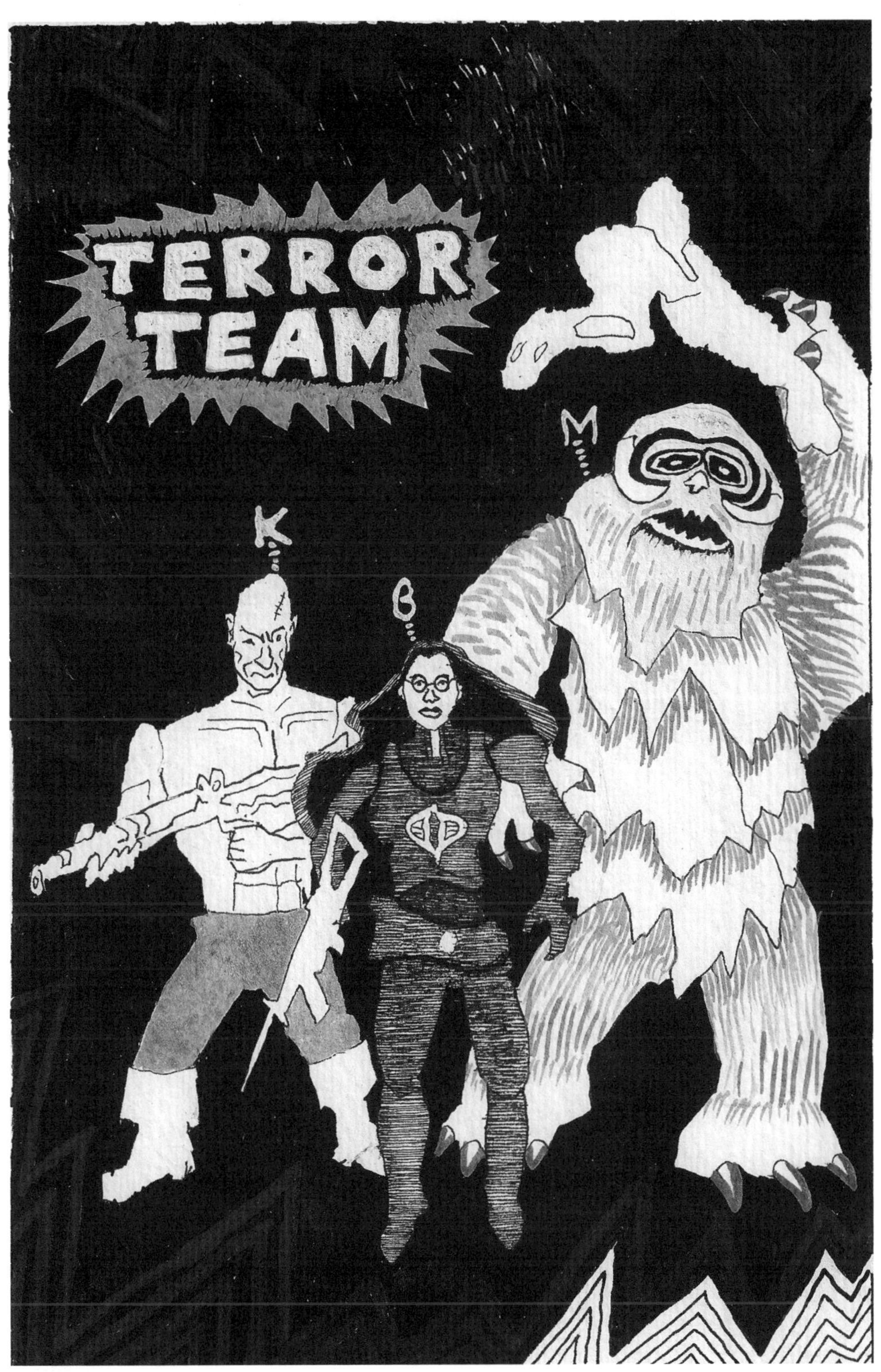
TERROR TEAM
K
B
M

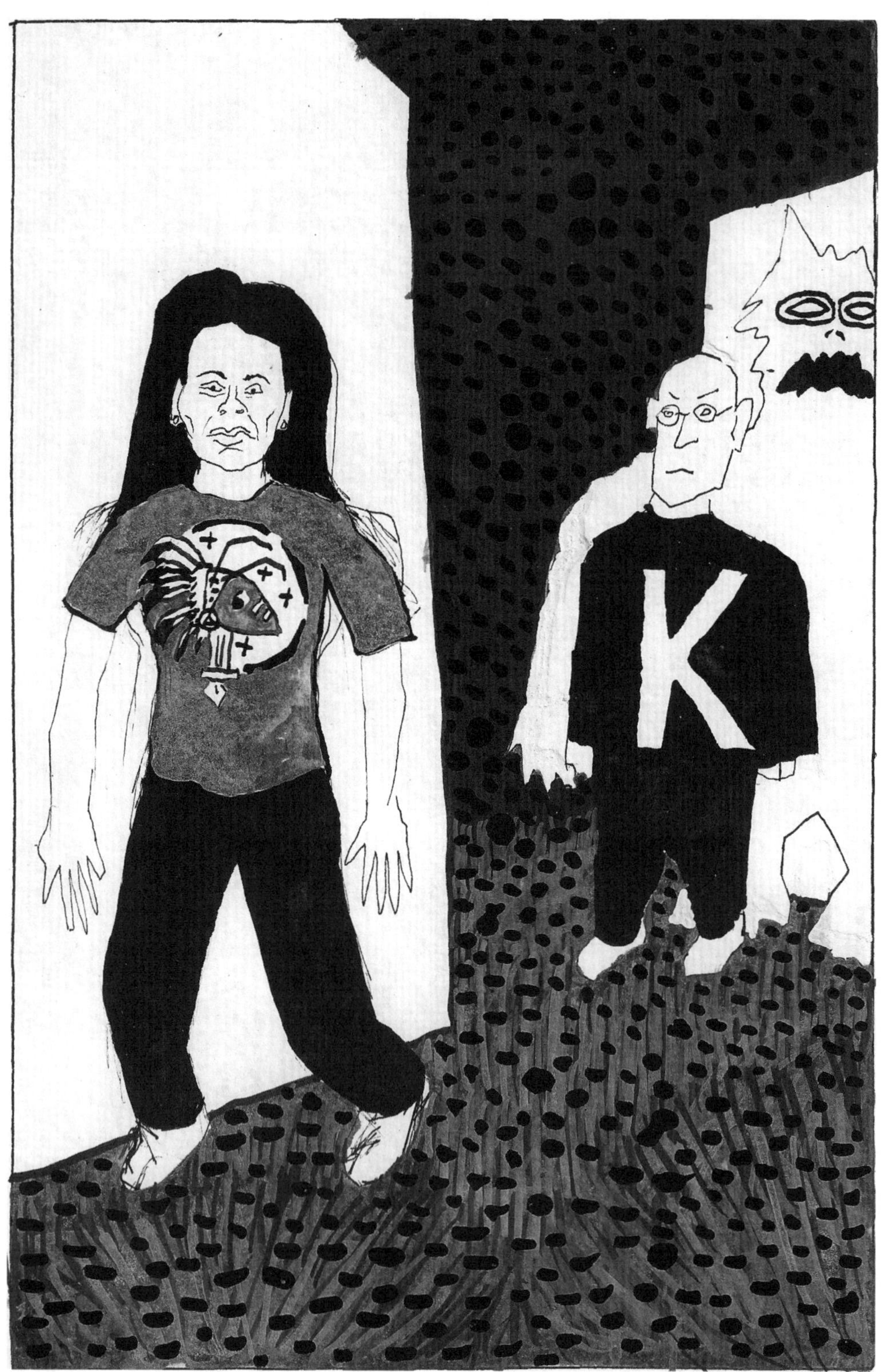
K

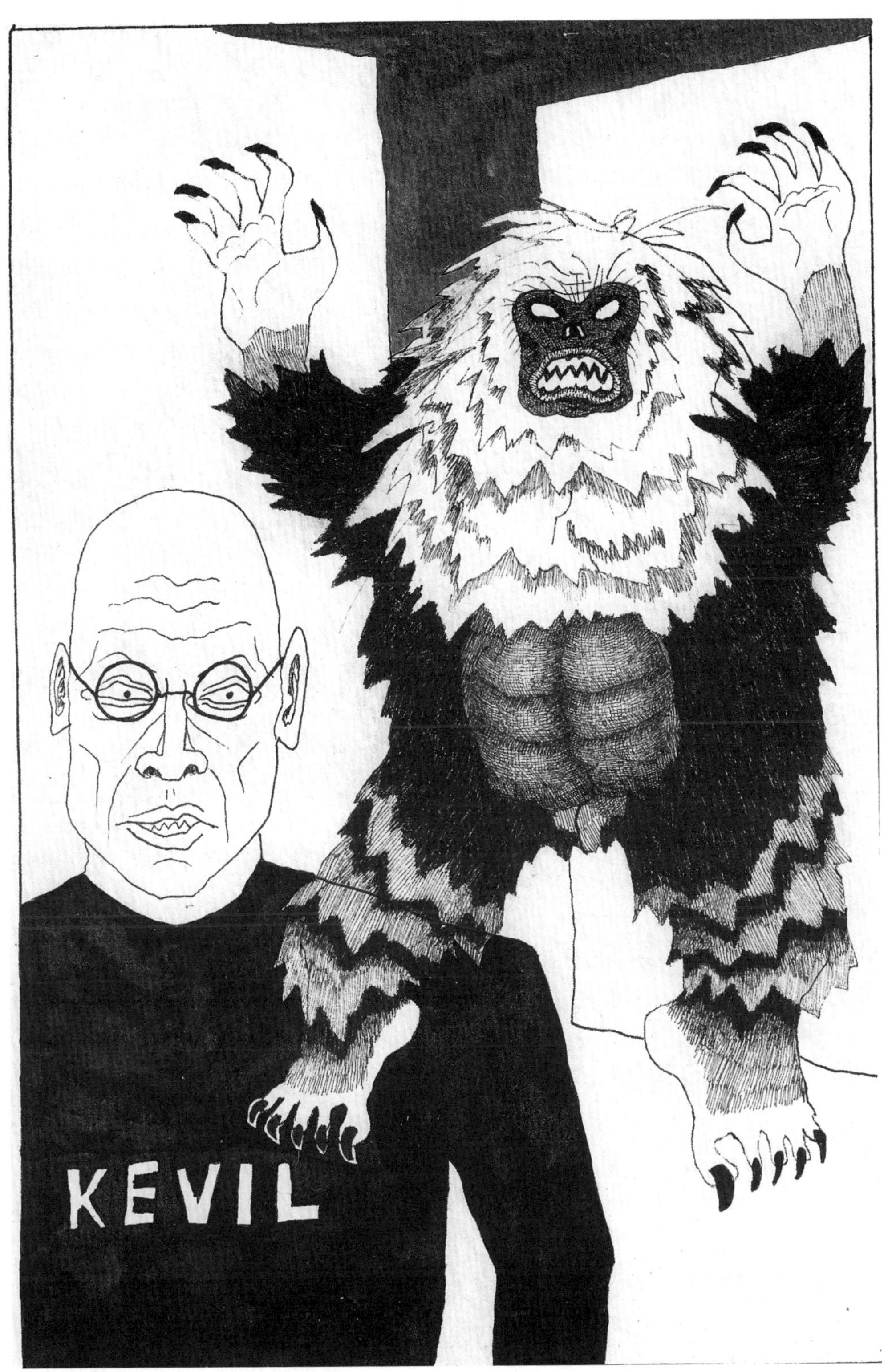
KEVIL

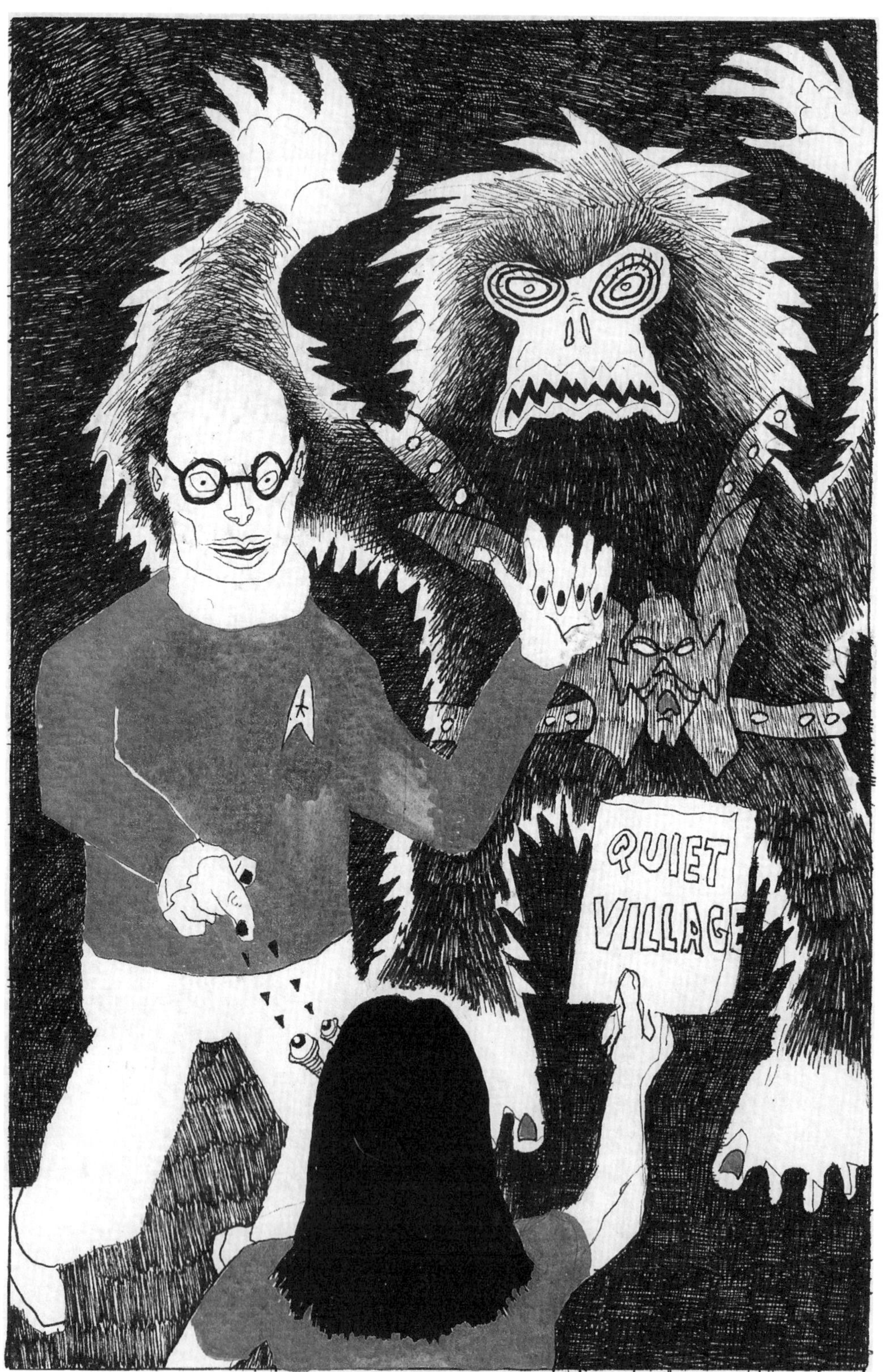
QUIET VILLAGE

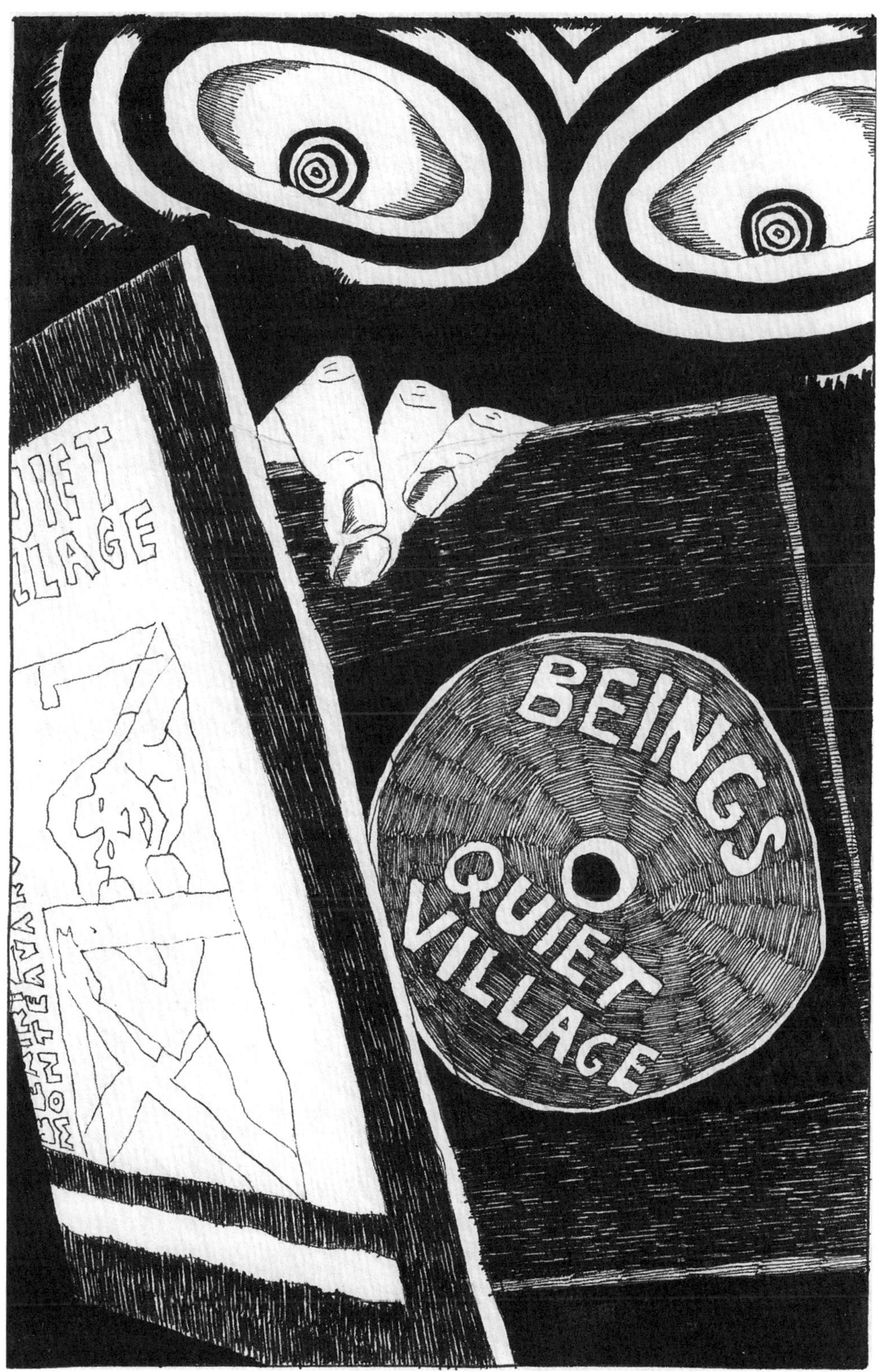
BEINGS
QUIET
VILLAGE

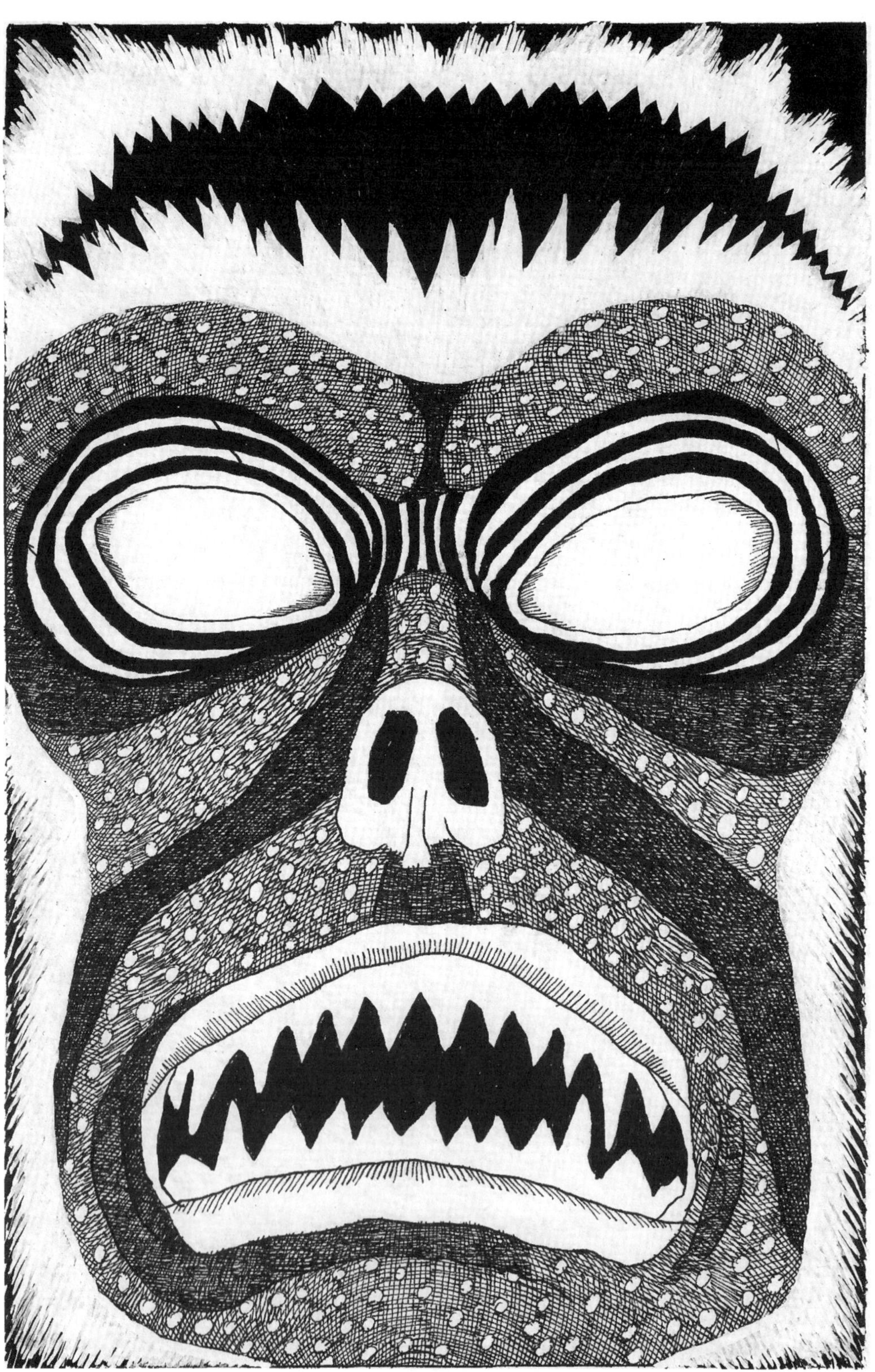

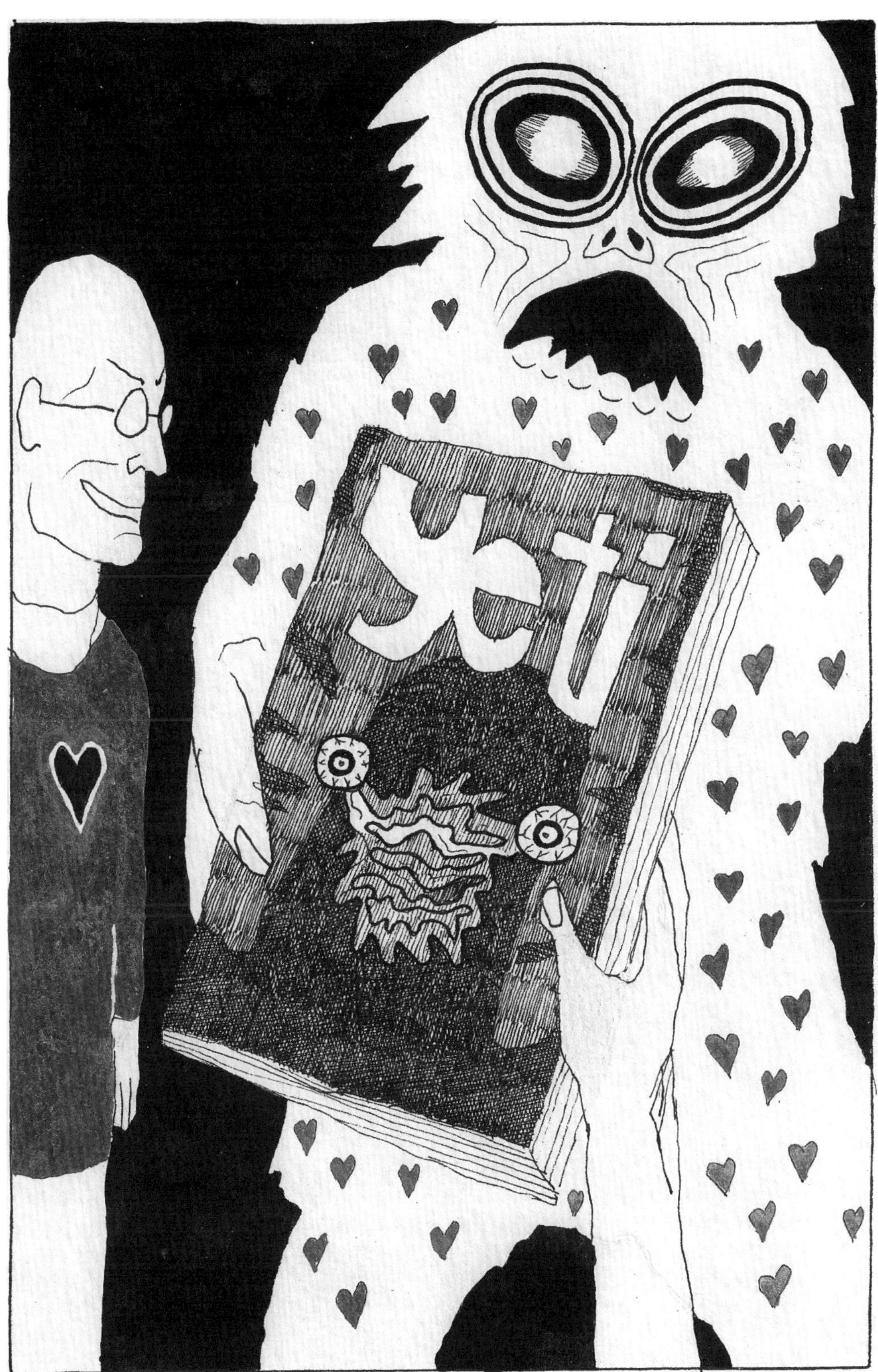
Yeti

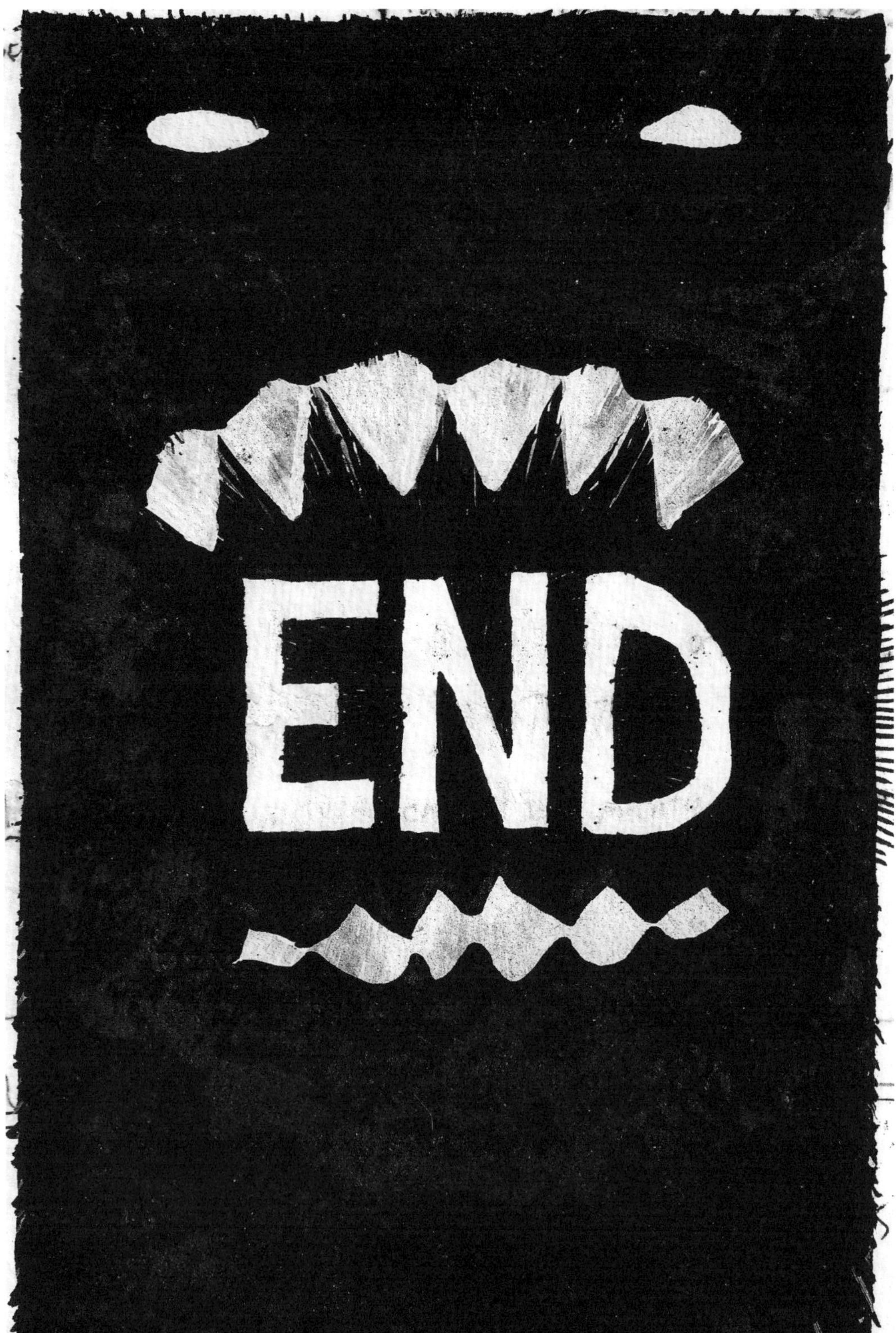
END

CONTRIBUTORS

DREW CHRISTIE has been making animations and drawings since he was a kid. More recently, he has been doing illustrations for Light in the Attic Records, *City Arts* magazine, and his own *Illustrated Guide to Old-Time Folk Instruments*. He just finished the animations for the upcoming Michael Hurley documentary, *Elwood Snock & The Land of Lo-Fi*. He lives in Seattle, WA. democracyforthecartoons.blogspot.com . . . **ERIK DAVIS** posts regularly at techgnosis.com. His last book was *The Visionary State: A Journey through California's Spiritual Landscape*, which includes lots of pretty pictures. His next book, *Nomad Codes: Adventures in Modern Esoterica*, will be published by YETI in fall 2010 . . . **LORI D.** lives and works in Portland, Oregon where she makes these things with her hands: paintings, animations, zines, films, quilts, gardens, miniature sweaters, and pies. She directs the animation department for the Cal State Summer School for the Arts and volunteers at the Independent Publishing Resource Center. She also has a monthly column called "The Learnings of" in *The Skateboard Mag*. She is finishing a humongous independent animation that has been in the works for 8 years and hopes to bring it to a neighborhood near you on an upcoming cross-country animation tour. More info: lori-d.com . . . Also known as "the James Bond of Improvised Music", **ARRINGTON DE DIONYSO** (b. January 4, 1975) throat-sings through a bass clarinet and plays the bass clarinet like a paintbrush. His latest album is called *Malaikat dan Singa* (K Records), on which every song is a Bahasa Indonesian "mis-translation" of half-remembered quotes from William Blake and the Zohar. He recently exhibited at La Fabrica Fluxus in Bari, Italy. . . . **JESS FOGEL** is an artist and curator who lives in Portland, Oregon. . . . **GILBERT ALTER-GILBERT** is a critic, translator, and literary historian whose work has appeared in numerous magazines and journals. His book-length translations include *The Mirror of Lida Sal* by Miguel Ángel Asturias and *Streetcorners: Prose Poems of the Demi-Monde* by Francis Carco. He's at work on translations of work by Leon Bloy, Francis Picabia, Massimo Bontempelli and Alberto Savinio. . . . **DR. ELIOT HANDELMAN** is a composer who turned against music and became a writer/theorist on the radical mediation of process perception, simulation, and induction of auditory consciousness; took a PhD at Princeton; dabbled in neuroscience; was invited to join the core research group at a Sony media lab; and is the author of Jack & Jill, an AI program that composes music autonomously . . . **LIZZ HICKEY** is an artist who lives in Brooklyn, where she sometimes sells cupcakes to people. . . . **PEDRO LOURENÇO** is a visual artist who lives in Lisboa, Portugal. He sometimes blogs at ink-and-paper.blogspot.com . . . **MIKE MCGONIGAL** lives in Portland where he edits *YETI*. Recently, he produced a full-length documentary for VBS on the "new garage rock" scene. His 4-hour set *Fire in My Bones: Raw, Rare & Otherworldly African-American Gospel, 1944-2007* was released by Tompkins Square last year. . . . **ROBERT MILLIS** is a founding member of Climax Golden Twins and AFCGT. Lately he's worked on releases for Dust-to-Digital and Parlortone, including *Victrola Favorites, Strings, Take Me To The Water*, and *Au Claire de la Lune* (the earliest recording of the human voice). His first solo record, *120,* came out last year on Etude Records. He is also a frequent contributor to the Sublime Frequencies label. "The material for the interview with VAK Ranga Rao was gathered during an extended trip through India in 2008. Trying to carry back the stack of 78 rpm records I bought was ridiculous, with many raised eyebrows and confused looks from airplane security and customs. I figured the airplane's overhead compartment was going to sheer off due to the weight." . . . **BEATRIZ MONTEAVARO** was born in Cuba. She received a BFA from the Tyler School of Art. Her work has been exhibited all over the world in group and solo exhibitions. She was selected by Gean Moreno to publish an artist book through [NAME] Publications, *Quiet Village* (2009). Monteavaro has been playing drums in bands since 1991 including The Human Oddites, Floor and Cavity. Her present band is called Beings and will be releasing a 12-inch through Amnesian Records this year. Beatriz lives and works in Miami. . . . **DAVID NICHOLS** is a historian who lives in Melbourne, Australia. He was in frequent contact with Pip Proud during the last fifteen years of Proud's life. The first volume of his history of Australian popular music since 1960, a chapter of which is adapted for the article included here, will be published by Verse Chorus Press in 2011. . . . **FRANK J. OTERI** is the Composer Advocate at the American Music Center and the founding editor of its web magazine NewMusicBox, which has been online since May of 1999. A crusader for new music and the breaking down of barriers between genres, Frank has written for publications including *BBC Music, Chamber Music, Ear Magazine, Stagebill/Playbill, Symphony, Time Out New York* and the *Revised New Grove Dictionary of Music and Musicians.* Frank holds a B.A. and a M.A. (in Ethnomusicology) from Columbia University, where he served as Classical Music Director and World Music Director for WKCR-FM. . . . **E*ROCK** is an artist/musician living in Portland, Oregon where he can often be found creating art/music, or sometimes not doing those things at all. e--rock.com . . . **TARA SINN** is an artist from Northern California. She lives in New York City with Pickles, Willy, and Jesse. Her website is here: babydinosaureyes.com . . . **SYLVIE SPENCER** is a visual artist who resides in Southern California. . . . **JAMES TUREK** studied the fine high art of oil painting until one day a crystal meth addict walked up to him and gave him, for no apparent reason, an entire box of indie comics from the '60s to the '90s! "The oil paints went in the trash! A sable brush, a bottle of black ink, and a set of Microns was purchased! The rest is history . . . My god, what have I done." . . . **DEAN WAREHAM** was a member of Galaxie 500 and Luna. His latest release is Dean & Britta's *13 Most Beautiful: Songs for Andy Warhol's Screen Tests*. . . . **ALISHA WESSLER** received her BFA from the School of the Art Institute of Chicago in 2006 and the range of her work includes otherworldly installation, soft sculpture, painting and illustration. She lives and works in Portland, Oregon and has shown her work in galleries nationally and internationally. alishawessler.com

ADVERTISEMENTS

YOU DON'T DESERVE ROCK'N'ROLL.

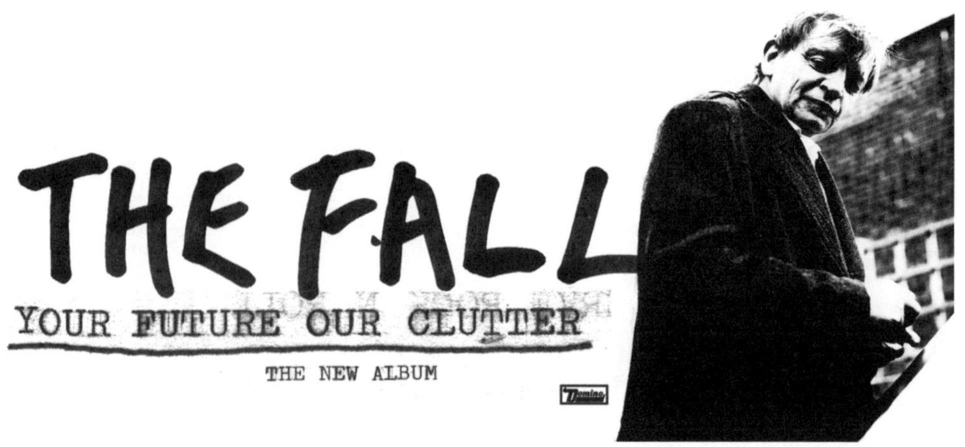

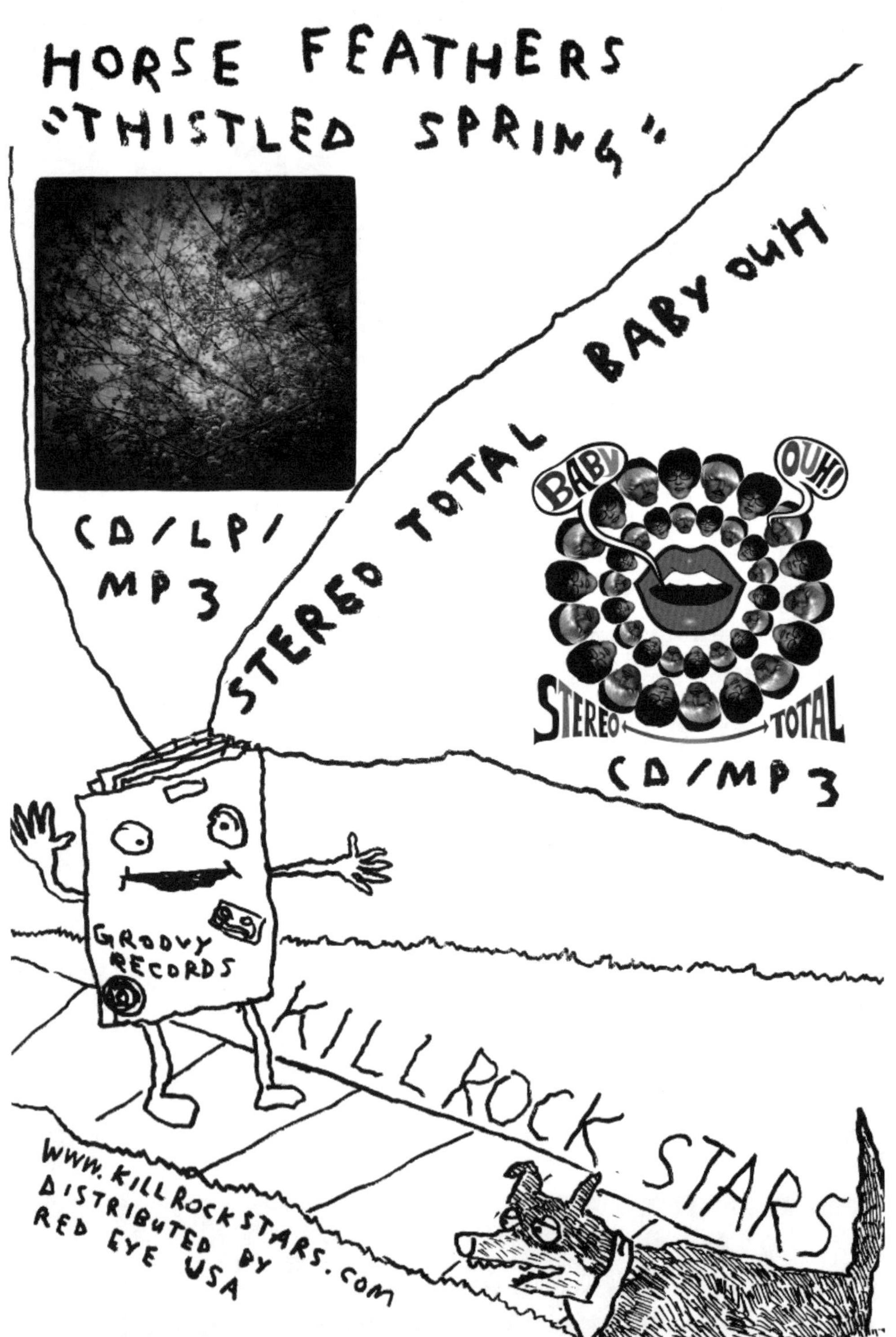
HORSE FEATHERS
"THISTLED SPRING"
CD/LP/
MP3
STEREO TOTAL BABY OUH
BABY
OUH!
STEREO
TOTAL
CD/MP3
GROOVY
RECORDS
KILL ROCK STARS
WWW.KILLROCKSTARS.COM
DISTRIBUTED BY
RED EYE USA

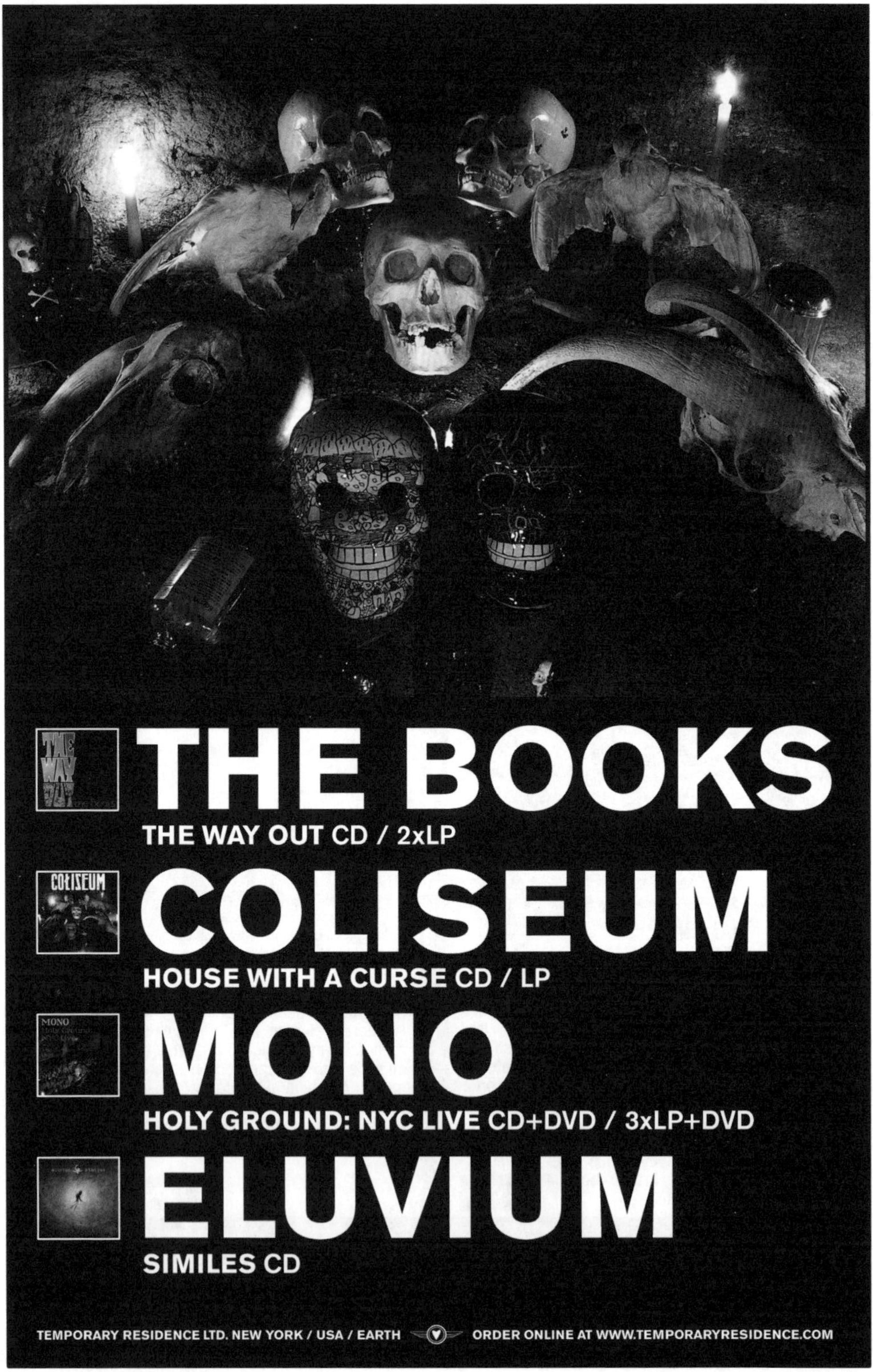

Trembling Bells
Abandoned Love
Pan Symphony in E Minor
William Nowik

CARIBOU *Swim*

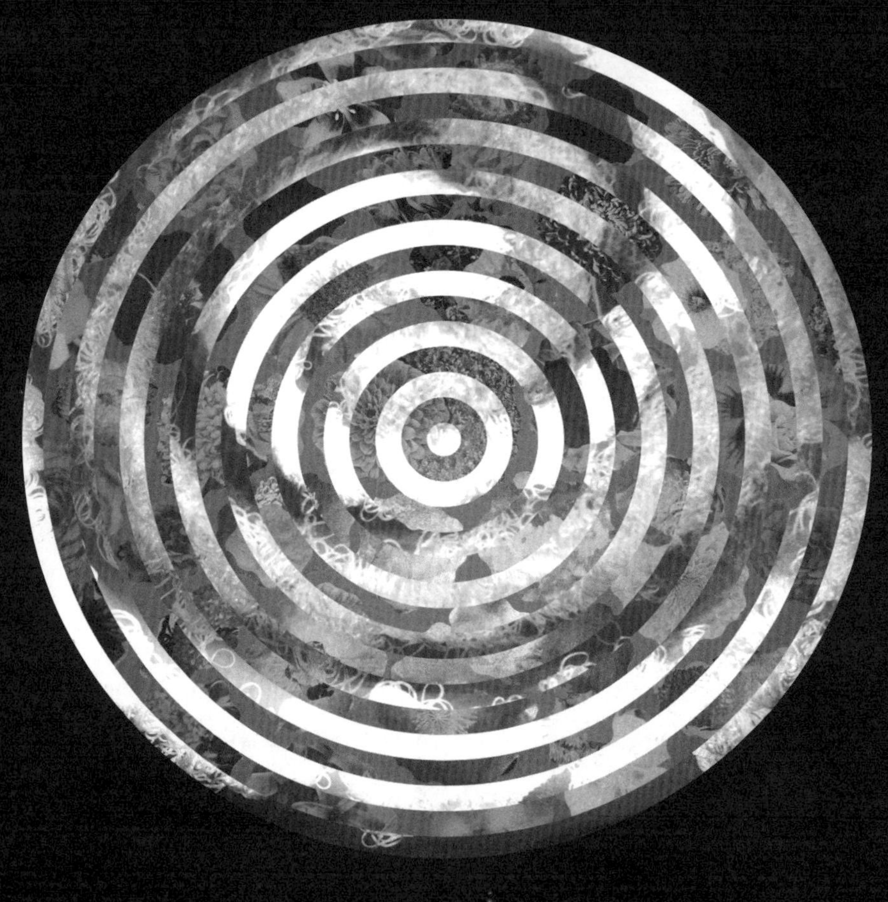

MERGE RECORDS

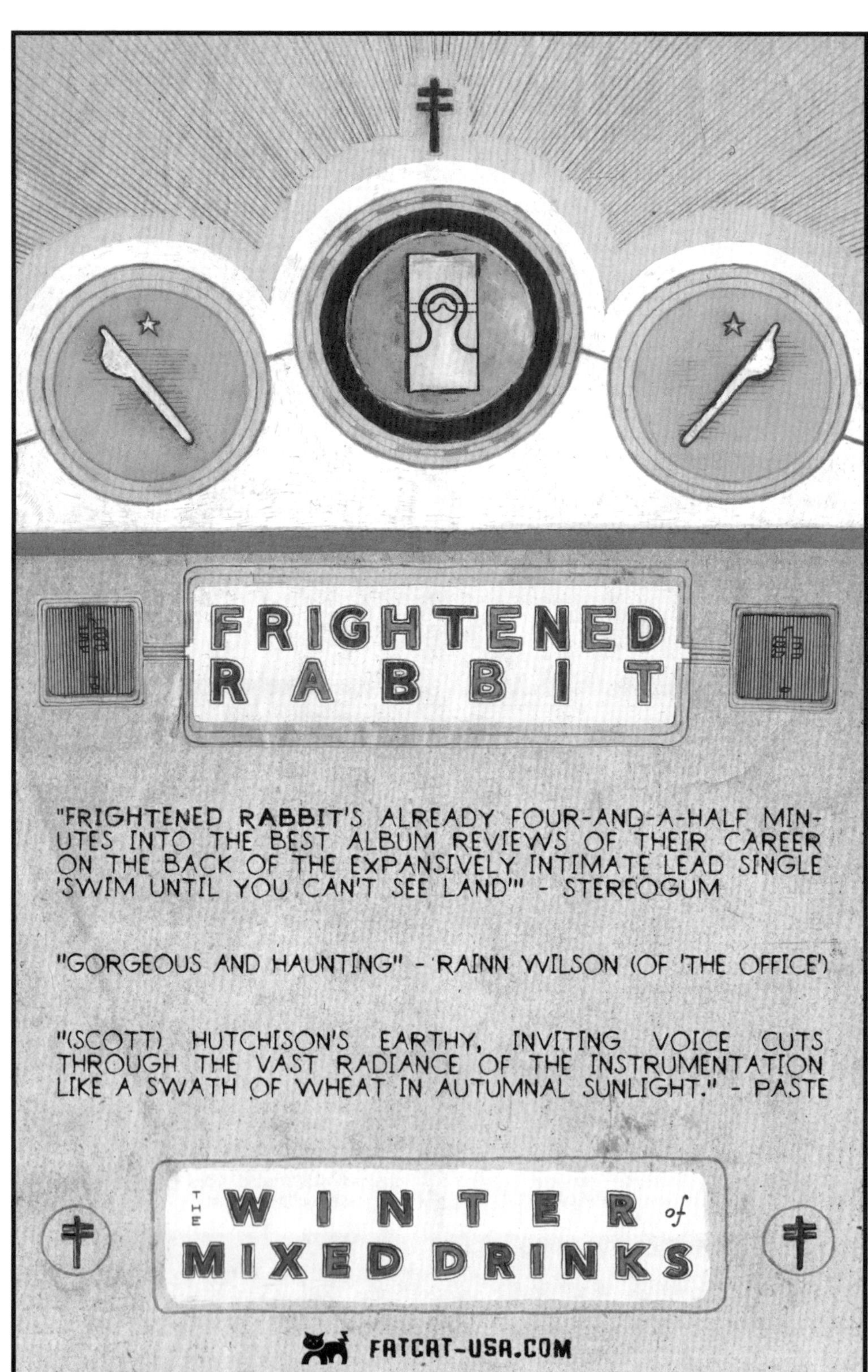
FRIGHTENED
RABBIT
"FRIGHTENED RABBIT'S ALREADY FOUR-AND-A-HALF MINUTES INTO THE BEST ALBUM REVIEWS OF THEIR CAREER ON THE BACK OF THE EXPANSIVELY INTIMATE LEAD SINGLE 'SWIM UNTIL YOU CAN'T SEE LAND'" - STEREOGUM
"GORGEOUS AND HAUNTING" - RAINN WILSON (OF 'THE OFFICE')
"(SCOTT) HUTCHISON'S EARTHY, INVITING VOICE CUTS THROUGH THE VAST RADIANCE OF THE INSTRUMENTATION LIKE A SWATH OF WHEAT IN AUTUMNAL SUNLIGHT." - PASTE
THE WINTER of
MIXED DRINKS
FATCAT-USA.COM

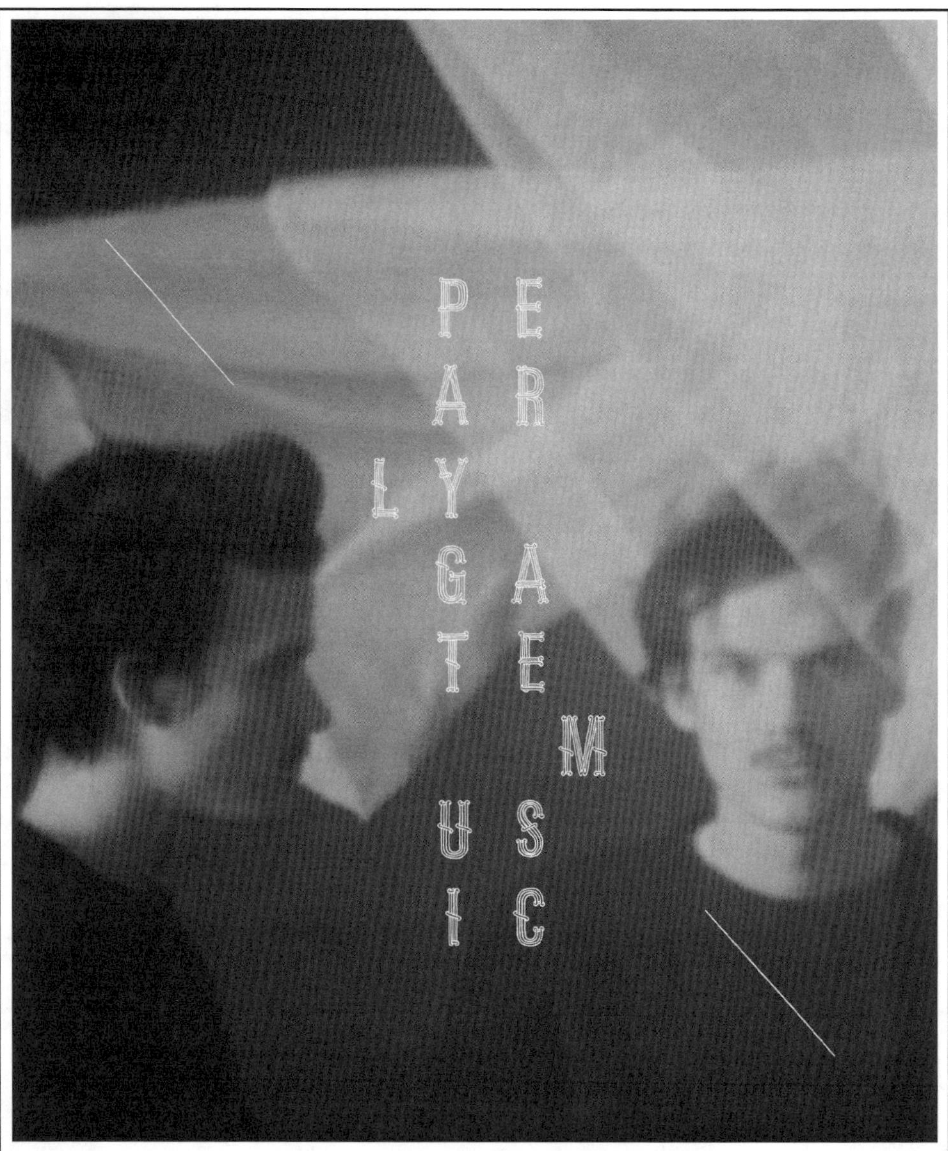

Pearly Gate Music is Zach Tillman.
The self-titled debut album is available now on CD / LP / MP3

"A heavenly offering from Seattle's Zach Tillman...When the Grim Reaper finally takes his swing and we scamper up that golden staircase to stand before St Peter we hope that the harp-strains that catch our ears are as beautiful as this debut." - ***NME***

"Lo-fi, high-octane. Tillman is a character on fire." (★★★★) - ***MOJO***

www.pearlygatemusic.com

barsuk records

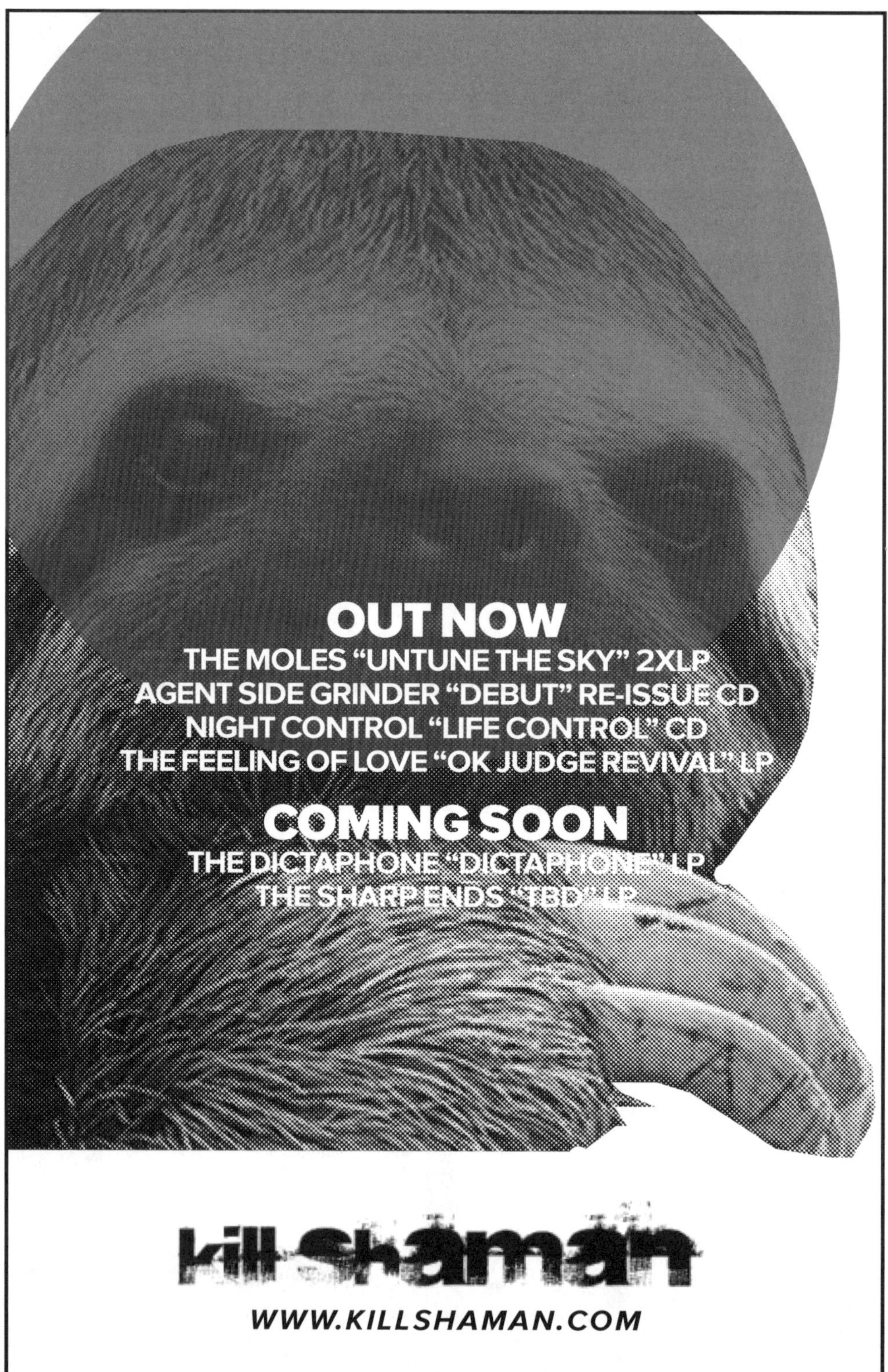
OUT NOW
THE MOLES "UNTUNE THE SKY" 2XLP
AGENT SIDE GRINDER "DEBUT" RE-ISSUE CD
NIGHT CONTROL "LIFE CONTROL" CD
THE FEELING OF LOVE "OK JUDGE REVIVAL" LP
COMING SOON
THE DICTAPHONE "DICTAPHONE" LP
THE SHARP ENDS "TBD" LP
kill shaman
WWW.KILLSHAMAN.COM

The Carpark Family of Labels
www.carparkrecords.com
www.paw-tracks.com
www.acuterecords.com

Coming Soon
Toro Y Moi album #2, Panda Bear *Tomboy*, Ear Pwr and more

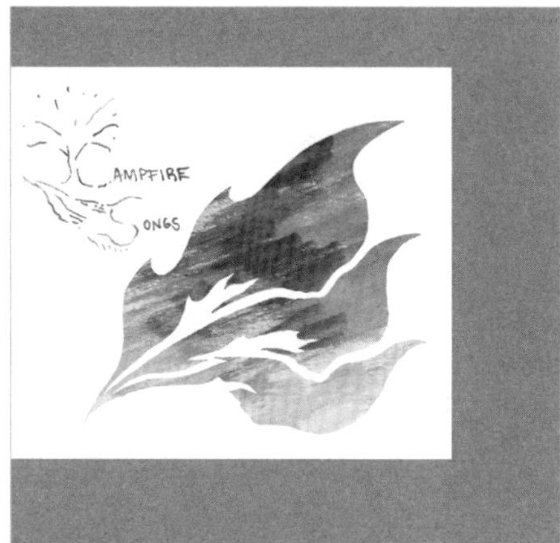

Animal Collective *Campfire Songs* CD/digital
Paw Tracks is proud to present the reissue of Animal Collective's 2003 album, an escape from the clutter and electronic assault of the group's previous records.
Out now on Paw Tracks

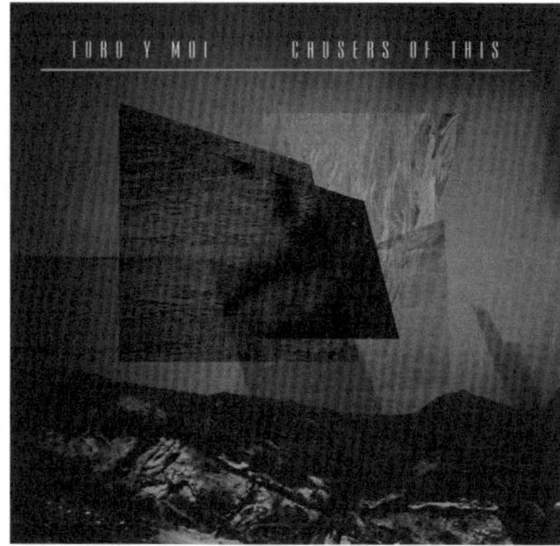

Toro Y Moi *Causers of This* CD/LP/digital
Toro Y Moi (a.k.a. Chaz Bundick) gathers up the best musical elements from around the globe – R&B, Indie Rock, Electronic Dance and Psychedelica – and spins them round and round.
Out now on Carpark

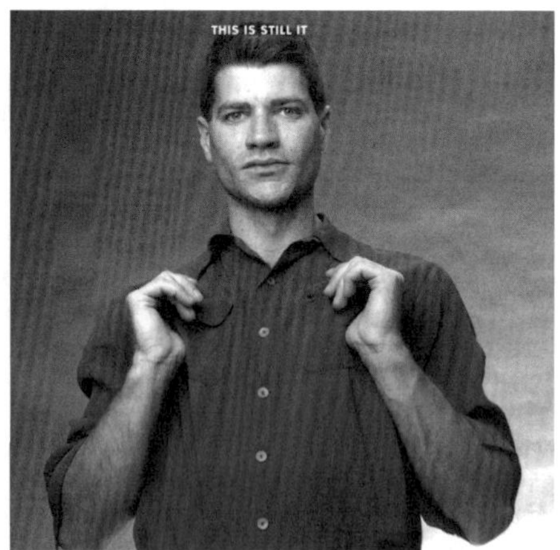

The Method Actors *This Is Still It* CD/digital
The Method Actors were one of the first bands to emerge from the scene that produced The B-52s, R.E.M., Pylon. *This Is Still It* revisits the legendary duo's early years. "Best new reissue" Pitchfork.
Out now on Acute

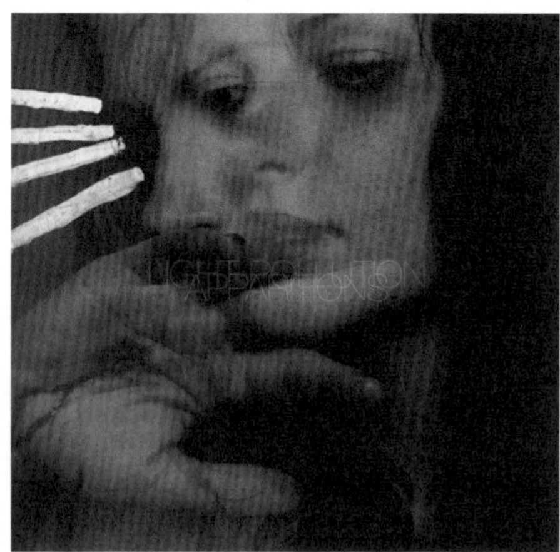

Light Pollution *Apparitions* CD/LP/digital
Swirling analog synths, shimmering arpeggios, and washed out tape noise create a perfect hybrid of moody indie pop and psychedelia.
Out June on Carpark

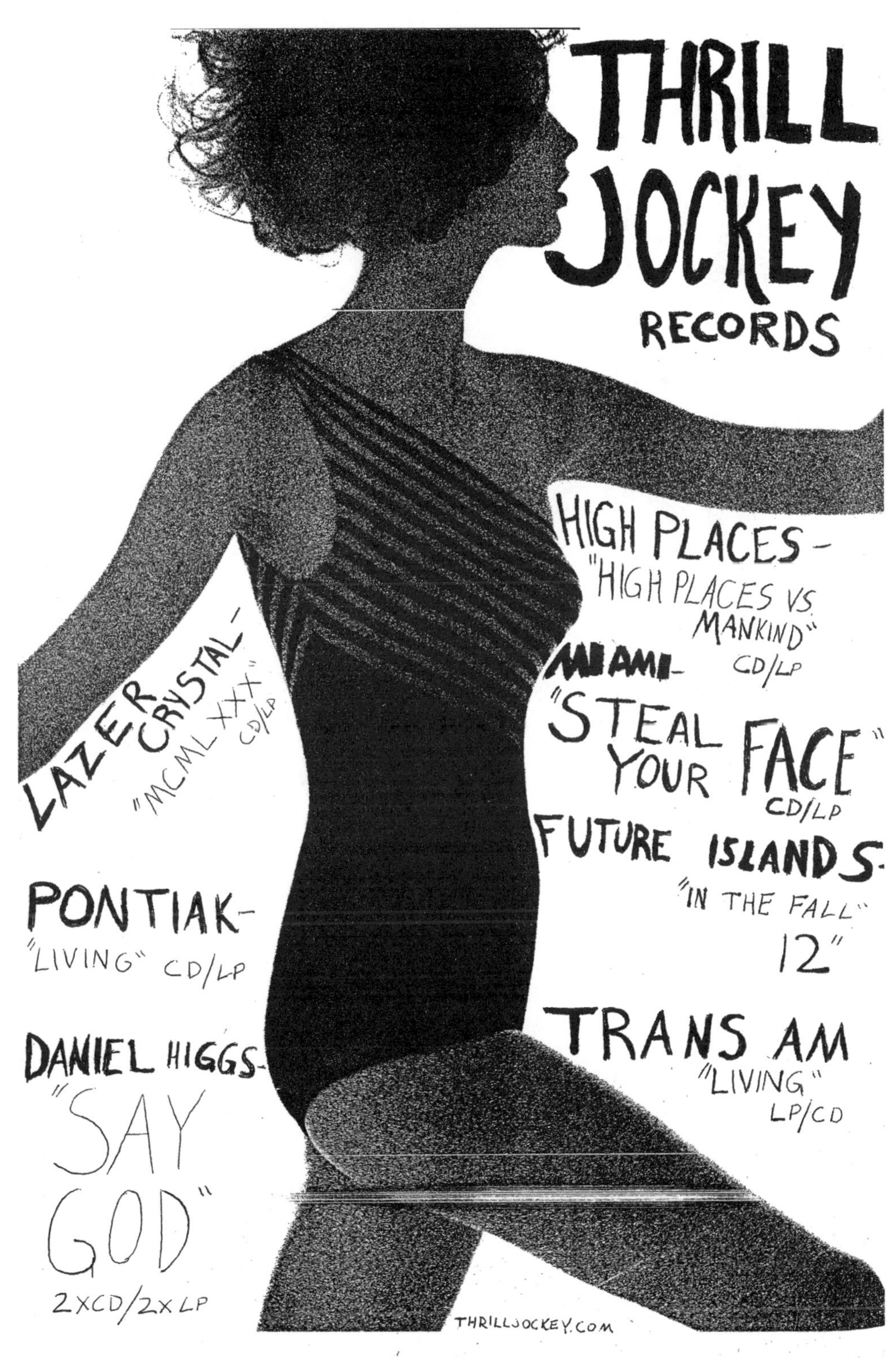

THRILL JOCKEY
RECORDS
HIGH PLACES -
"HIGH PLACES VS MANKIND"
CD/LP
MIAMI -
"STEAL YOUR FACE"
CD/LP
FUTURE ISLANDS -
"IN THE FALL"
12"
TRANS AM
"LIVING"
LP/CD
LAZER CRYSTAL -
"MCMLXXX"
CD/LP
PONTIAK -
"LIVING" CD/LP
DANIEL HIGGS -
"SAY GOD"
2XCD/2XLP
THRILLJOCKEY.COM

BOOKS FROM yeti

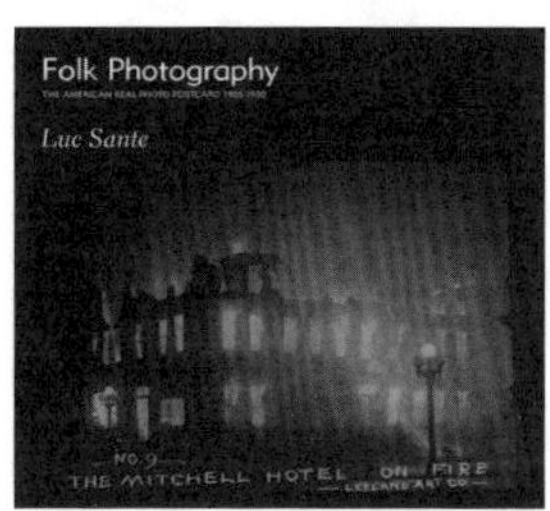

LUC SANTE

Folk Photography
The American Real-Photo Postcard, 1905–1930

Reproductions of 127 postcards, plus a groundbreaking critical essay. "Sante's deep preoccupation is an outlaw history of Modernism in which avant-gardists and roustabouts sync up. With each new old thing his eye and phrasing fall on, Sante picks up a mystery to unfold, smooth out and trickily refold. He claims it, and hands it on."**—THE NATION**

THE ART OF TOURING

Edited by Sara Jaffe and Mia Clarke

A book of art, photographs, and writing reflecting life on the road, plus a DVD of live footage. Over 50 contributors, including: Devendra Banhart, Carla Bozulich, Jem Cohen, Electrelane, Erase Errata, the Ex, Explosions in the Sky, Le Tigre, Matmos, Tara Jane ONeil, Sonic Youth, Yeah Yeah Yeahs

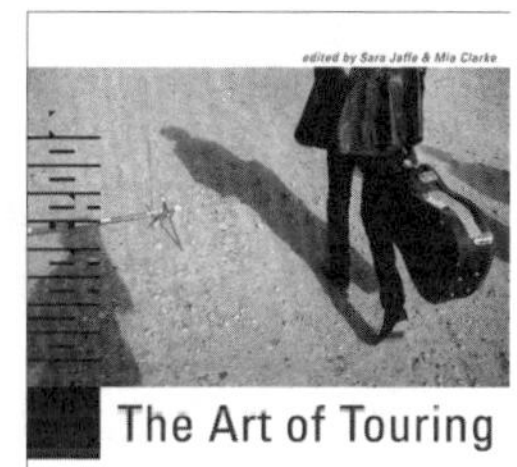

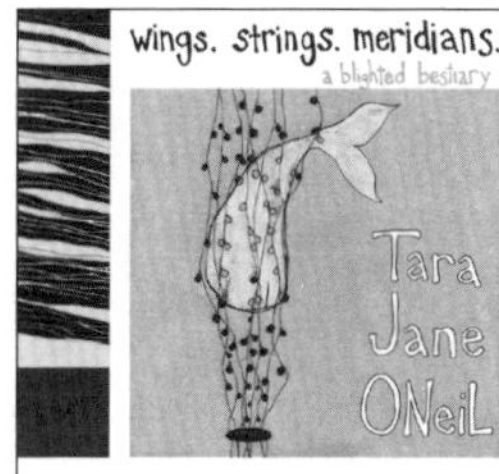

TARA JANE ONEIL

Wings. Strings. Meridians.

Art and music together in one beautiful six-inch-square package. 96 pages of paintings and drawings, plus a CD of live songs, home recordings and film scores.

LUC SANTE

Kill All Your Darlings

"Tough in his thinking, empathic in his analysis, and liberated in expression, Sante selects barbed details, tunes in to danger and suspense, and dispenses wry humor and sure insight."**—BOOKLIST**

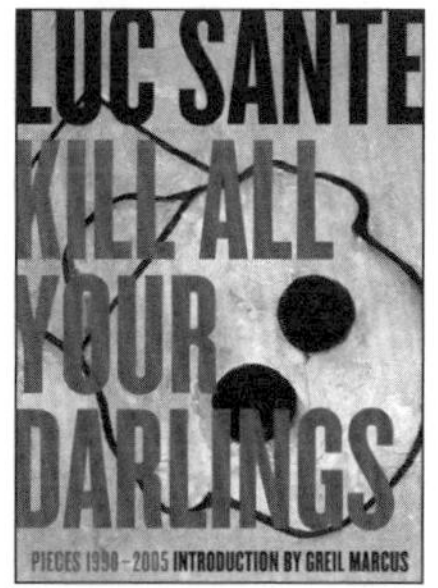

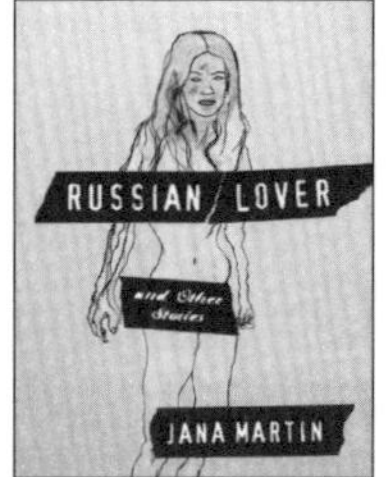

JANA MARTIN

Russian Lover and other stories

If you've read Jana's contributions to YETI, you already know how great her stories are. Sam Lipsyte called them "tough, funny stories from a writer wise enough to know that wisdom doesn't always come with experience."

Coming this fall:
NOMAD CODES: ADVENTURES IN MODERN ESOTERICA, by ERIK DAVIS

yetipublishing.com

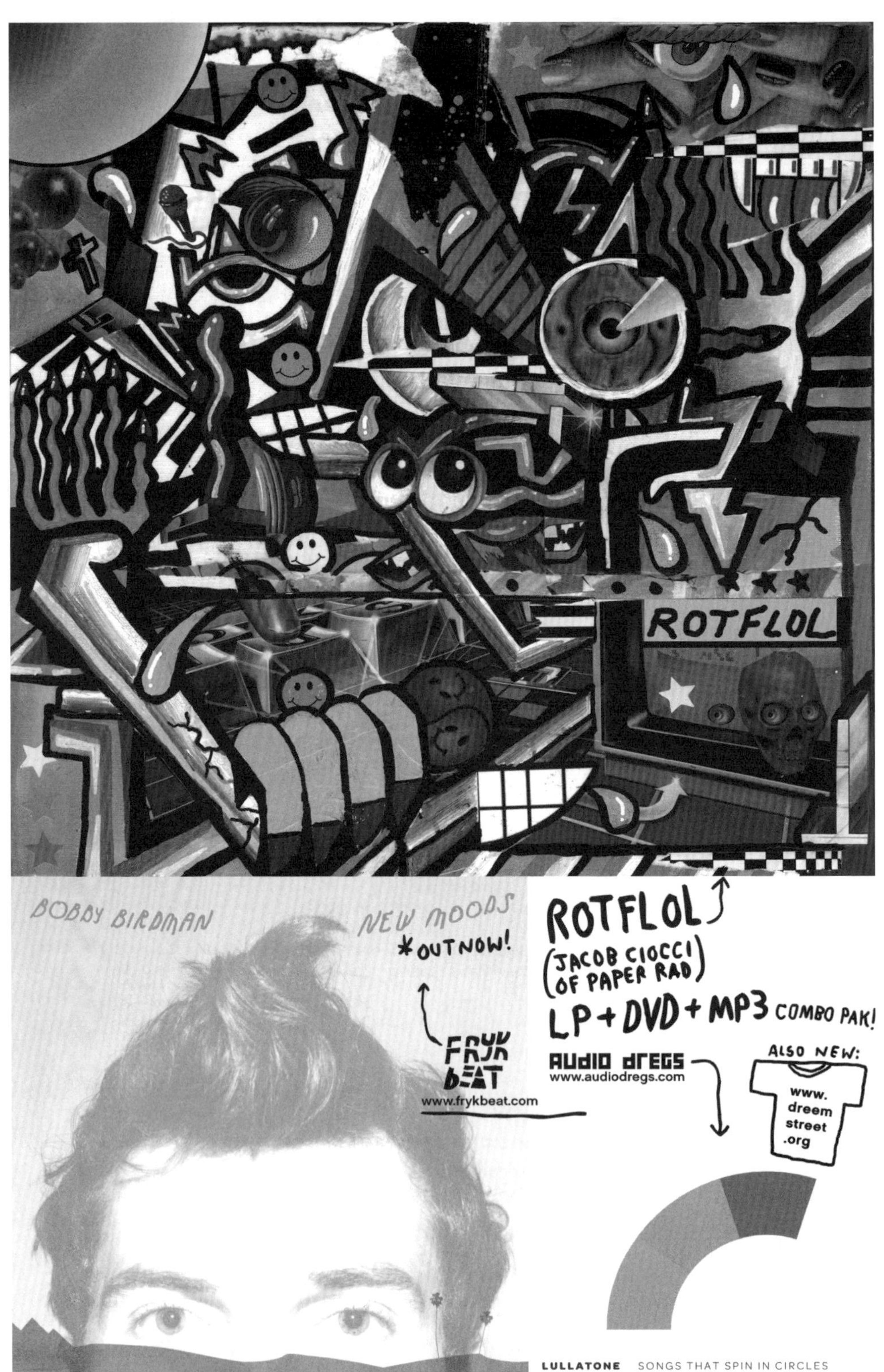
ROTFLOL
BOBBY BIRDMAN
NEW MOODS
*OUT NOW!
FRYK BEAT
www.frykbeat.com
ROTFLOL
(JACOB CIOCCI OF PAPER RAD)
LP + DVD + MP3 COMBO PAK!
AUDIO DREGS
www.audiodregs.com
ALSO NEW:
www.dreemstreet.org
LULLATONE SONGS THAT SPIN IN CIRCLES

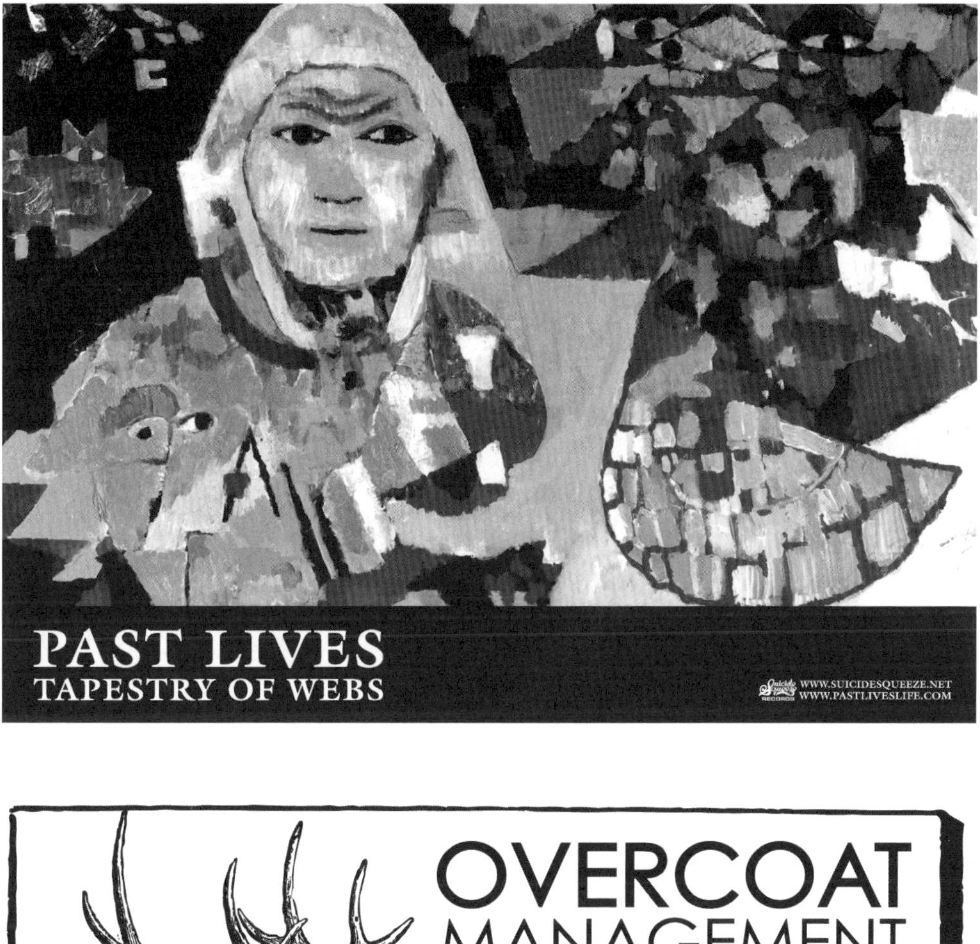

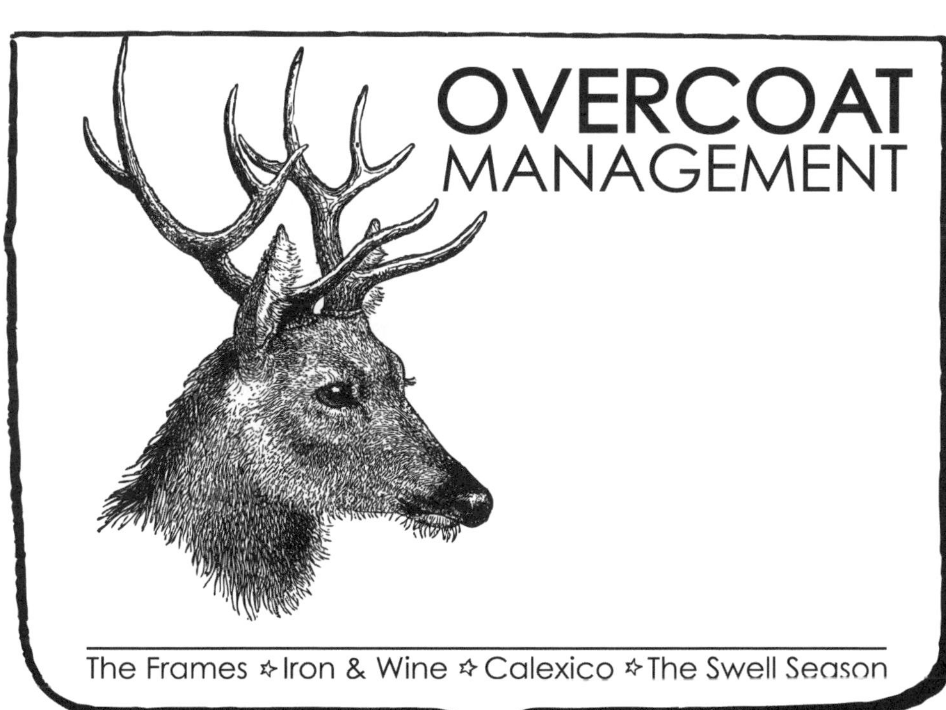
OVERCOAT
MANAGEMENT
The Frames ✩ Iron & Wine ✩ Calexico ✩ The Swell Season

Soft Abuse

SAB 034
TOMORROW IS ALRIGHT
SAB 039
SAB 036
SAB 038
Soft Abuse
SAB 040

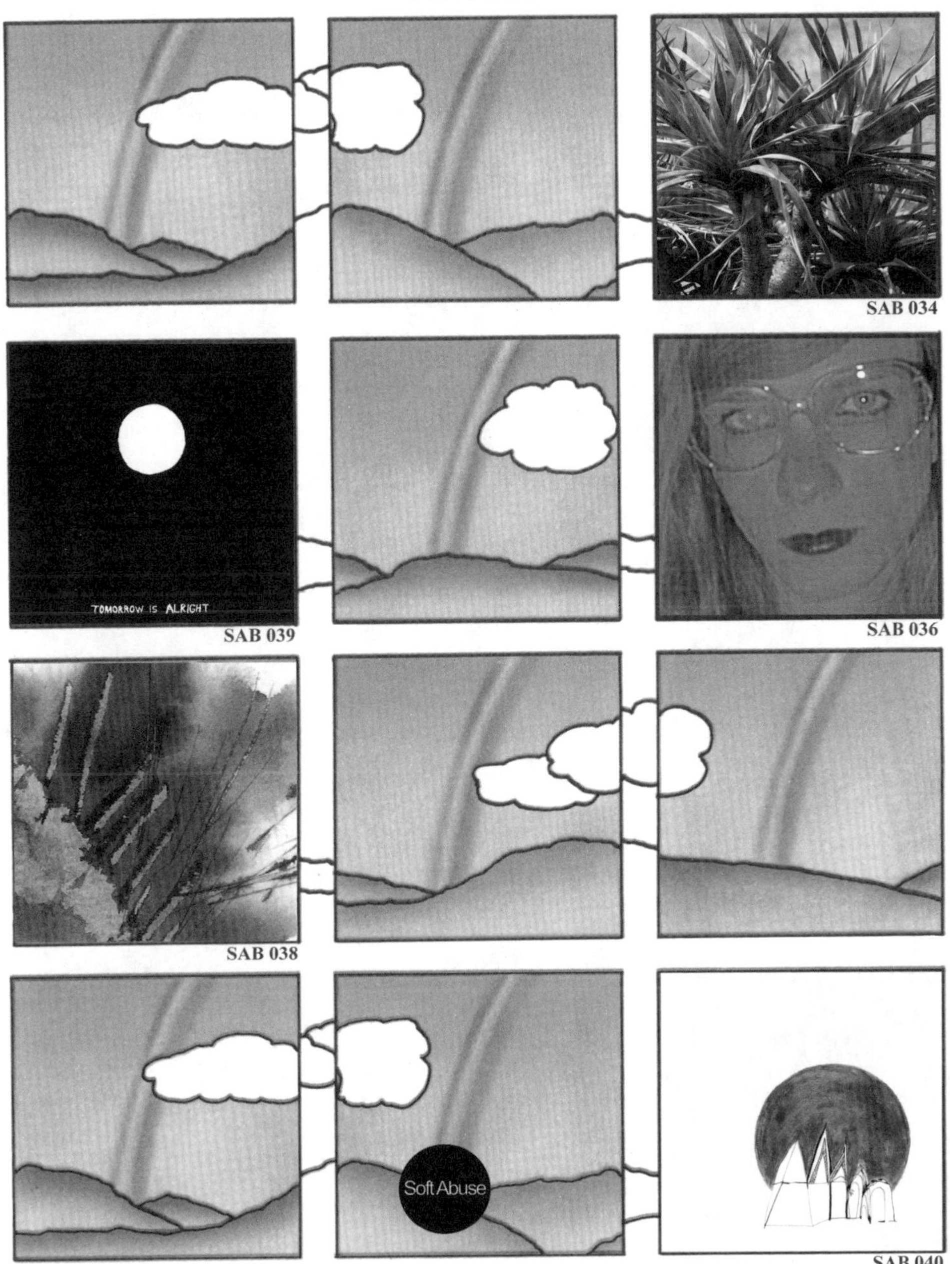

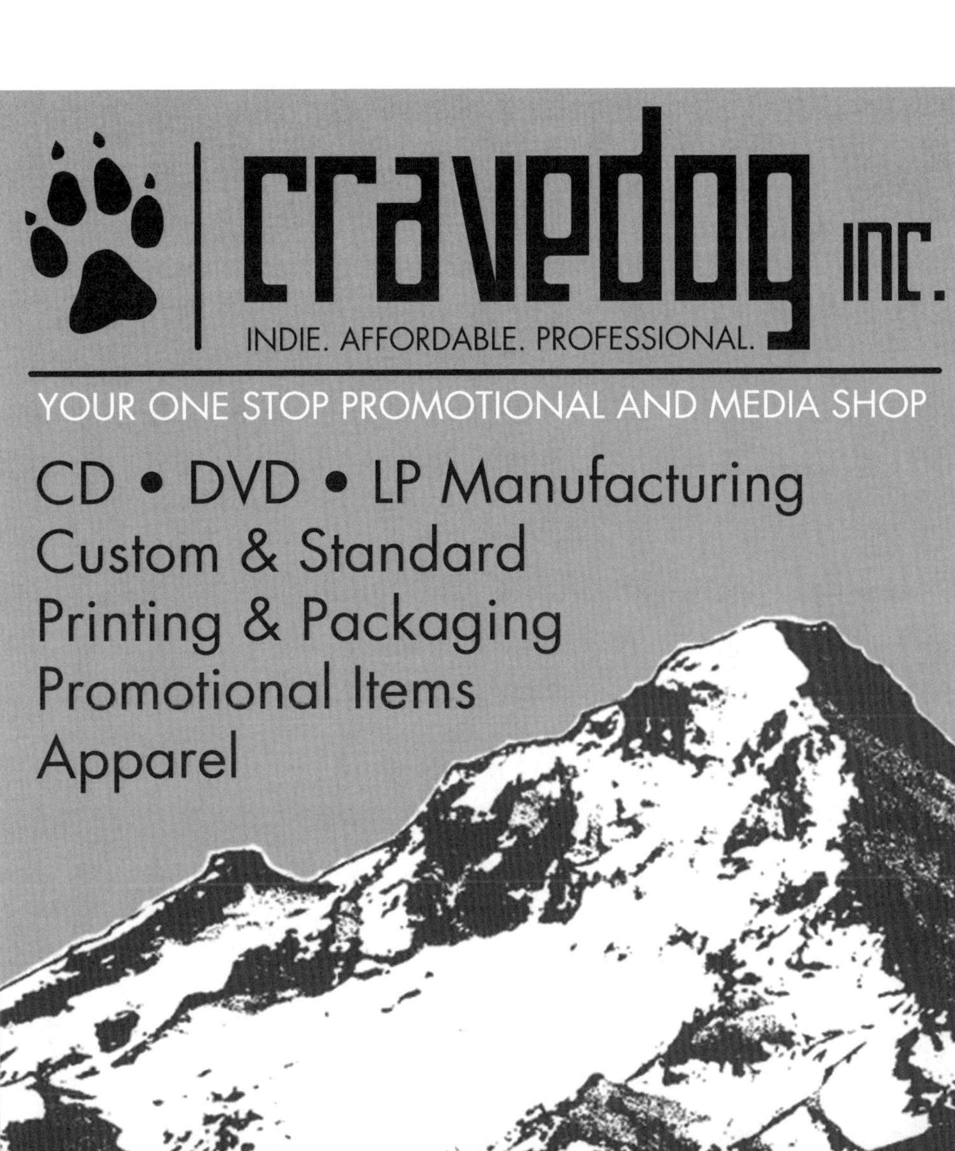
cravedog inc.
INDIE. AFFORDABLE. PROFESSIONAL.
YOUR ONE STOP PROMOTIONAL AND MEDIA SHOP
CD • DVD • LP Manufacturing
Custom & Standard
Printing & Packaging
Promotional Items
Apparel
412 NW Couch St #203
Portland, OR 97209
503-233-7284
CRAVEDOG.COM

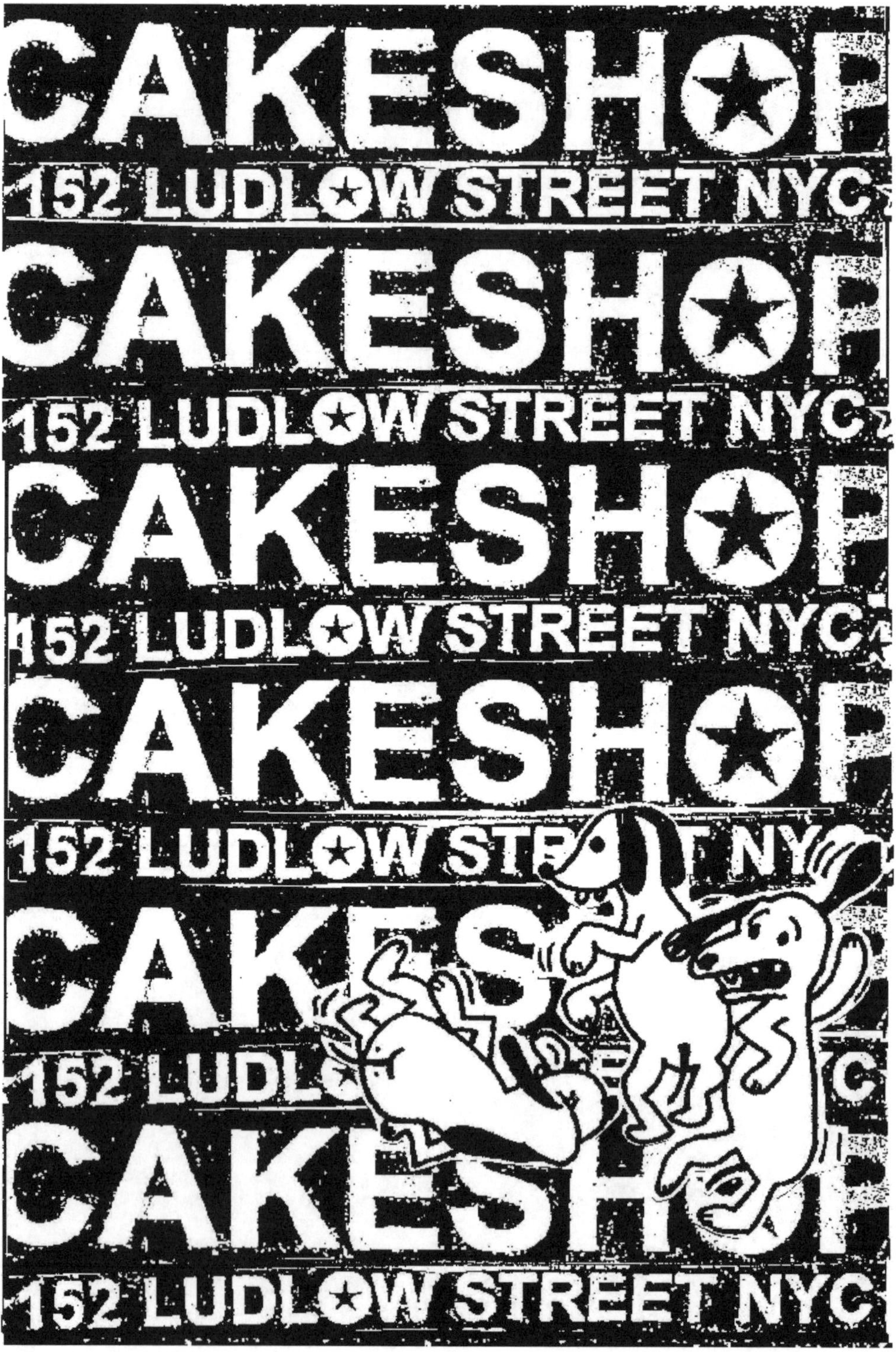

CAKESHOP

152 LUDLOW STREET NYC

CAKESHOP

152 LUDLOW STREET NYC

CAKESHOP

152 LUDLOW STREET NYC

CAKESHOP

152 LUDLOW ST NY

CAK S

152 LUDL C

CAKESH

152 LUDLOW STREET NYC

Upcoming Releases from

GOBBLE GOBBLE

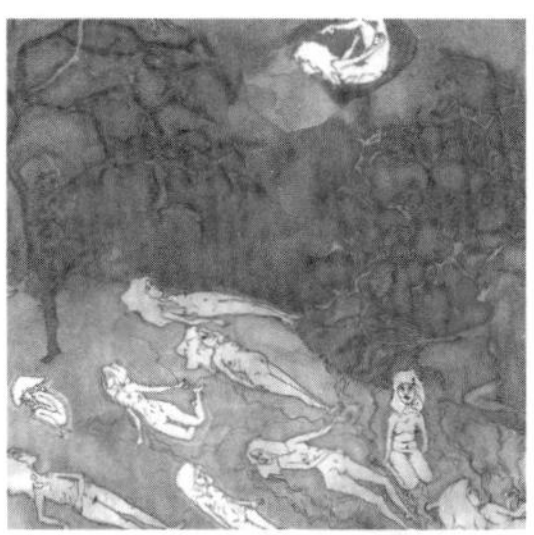

July 13:
RRFR-020
Neon Graveyard
12" / Mp3 LP

"...a carnal **carnival**, vivid and painful but **ultimately glittering** with the **happiness** that is **lurking** behind all **desolation.**"

- LoFi Disguise

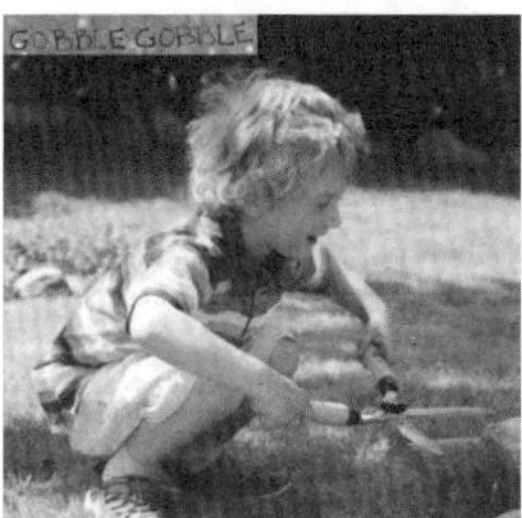

August 17:
RRFR-023:
Lawn Knives / End of Days
7" / Mp3 Single

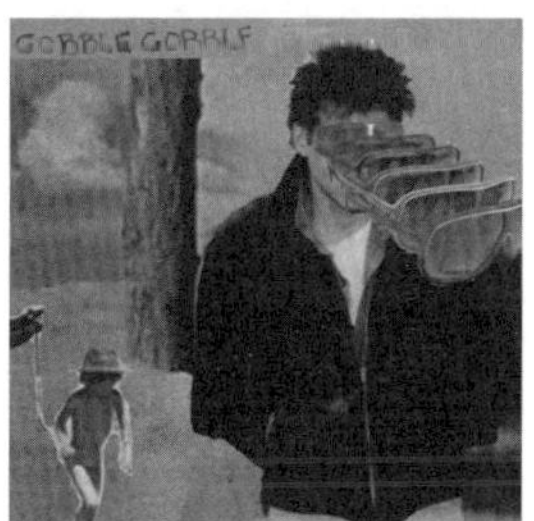

September 14:
RRFR-024:
Wrinklecarver / Nemo
Mp3 Single / 7"
on National Archive of Records

from your friends at

Royal Rhino Flying Records

230 Waitman Street
Morgantown, WV 26501

royalrhinoflying.wordpress.com
flyingrecords@gmail.com

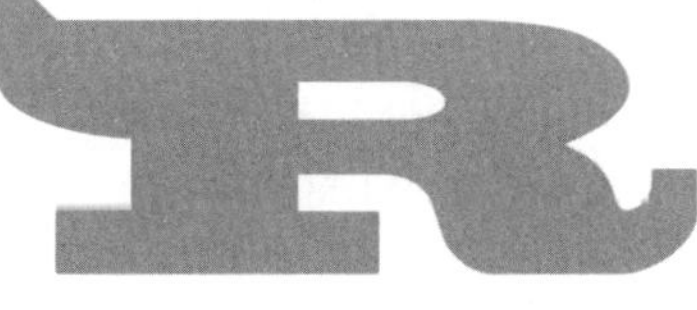

DON'T NOT LOOK BACK!

Liner Notes to the YETI Nine CD

by Mike McGonigal

ILLUSTRATION BY JESS FOGEL

This was a tough one to sequence. Apologies if that one really awkward segue made you drop your Coke Zero or run right into the curb. It was not so easy to weave together the Pip Proud tracks, the "outtakes" from *Fire in My Bones* and tracks assembled from Indian record collector Ranga Rao with the usual *YETI* mixture of weirdo garage pop, left-handed ventriloquist jazz, tasteful coffee-shoppe folk and outsider boogie drone. Though, next time, it'll hopefully all be outsider boogie drone!

I want to briefly address a problem that affects both young people and those folks who saw Honor Role play those CBGBs shows when Penn Rollings forgot to put his sneakers on. I'm talking about ARRS (Alt-Rock Reunion Syndrome).Today, more than ever, bands need to stay broken up. This is even more of a problem than the chillwave epidemic. No, wait, sorry, that never even happened really (chillwave). It was just some prank pulled by blog nerds. Psyche!

I'd like every group, especially ones that I love, to sign a contract stating they'll never ever get back together unless it's at a private affair, such as a wedding none of us are invited to (as in that amazing *SNL* hardcore skit from last year). We should all pool our funds to prevent rock and roll reunions. Let's make it not only morally but *fiscally* responsible for folks to resist this . . . necrophilic nostalgia. We could throw in a special bonus for acts that turn down the offer to play their *most seminal* release from start to finish. Seriously. It's super creepy when that shit happens.

1. FANTASTIC PALACE, "And Now, This"—Fantastic Palace is the one-man musical project of visual artist Alexander Ross. The first time I tried to have a record label (See Eye, early '90s), I released some of his tracks on a four-band collection called *Chinny Chin Chin*. That release was modeled on the Flying Nun's *Dunedin Double*, because it made sense at the time. Anyway, Fantastic Palace music is circus-like and fully amazing.

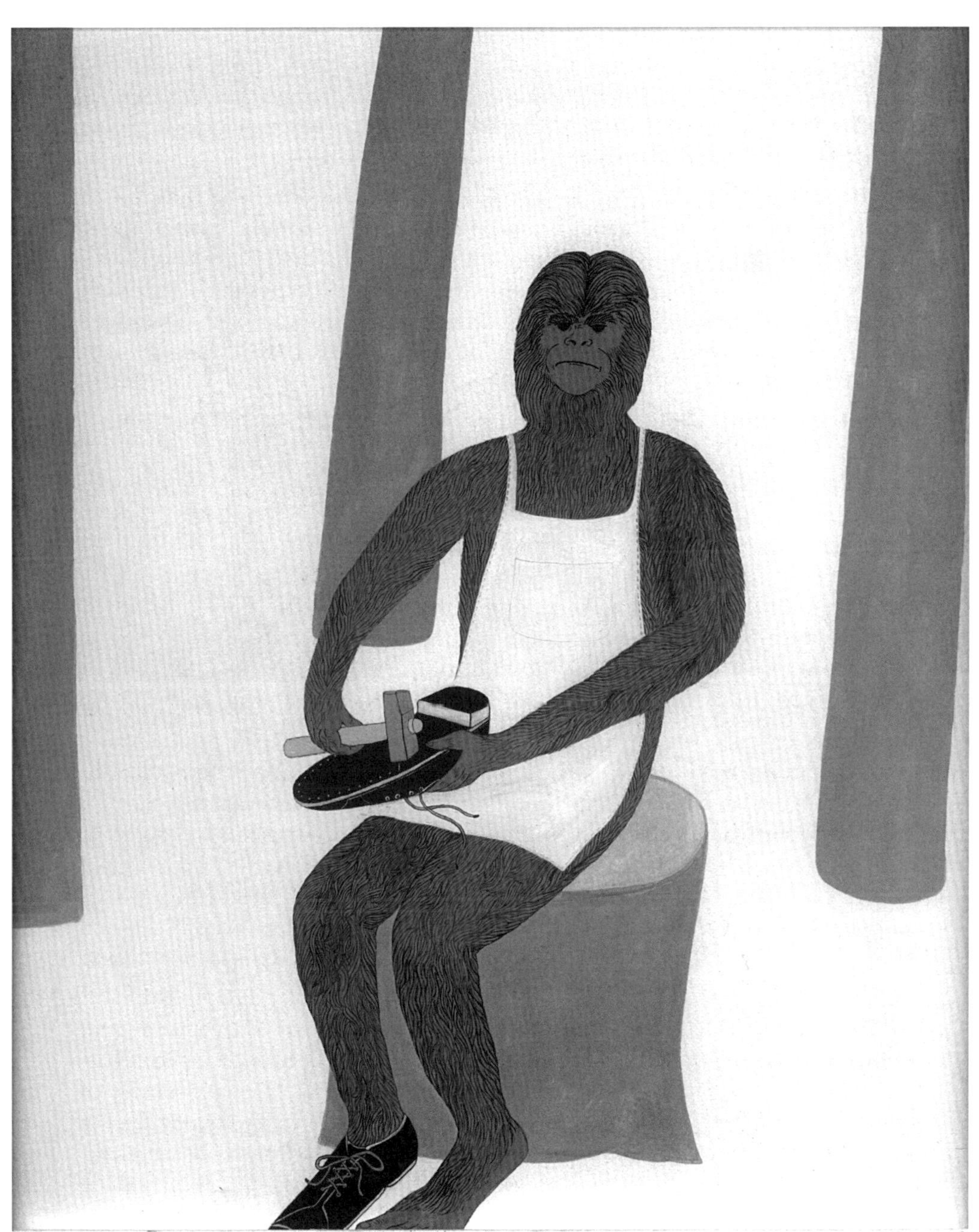

It's finally going to be released on vinyl within the next year, by our friends at Audio Dregs. There will hopefully be two volumes, the first collecting songs recorded between the late 1980s and 1990. This song is from a self-released 1990 cassette, *Ringlets and Gaskets*. "There's one track in particular that I think encapsulates what I was trying to get at with a lot the happier recordings, the third track from *Ringlets and Gaskets*, called 'And Now, This.' Ecstatic and childlike enthusiasm," Ross writes. The funny thing is that it's the song I'd picked before I got that note from him! Yay.

2. THE ART MUSEUMS, "(I'm Always Touched) By Your Presence Dear"—Not much to say here; I cold-emailed the group on MySpace for a song and got one! Glenn from the band said, "Sure," and then wrote "I hope you don't mind if it's a cover? It's a Blondie tune." And here you have it. MySpace has to be good for something aside from hitting on teenagers, and it is! Bands still use MySpace, because musicians are always a decade behind the times. The Art Museums are from the Bay Area and have a terrific record out on Woodsist.

3. KO + FRIENDS, "Hiding"—Ko Melina is one of the raddest people alive. She plays baritone guitar in the Dirtbombs and has her own satellite radio program. In a marginally just world, Ko would be hired by the city of Detroit to serve as a full time cultural ambassador. "Song writing credit goes to Fred Thomas," Ko writes. "We kinda worked on it together but he did the brunt of the writing work."

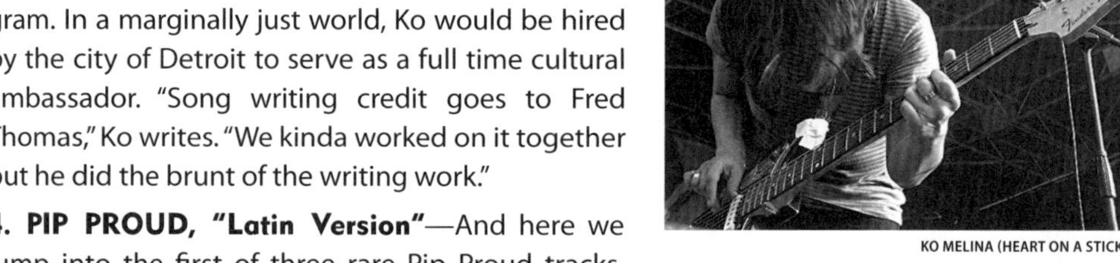
KO MELINA (HEART ON A STICK)

4. PIP PROUD, "Latin Version"—And here we jump into the first of three rare Pip Proud tracks. Many thanks to David Nichols (formerly of excellent rock-and-roll band the Cannanes, whose output you need to hear). David not only let us run that excerpt from his forthcoming history of Australian rock in this issue but he got us these tracks, with the permission of Proud's family. Pip Proud passed away while we were assembling the issue, and had already approved the release of this material here. Nichols writes: "This is 'Latin Version,' a song from his first album *De Da De Dum*, which was later rerecorded for *Adreneline and Richard*. The song's from the original master tape, not the vinyl." Someone seriously needs to reissue this thing; it was originally released as a private demonstration record on Pip's own label Grendel in 1967.

5. BOBBY CHARLES, "Homemade Songs"—This is the only known outtake from Louisiana born-and-bred singer-songwriter Bobby Charles's self-titled LP for Bearsville. Recorded in 1971, *Bobby Charles* is a delightful, laid-back, incredibly smart swamp-soul record. I'm in love with the production and playing on the thing. If it sounds like the Band to you, well, those guys are all over the record (Dr. John too) and their same producer, John Simon, produced it. Charles was born in 1938 and passed away on January 14, 2010.

6. RHYTHMICAL WRIGHT SINGERS, "When He Comes Again"—This song appears courtesy Andrew Yeomanson, aka DJ Le Spam. Andrew is the founding member of Miami's infamous Spam All-Stars and a great DJ with one of the sickest record collections you'll ever see, especially if you're into Afro-Cuban jams and Miami funk. As soon as he played this one for me, I got super excited; it's such a lovely modal shuffle! Initially, we thought these Wright Singers might be related to the great Miami soul singer Betty Wright, but that turned out to be a dead end. It is known that the Miami-based Rhythmical Wright Singers released two singles for the Spirit label in the late 1960s.

7. REV. LONNIE FARRIS, "What Mother Can Do"—This L.A.-based lap-steel player released eight singles on his own Farris label in the early 1960s. Social Music plans to release an LP of the material within the year.

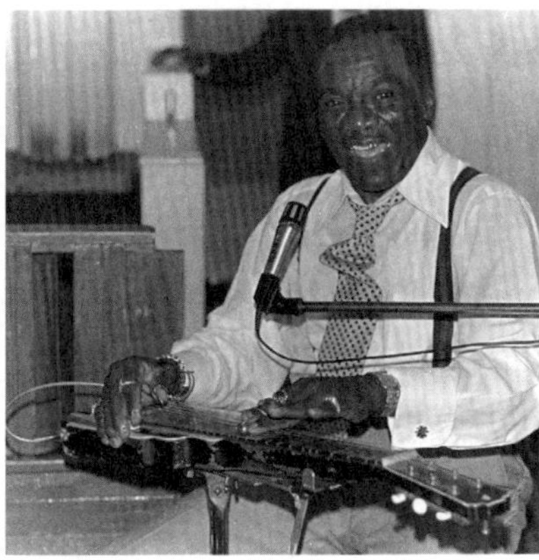
REV. LONNIE FARRIS,1977 (MARK WEBER JAZZ COLLECTION, UCLA)

8. BISHOP R. MCDANIEL, "Swing Low Sweet Chariot"—I have a double album and a weird country-rap (really!) 7-inch by Bishop R. McDaniel, but I haven't tracked down the artist himself. I know he's from Austin. I've been to where his Guiding Angel Church used to be, spoken to his neighbors, sent letters to his last known address—no luck yet. His track on the *Fire in My Bones* set I compiled for Tompkins Square was one of the most loved tracks on there, and for good reason. You've never heard anything quite like this, have you?

9. PUPPY HEARTS, "Kingdom Come"—All rock and roll songs should make you fantasize about being in the band and being cool as you play the song to a room full of adoring people. Or else starring in the video. This song is from the self titled 7" on Dead Pizza by this Huntsville, Alabama-based band.

10. AIAS, "La Truita"—Aias is a trio from Barcelona, Spain. Gaia writes that "the band was formed in April 2009; very recent creation! Here are the people who play in the band: guitar and first voice: Gaia Bihr; drums and second voice: Laia Aubia; bass guitar: Miriam Garcia. We made it, Laia and me, first, for a surprise birthday party. The challenge was the following: I play keyboard and sing in another band, but almost never played or composed with guitar. And Laia never played drums. In two weeks we made seven songs, and performed. Our friends really liked the concert so we decided to follow with this little project. As we are very very amateur and spontaneous, and no-musician, we had almost no hope that a label would release this album. Miraculously, Mike from Captured Tracks appeared and proposed to release the LP. We needed about a week to believe that it was real... it seemed like a cute indie movie -- where a small and totally unknown , non-musician band receive a proposal from Brooklyn."

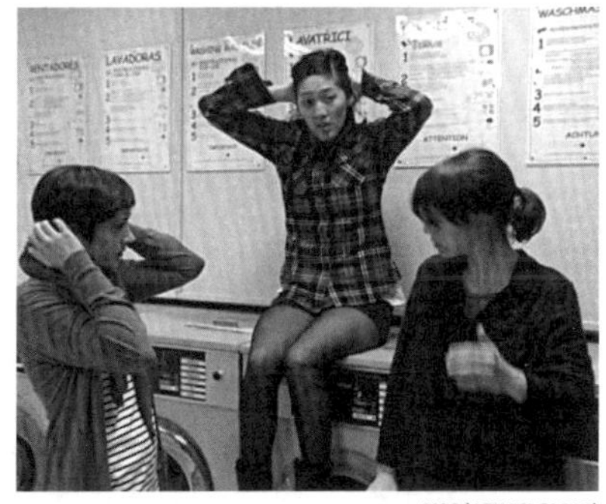
AIAS (IGNASI CASAS)

11. ARRINGTON DE DIONYSO'S MALAIKAT DAN SINGA, "Kargyraa Locked Groove (Edit)"—A very brief snippet from the locked-groove ending of one of Arrington's home-made records. "I have a Recordio home-use model record lathe, probably from the late '40s or early '50s," Mr. Dionyso explains. "It has a microphone attached and it's about the size of those old schoolhouse record players, except it has two arms—one for playing records, one for cutting. The needles are expensive and break easily. I cut records onto plastic picnic plates from Safeway. As long as I use a good needle, the sound is amazing. Frequencies distort in a completely different pattern than when recording with tape. Low-end frequencies are particularly rich and throbbing, so it's great for my throat singing and bass clarinet work. It's also very easy to create a lock groove simply by lifting up the needle while it is still cutting," he says. "I sometimes employ a primitive "overdubbing" technique by playing a locked-groove record on another stereo and rerecording myself playing along with it to make another record." You can buy these records from him, each completely one of a kind. "And I make original color paintings on the covers of each one," he further tantalizes.

12. TEENAGE PANZERKORPS, "Turn Out Your Lights"—Edmund Xavier wrote to say:" Credits: DER TPK: Catholic Pat: drums; Bunker Wolf: vocals; Boy True: bass; Edmund Xavier: guitar, bass, Casio," adding: "Please do not fuck with in mastering, except to make *louder* if necessary." It's good when bands know exactly what they want. This song might scare you a little.

13. US GIRLS, "Take Over Dynamix"—Because this issue took a while to come out, this song is now available as the B-side to a 7" on Atelier Ciseaux, in an edition of 300 copies on recycled paper with screenprinted art by Meghan Remy (the US Girl herself).

14. PIP PROUD, "The Love I Gave You Was All I Was"—David Nichols writes that this is "a song from the late 1990s, recorded (digitally) in Tenterfield." It's never been released before.

15. GEOFF SOULE "2009-12-22"—Solo acoustic guitar piece by this Portland-based member of Fuck and Sad Horse. Cryptic numbers in the title need deciphering.

AWESOME INDIAN MUSIC FROM VAK RANGA RAO'S 78 COLLECTION, SELECTED BY ROB MILLIS

16. VAK RANGA RAO, Interview Excerpt—We never do this and I don't know why. Here's what Ranga Rao sounds like. And as he is talking about a Bollywood musical, let's then here a song from a musical right afterwards.

17. MUKESH, "Mere Man Ki Ganga"—This track is from the film *Sangam* performed by Mukesh in 1964. Millis writes that "*Sangam* was a big hit film; this record was given to me by Ranga Rao—he had duplicates."

18. TIRUVASANALIUR NARAYANASAMI IYER, "Sankarabharanam Adi Talam"—"Religious tracks, sung in Sanskrit. Also in the Sankarabharanam raga. Adi Talam is the rhythm, recorded in Thanjavur, Tamil Nadu, 1907."

19. SEMBANNARKOVIL RAMASWAMY PILLAY, "Sankarabharanam-Rupakam"—"Probably recorded in Madras, circa 1910. Improvisation in the Sankarabharanam raga or mode; Rupakam is the rhythm."

20. SPENCER MOODY, "Wreck of the Medusa"—This solo track by the Seattle, WA-based Triumph of Lethargy/Murder City Devil frontperson was recorded with Daniel Pirone at the tail end of 2009. "Ya, stoked sounds good," Spencer adds.

21. PLANKTON WAT, "Pathways to Spaceways"—Plankton Wat is Dewey Mahood of Portland, Oregon. "I used harmonium, drum machine, voice, drums and bass," he writes. Dewey is in Eternal Tapestry, so you know he knows how to bring the boogie. He himself described the vibe of this one as "raga shoegaze," and that's about right.

22. READING RAINBOW, "Empty Without You"—Reading Rainbow is a pretty killer duo from Philadelphia, but you probably know that already. "We just sent an mp3 of a new song we just recorded over the past few nights," Rob writes. "SXSW was both amazingly awesome and grueling. It definitely kicked both of our asses. Sarah has coughed up blood the past couple mornings. She's sipping on that codeine now. Hope you like the song!"

23. HUMAN EYE, "Slop Cult"—Human Eye is based in and around Detroit, MI. The group lists their lineup as: "Alien pianos: Johnny Lzr; drums/percussion/sax: Hurricane William; guitar/vocals-Timmy Lampinen; bass: Brad Hales." Timmy (aka Timmy Vulgar from Clone Defects) is an ideal front-man. Dude makes elaborate costumes, hand-draws exquisite flyers and shoots glitter onto the audience. Ohh, he writes pretty great songs as well. They explore that long since burnt bridge between punk and prog. If you wanted to write the sticker on the front of their next record, one might say that Human Eye is what the members of Chrome, Alice Cooper, and Crime would have sounded like if you'd locked them up together in a studio in 1977. From what I can tell, Timmy is part born-out-of-time possessed punk psycho and part sweet, soul-of-a-kitten introverted visionary artiste. He's not "fronting," though. Like, he's not only the kind of person who'll sit in front of your house on Christmas day at your party, eat half the Christmas tree, and then shit it back on your front lawn later that night. But, he's the person who actually did that, at least once—scout's honor! I could go off on each member of Human Eye as well, but I ran out of space.

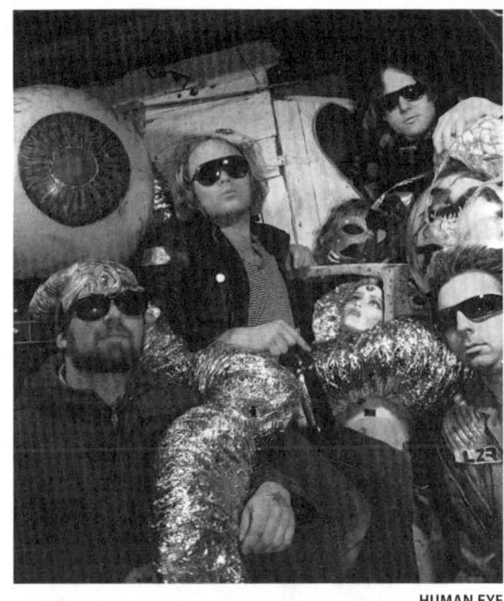
HUMAN EYE

24. X-RAY EYEBALLS, "Nightwalkers"—O.J. San Felipe (whose band Golden Triangle is getting some deserved attention) sent in this song from his solo project. "Well it's a full band now that we are playing live," he says. "This is one of the songs that we recorded in Kayrock Screenprinting's recording studio in October, 2009. I work at this shop during the day too, printing posters and shirts mostly for bands. X-Ray Eyeballs is a project consisting of Rop from Rice, Jay High and Carly from Golden Triangle, and Jack from Georgiana Starlington. All these songs are just ideas me and Carly had for Golden Triangle songs that never became GT songs, but I didn't want to forget them, and have these ideas go to waste- so I fleshed out these ideas into full songs, and recorded them myself. First with pre-recorded drum beats, then later with Jack drumming. We made a cassette for Shawn from Night-People Records sometime in 2009. Pretty soon after that people started demanding X-Ray to play, so I rounded up this motley cast of characters. Everyone in this project is in another band, so this is just something we do for fun. We play shows if people ask us, and only if we all happen to be free from our other bands."

25. ARRINGTON DE DIONYSO'S MALAIKAT DAN SINGA, "Nadasuaram Solo"—Here's a full track recorded live to plastic plate on Arrington's home recording machine.

26. MODERN WOMEN, "Nu Witch"—Modern Women is a band comprised of West Coast visual artist/musician/awesome party-thrower Sarah Gottesdie-ner and various friends. On this song, Radio Sloan plays guitar "and she also recorded it at the Rock 'n' Roll Camp for Girls; me: everything else," Sarah says.

27. PIP PROUD, "Bedwrecker"—"This is one [Pip] was particularly pleased with," David Nichols writes. It's "from July 1996, recorded with Nic Dalton and me. Nic produced. I don't think it has been released anywhere before."

28. MARISA ANDERSON, "Drop Down"—The Portland-based guitarist writes that "this song is the first track on my new record which consists of twelve solo improvisations for guitar and lap steel . . . The record doesn't have a name yet. I think [the album] is mostly inspired by listening to blues and gospel records, time spent with my dad, and going to Sunday school and singing Presbyterian hymns at the top of my lungs when I was a kid. The record will be out in fall 2010 on Mississippi Records." Marisa can be found online at myspace.com/marisaandersonmusic.

CD TRACK LISTING (CLIFFS NOTES VERSION)

1. FANTASTIC PALACE, "And Now, This" — 2. THE ART MUSEUMS, "(I'm Always Touched) By Your Presence Dear" — 3. KO + FRIENDS, "Hiding" — 4. PIP PROUD, "Latin Version" — 5. BOBBY CHARLES, "Homemade Songs" — 6. RHYTHMICAL WRIGHT SINGERS, "When He Comes Again" — 7. REV. LONNIE FARRIS, "What Mother Can Do" — 8. BISHOP R. MCDANIEL, "Swing Low Sweet Chariot" — 9. PUPPY HEARTS, "Kingdom Come" — 10. AIAS, "La Truita" — 11. ARRINGTON DE DIONYSO'S MALAIKAT DAN SINGA, "Kargyraa Locked Groove (Edit)" — 12. TEENAGE PANZERKORPS, "Turn Out Your Lights" — 13. US GIRLS, "Take Over Dynamix" — 14. PIP PROUD, "The Love I Gave You Was All I Was" — 15. GEOFF SOULE "2009-12-22" — 16. VAK RANGA RAO, Interview Excerpt — 17. MUKESH, "Mere Man Ki Ganga" — 18. TIRUVASANALIUR NARAYANASAMI IYER, "Sankarabharanam Adi Talam" — 19. SEMBANNARKOVIL RAMASWAMY PILLAY, "Sankarabharanam-Rupakam" —20. SPENCER MOODY, "Wreck of the Medusa" — 21. PLANKTON WAT, "Pathways to Spaceways" — 22. READING RAINBOW, "Empty Without You" —23. HUMAN EYE, "Slop Cult" — 24. X-RAY EYEBALLS, "Nightwalkers" — 25. ARRINGTON DE DIONYSO'S MALAIKAT DAN SINGA, "Nadasuaram Solo" — 26. MODERN WOMEN, "Nu Witch" — 27. PIP PROUD, "Bedwrecker" — 28. MARISA ANDERSON, "Drop Down"